Reclaiming the State

Reclaiming the State

A Progressive Vision of Sovereignty for a Post-Neoliberal World

William Mitchell and Thomas Fazi

PLUTO  PRESS

First published 2017 by Pluto Press
345 Archway Road, London N6 5AA

www.plutobooks.com

Copyright © William Mitchell and Thomas Fazi 2017

The right of William Mitchell and Thomas Fazi to be identified as
the authors of this work has been asserted by them in accordance
with the Copyright, Designs and Patents Act 1988.

British Library Cataloguing in Publication Data
A catalogue record for this book is available from the British Library

ISBN   978 0 7453 3733 3   Hardback
ISBN   978 0 7453 3732 6   Paperback
ISBN   978 1 7868 0148 7   PDF eBook
ISBN   978 1 7868 0150 0   Kindle eBook
ISBN   978 1 7868 0149 4   EPUB eBook

Typeset by Stanford DTP Services, Northampton, England
Printed and bound by CPI Group (UK) Ltd, Croydon, CR0 4YY

Contents

Acknowledgements

Both authors would like to specially acknowledge the valuable administrative and editorial assistance they received from Melinda Hannan (at CofFEE). Thomas Fazi would also like to thank Cristina for her love and patience.

The overall project is dedicated however to the millions of nameless unemployed workers who have been denied the opportunity to live fulfilled lives by the implementation of neoliberal economic policies abetted by orthodox economists who, unfortunately, bear none of the costs of their folly.

While many have offered help and advice, all errors remain the responsibility of the authors.

Introduction:
Make the Left Great Again

The West is currently in the midst of an anti-establishment revolt of historic proportions.

The Brexit vote in the United Kingdom, the election of Donald Trump in the United States, the rejection of Matteo Renzi's neoliberal constitutional reform in Italy, the EU's unprecedented crisis of legitimation: although these interrelated phenomena differ in ideology and goals, they are all rejections of the (neo)liberal order that has dominated the world – and in particular the West – for the past 30 years.

Even though the system has thus proven capable (for the most part) of absorbing and neutralising these electoral uprisings,[1] there is no indication that this anti-establishment revolt is going to abate any time soon. Support for anti-establishment parties in the developed world is at the highest level since the 1930s – and growing.[2] At the same time, support for mainstream parties – including traditional social-democratic parties – has collapsed.

The reasons for this backlash are rather obvious. The financial crisis of 2007–9 laid bare the scorched earth left behind by neoliberalism, which the elites had gone to great lengths to conceal, in both material (financialisation) and ideological ('the end of history') terms. As credit dried up, it became apparent that for years the economy had continued to grow primarily because banks were distributing the purchasing power – through debt – that businesses were not providing in salaries. To paraphrase Warren Buffett, the receding tide of the debt-fuelled boom revealed that most people were, in fact, swimming naked.

The situation was (is) further exacerbated by the post-crisis policies of fiscal austerity and wage deflation pursued by a number of Western governments, particularly in Europe, which saw the financial crisis as an opportunity to impose an even more radical neoliberal regime and to push through policies designed to suit the financial sector and the wealthy, at the expense of everyone else. Thus, the unfinished agenda of privatisation, deregulation and welfare state retrenchment –

2 · RECLAIMING THE STATE

temporarily interrupted by the financial crisis – was reinstated with even greater vigour.

Amid growing popular dissatisfaction, social unrest and mass unemployment (in a number of European countries), political elites on both sides of the Atlantic responded with business-as-usual policies and discourses. As a result, the social contract binding citizens to traditional ruling parties is more strained today than at any other time since World War II – and in some countries has arguably already been broken.

Of course, even if we limit the scope of our analysis to the post-war period, anti-systemic movements and parties are not new in the West. Up until the 1980s, anti-capitalism remained a major force to be reckoned with. The novelty is that today – unlike 20, 30 or 40 years ago – it is movements and parties of the right and extreme right (along with new parties of the neoliberal 'extreme centre', such as the new French president Emmanuel Macron's party En Marche!) that are leading the revolt, far outweighing the movements and parties of the left in terms of voting strength and opinion-shaping. With few exceptions, left parties – that is, parties to the left of traditional social-democratic parties – are relegated to the margins of the political spectrum in most countries. Meanwhile, in Europe, traditional social-democratic parties are being 'pasokified' – that is, reduced to parliamentary insignificance, like many of their centre-right counterparts, due to their embrace of neoliberalism and failure to offer a meaningful alternative to the status quo – in one country after another. The term refers to the Greek social-democratic party PASOK, which was virtually wiped out of existence in 2014, due to its inane handling of the Greek debt crisis, after dominating the Greek political scene for more than three decades. A similar fate has befallen other former behemoths of the social-democratic establishment, such as the French Socialist Party and the Dutch Labour Party (PvdA). Support for social-democratic parties is today at the lowest level in 70 years – and falling.[3]

How should we explain the decline of the left – not just the electoral decline of those parties that are commonly associated with the left side of the political spectrum, regardless of their effective political orientation, but also the decline of core left values within those parties and within society in general? Why has the anti-establishment left proven unable to fill the vacuum left by the collapse of the establishment left? More broadly, how did the left come to count so little in global politics? Can the left, both culturally and politically, become a major force in our societies again? And if so, how? These are some of the questions that we attempt to answer in this book.

Though the left has been making inroads in some countries in recent years – notable examples include Bernie Sanders in the United States, Jeremy Corbyn in the UK, Podemos in Spain and Jean-Luc Mélenchon in France – and has even succeeded in taking power in Greece (though the SYRIZA government was rapidly brought to heel by the European establishment), there is no denying that, for the most part, movements and parties of the extreme right have been more effective than left-wing or progressive forces at tapping into the legitimate grievances of the masses – disenfranchised, marginalised, impoverished and dispossessed by the 40-year-long neoliberal class war waged from above. In particular, they are the only forces that have been able to provide a (more or less) coherent response to the widespread – and growing – yearning for greater territorial or national sovereignty, increasingly seen as the only way, in the absence of effective supranational mechanisms of representation, to regain some degree of collective control over politics and society, and in particular over the flows of capital, trade and people that constitute the essence of neoliberal globalisation.

Given neoliberalism's war against sovereignty, it should come as no surprise that 'sovereignty has become the master-frame of contemporary politics', as Paolo Gerbaudo notes.[4] After all, as we argue in Chapter 5, the hollowing out of national sovereignty and curtailment of popular-democratic mechanisms – what has been termed depoliticisation – has been an essential element of the neoliberal project, aimed at insulating macroeconomic policies from popular contestation and removing any obstacles put in the way of economic exchanges and financial flows. Given the nefarious effects of depoliticisation, it is only natural that the revolt against neoliberalism should first and foremost take the form of demands for a *repoliticisation* of national decision-making processes.

The fact that the vision of national sovereignty that was at the centre of the Trump and Brexit campaigns, and that currently dominates the public discourse, is a reactionary, quasi-fascist one – mostly defined along ethnic, exclusivist and authoritarian lines – should not be seen as an indictment of national sovereignty *as such*. History attests to the fact that national sovereignty and national self-determination are not *intrinsically* reactionary or jingoistic concepts – in fact, they were the rallying cries of countless nineteenth- and twentieth-century socialist and left-wing liberation movements.

Even if we limit our analysis to core capitalist countries, it is patently obvious that virtually all the major social, economic and political advancements of the past centuries were achieved *through the institutions of the democratic nation state*, not through international, multilateral or supranational institutions, which in a number of ways have, in fact, been used to *roll back* those very achievements, as we have seen in the context of the euro crisis, where supranational (and largely unaccountable) institutions such as the European Commission, Eurogroup and European Central Bank (ECB) used their power and authority to impose crippling austerity on struggling countries. The problem, in short, is not national sovereignty as such, but the fact that the concept in recent years has been largely monopolised by the right and extreme right, which understandably sees it as a way to push through its xenophobic and identitarian agenda. It would therefore be a grave mistake to explain away the seduction of the 'Trumpenproletariat' by the far right as a case of false consciousness, as Marc Saxer notes;[5] the working classes are simply turning to the only movements and parties that (so far) promise them some protection from the brutal currents of neoliberal globalisation (whether they can or truly intend to deliver on that promise is a different matter).

However, this simply raises an even bigger question: why has the left not been able to offer the working classes and increasingly proletarianised middle classes a credible alternative to neoliberalism and to neoliberal globalisation? More to the point, why has it not been able to develop a *progressive view of national sovereignty*? As we argue in this book, the reasons are numerous and overlapping. For starters, it is important to understand that the current existential crisis of the left has very deep historical roots, reaching as far back as the 1960s. If we want to comprehend how the left has gone astray, that is where we have to begin our analysis.

Today the post-war 'Keynesian' era is eulogised by many on the left as a golden age in which organised labour and enlightened thinkers and policymakers (such as Keynes himself) were able to impose a 'class compromise' on reluctant capitalists that delivered unprecedented levels of social progress, which were subsequently rolled back following the so-called neoliberal counter-revolution. It is thus argued that, in order to overcome neoliberalism, all it takes is for enough members of the establishment to be swayed by an alternative set of ideas. However, as we note in Chapter 2, the rise and fall of Keynesianism cannot simply be explained in terms of working-class strength or the victory of one ideology over another, but should instead be viewed as the outcome of the fortuitous confluence, in the aftermath of World War II, of a number of social, ideological, political, economic, technical and institutional conditions.

To fail to do so is to commit the same mistake that many leftists committed in the early post-war years. By failing to appreciate the extent to which the class compromise at the base of the Fordist-Keynesian system was, in fact, a crucial component of that history-specific regime of accumulation – actively supported by the capitalist class insofar as it was conducive to profit-making, and bound to be jettisoned once it ceased to be so – many socialists of the time convinced themselves 'that they had done much more than they actually had to shift the balance of class power, and the relationship between states and markets'.[6] Some even argued that the developed world had already entered a post-capitalist phase, in which all the characteristic features of capitalism had been permanently eliminated, thanks to a fundamental shift of power in favour of labour vis-à-vis capital, and of the state vis-à-vis the market. Needless to say, that was not the case. Furthermore, as we show in Chapter 3, monetarism – the ideological precursor to neoliberalism – had already started to percolate into left-wing policymaking circles as early as the late 1960s.

Thus, as argued in Chapters 2 and 3, many on the left found themselves lacking the necessary theoretical tools to understand – and correctly respond to – the *capitalist* crisis that engulfed the Keynesian model in the 1970s, convincing themselves that the distributional struggle that arose at the time could be resolved within the narrow limits of the social-democratic framework. The truth of the matter was that the labour–capital conflict that re-emerged in the 1970s could only have been resolved one way or another: on capital's terms, through a reduction of labour's bargaining power, or on labour's terms, through an extension of the state's control over investment and production. As we show in Chapters 3 and 4, with regard to the experience of the social-democratic governments of Britain and France in the 1970s and 1980s, the left proved unwilling to go this way. This left it (no pun intended) with no other choice but to 'manage the capitalist crisis on behalf of capital', as Stuart Hall wrote, by ideologically and politically legitimising neoliberalism as the only solution to the survival of capitalism.[7]

In this regard, as we show in Chapter 3, the Labour government of James Callaghan (1974–9) bears a very heavy responsibility. In an (in)famous speech in 1976, Callaghan justified the government's programme of spending cuts and wage restraint by declaring Keynesianism dead, indirectly legitimising the emerging monetarist (neoliberal) dogma and effectively setting up the conditions for Labour's 'austerity lite' to be refined into an all-out attack on the working class by Margaret Thatcher. Even worse, perhaps, Callaghan popularised the notion that austerity was the only solution to the economic crisis of the 1970s, anticipating Thatcher's 'there is no alternative' (TINA) mantra, even though *there were radical alternatives available at the time*, such as those put forward by Tony Benn and others. These, however, were 'no longer perceived to exist'.[8]

In this sense, the dismantling of the post-war Keynesian framework cannot simply be explained as the victory of one ideology ('neoliberalism') over another ('Keynesianism'), but should rather be understood as the result of a number of overlapping ideological, economic and political factors: the capitalists' response to the profit squeeze and to the political implications of full employment policies; the structural flaws of 'actually existing Keynesianism'; and, importantly, the left's inability to offer a coherent response to the crisis of the Keynesian framework, let alone a radical alternative. These are all analysed in-depth in the first chapters of the book.

Furthermore, throughout the 1970s and 1980s, a new (fallacious) left consensus started to set in: that economic and financial internationalisation – what today we call 'globalisation' – had rendered the state increasingly powerless vis-à-vis 'the forces of the market', and that therefore countries had little choice but to abandon national economic strategies and all the traditional instruments of intervention in the economy (such as tariffs and other trade barriers, capital controls, currency and exchange rate manipulation, and fiscal and central bank policies), and hope, at best, for transnational or supranational forms of economic governance. In other words, government intervention in the economy came to be seen not only as ineffective but, increasingly, as outright impossible. This process – which was generally (and erroneously, as we shall see) framed as a shift from the state to the market – was accompanied by a ferocious attack on the very idea of national sovereignty, increasingly vilified as a relic of the past. As we show, the left – in particular the European left – played a crucial role in this regard as well, by cementing this ideological shift towards a *post-national* and *post-sovereign* view of the world, often anticipating the right on these issues.

One of the most consequential turning points in this respect, which is analysed in Chapter 4, was Mitterrand's 1983 turn to austerity – the so-called *tournant de la rigueur* – just two years after the French Socialists' historic victory in 1981. Mitterrand's election had inspired the widespread belief that a radical break with capitalism – at least with the extreme form of capitalism that had recently taken hold in the Anglo-Saxon world – was still possible. By 1983, however, the French Socialists had succeeded in 'proving' the exact opposite: that neoliberal globalisation was an inescapable and inevitable reality. As Mitterrand stated at the time: 'National sovereignty no longer means very much, or has much scope in the modern world economy. … A high degree of supra-nationality is essential.'[9]

The repercussions of Mitterrand's about-turn are still being felt today. It is often brandished by left-wing and progressive intellectuals as proof of the fact that globalisation and the internationalisation of finance has ended the era of nation states and their capacity to pursue policies that are not in accord with the diktats of global capital. The claim is that if a government tries autonomously to pursue full employment and a progressive/redistributive agenda, it will inevitably be punished by the amorphous forces of global capital. This narrative claims that Mitterrand had no option but to abandon his agenda of radical reform. To most modern-day leftists, Mitterrand thus represents a pragmatist who was cognisant of the international capitalist forces he was up against and responsible enough to do what was best for France.

In fact, as we argue in the second part of the book, sovereign, currency-issuing states – such as France in the 1980s – far from being helpless against the power of global capital, still have the capacity to deliver full employment and social justice to their citizens. So how did the idea of the 'death of the state' come to be so ingrained in our collective consciousness? As we explain in Chapter 5, underlying this post-national view of the world was (is) a failure to understand – and in some cases an explicit attempt to conceal – on behalf of left-wing intellectuals and policymakers that 'globalisation' was (is) not the result of inexorable economic and technological changes but was (is) largely the product of state-driven processes. All the elements that we associate with neoliberal globalisation – delocalisation, deindustrialisation, the free movement of goods and capital, etc. – were (are), in most cases, the result of choices made by governments. More generally, states continue to play a crucial role in promoting, enforcing and sustaining a (neo)liberal international framework – though that would appear to be changing, as we discuss in Chapter 6 – as well as establishing the domestic conditions for allowing global accumulation to flourish.

The same can be said of neoliberalism *tout court*. There is a widespread belief – particularly among the left – that neoliberalism has involved (and involves) a 'retreat', 'hollowing out' or 'withering away' of the state, which in turn has fuelled the notion that today the state has been 'overpowered' by the market. However, as we argue in Chapter 5, neoliberalism has not entailed a retreat of the state but rather a reconfiguration of the state, aimed at placing the commanding heights of economic policy 'in the hands of capital, and primarily financial interests'.[10]

It is self-evident, after all, that the process of neoliberalisation would not have been possible if *governments* – and in particular social-democratic governments – had not resorted to a wide array of tools to promote it: the liberalisation of goods and capital markets; the privatisation of resources and social services; the deregulation of business, and financial markets in particular; the reduction of workers' rights (first and foremost, the right to collective bargaining) and more generally the repression of labour activism; the lowering of taxes on wealth and capital, at the expense of the middle and working classes; the slashing of social programmes; and so on. These policies were systemically pursued throughout the West (and imposed on developing countries) with unprecedented determination, and with the support of all the major international institutions and political parties.

As noted in Chapter 5, even the loss of national sovereignty – which has been invoked in the past, and continues to be invoked today, to justify neoliberal policies – is largely the result of a willing and conscious limitation of state sovereign rights by national elites. The reason why governments chose willingly to 'tie their hands' is all too clear: as the European case epitomises, the creation of self-imposed 'external constraints' allowed national politicians to reduce the politics costs of the neoliberal transition – which clearly involved unpopular policies – by 'scapegoating' institutionalised rules and 'independent' or international institutions, which in turn were presented as an inevitable outcome of the new, harsh realities of globalisation.

Moreover, neoliberalism has been (and is) associated with various forms of authoritarian statism – that is, the opposite of the minimal state advocated by neoliberals – as states have bolstered their security and policing arms as part of a generalised militarisation of civil protest. In other words, not only does neoliberal economic policy require the presence of a strong state, but it requires the presence of an *authoritarian* state (particularly where extreme forms of neoliberalism are concerned, such as the ones experimented with in periphery countries), at both the domestic and international level (see Chapter 5). In this sense, neoliberal ideology, at least in its official anti-state guise, should be considered little more than a convenient alibi for what has been and is essentially a *political and state-driven project*. Capital remains as dependent on the state today as it was under 'Keynesianism' – to police the working classes, bail out large firms that would otherwise go bankrupt, open up markets abroad (including through military intervention), etc. The ultimate irony, or indecency, is that traditional left establishment parties have become standard-bearers for neoliberalism themselves, both while in elected office and in opposition.

In the months and years that followed the financial crash of 2007–9, capital's – and capitalism's – continued dependency on the state in the age of neoliberalism became glaringly obvious, as the governments of the US, Europe and elsewhere bailed out their respective financial institutions to the tune of trillions of euros/dollars. In Europe, following the outbreak of the so-called 'euro crisis' in 2010, this was accompanied by a multi-level assault on the post-war European social and economic model aimed at restructuring and re-engineering European societies and economies along lines more favourable to capital. This radical reconfiguration of European societies – which, again, has seen social-democratic governments at the forefront – is not based on a retreat of the state in favour of the market, but rather on a reintensification of state intervention on the side of capital.

Nonetheless, the erroneous idea of the waning nation state has become an entrenched fixture of the left. As we argue throughout the book, we consider this to be central in understanding the decline of the traditional political left and its acquiescence to neoliberalism. In view of the above, it is hardly surprising that the mainstream left is, today, utterly incapable of offering a positive vision of national sovereignty in response to neoliberal globalisation. To make matters worse, most leftists have bought into the macroeconomic myths that the establishment uses to discourage any alternative use of state fiscal capacities. For example, they have accepted without question the so-called household budget analogy, which suggests that currency-issuing governments, like households, are financially constrained, and that fiscal deficits impose crippling debt burdens on future generations – a notion that we thoroughly debunk in Chapter 8.

This has gone hand in hand with another, equally tragic, development. As discussed in Chapter 5, following its historical defeat, the left's traditional anti-capitalist focus on class slowly gave way to a liberal-individualist understanding of emancipation. Waylaid by post-modernist and post-structuralist theories, left intellectuals slowly abandoned Marxian class categories to focus, instead, on elements of political power and the use of language and narratives as a way of establishing meaning. This also defined new arenas of political struggle that were diametrically opposed to those defined by Marx. Over the past three decades, the left focus on 'capitalism' has given way to a focus on issues such as racism, gender, homophobia, multiculturalism, etc. Marginality is no longer described in terms of class but rather in terms of identity. The struggle against the illegitimate hegemony of the capitalist class has given way to the struggles of a variety of (more or less) oppressed and marginalised groups: women, ethnic and racial minorities, the LGBTQ community, etc. As a result, class struggle has ceased to be seen as the path to liberation.

In this new post-modernist world, only categories that transcend Marxian class boundaries are considered meaningful. Moreover, the institutions that evolved to defend workers against capital – such as trade unions and social-democratic political parties – have become subjugated to these non-class struggle foci. What has emerged in practically all Western countries as a result, as Nancy Fraser notes, is a perverse political alignment between 'mainstream currents of new social movements (feminism, anti-racism, multiculturalism, and LGBTQ rights), on the one side, and high-end "symbolic" and service-based business sectors (Wall Street, Silicon Valley, and Hollywood), on the other'.[11] The result is a *progressive neoliberalism* 'that mix[es] together truncated ideals of emancipation and lethal forms of financialization', with the former unwittingly lending their charisma to the latter.

As societies have become increasingly divided between well-educated, highly mobile, highly skilled, socially progressive cosmopolitan urbanites, and lower-skilled and less educated peripherals who rarely work abroad and face competition from immigrants, the mainstream left has tended to consistently side with the former. Indeed, the split between the working classes and the intellectual-cultural left can be considered one of the main reasons behind the right-wing revolt currently engulfing the West. As argued by Jonathan Haidt, the way the globalist urban elites talk and act unwittingly activates authoritarian tendencies in a subset of nationalists.[12] In a vicious feedback loop, however, the more the working classes turn to right-wing populism and nationalism, the more the intellectual-cultural left doubles down on its liberal-cosmopolitan fantasies, further radicalising the ethno-nationalism of the proletariat. As Wolfgang Streeck writes:

> Protests against material and moral degradation are suspected of being essentially fascist, especially now that the former advocates of the plebeian classes have switched to the globalization party, so that if their former clients wish to complain about the pressures of capitalist modernization, the only language at their disposal is the pre-political, untreated linguistic raw material of everyday experiences of deprivation, economic or cultural. This results in constant breaches of the rules of civilized public speech, which in turn can trigger indignation at the top and mobilization at the bottom.[13]

This is particularly evident in the European debate, where, despite the disastrous effects of the EU and monetary union, the mainstream left – often appealing to exactly the same arguments used by Callaghan and Mitterrand 30–40 years ago – continues to cling on to these institutions and to the belief that they can be reformed in a progressive direction, despite all evidence to the contrary, and to dismiss any talk of restoring a progressive agenda on the foundation of retrieved national sovereignty as a 'retreat into nationalist positions', inevitably bound to plunge the continent into 1930s-style fascism.[14] This position, as irrational as it may be, is not surprising, considering that European Economic and Monetary Union (EMU) is, after all, a brainchild of the European left (see Chapter 5). However, such a position presents numerous problems, which are ultimately rooted in a failure to understand the true nature of the EU and monetary union. First of all, it ignores the fact that the EU's economic and political constitution is structured to produce the results that we are seeing – the erosion of popular sovereignty, the massive transfer of wealth from the middle and lower classes to the upper classes, the weakening of labour and more generally the rollback of the democratic and social/economic gains that had previously been achieved by subordinate classes – and is designed precisely to impede the kind of radical reforms to which progressive integrationists or federalists aspire to.

More importantly, however, it effectively reduces the left to the role of defender of the status quo, thus allowing the political right to hegemonise the legitimate anti-systemic – and specifically anti-EU – grievances of citizens. This is tantamount to relinquishing the discursive and political battleground for a post-neoliberal hegemony – which is inextricably linked to the question of national sovereignty – to the right and extreme right. It is not hard to see that if progressive change can only be implemented at the global or even European level – in other words, if the alternative to the status quo offered to electorates is one between *reactionary nationalism* and *progressive globalism* – then the left has already lost the battle.

It needn't be this way, however. As we argue in the second part of the book, a progressive, emancipatory vision of national sovereignty that offers a radical alternative to both the right and the neoliberals – one based on popular sovereignty, democratic control over the economy, full employment, social justice, redistribution from the rich to the poor, inclusivity and the socio-ecological transformation of production and society – is possible. Indeed, it is necessary. As J. W. Mason writes:

> Whatever [supranational] arrangements we can imagine in principle, the systems of social security, labor regulation, environmental protection, and redistribution of income and wealth that in fact exist are national in scope and are operated by national governments. By definition, any struggle to preserve social democracy as it exists today is a struggle to defend national institutions.[15]

As we contend in this book, the struggle to defend the democratic sovereign from the onslaught of neoliberal globalisation is the only basis on which the left can be refounded (and the nationalist right challenged). However, this is not enough. The left also needs to abandon its obsession with identity politics and retrieve the 'more expansive, anti-hierarchical, egalitarian, class-sensitive, anti-capitalist understandings of emancipation' that used to be its trademark (which, of course, is not in contradiction with the struggle against racism, patriarchy, xenophobia and other forms of oppression and discrimination).[16]

Fully embracing a progressive vision of sovereignty also means abandoning the many false macroeconomic myths that plague left-wing and progressive thinkers. One of the most pervasive and persistent myths is the assumption that governments are revenue-constrained, that is, that they need to 'fund' their expenses through taxes or debt. This leads to the corollary that governments have to 'live within their means', since ongoing deficits will inevitably result in an 'excessive' accumulation of debt, which in turn is assumed to be 'unsustainable' in the long run. In reality, as we show in Chapter 8, monetarily sovereign (or currency-issuing) governments – which nowadays include most governments – are *never* revenue-constrained because they issue their own currency by legislative fiat and *always* have the means to achieve and sustain full employment and social justice.

In this sense, a progressive vision of national sovereignty should aim to reconstruct and redefine the national state as a place where citizens can seek refuge 'in democratic protection, popular rule, local autonomy, collective goods and egalitarian traditions', as Streeck argues, rather than a culturally and ethnically homogenised society.[17] This is also the necessary prerequisite for the construction of a new international(ist) world order, based on interdependent but independent sovereign states. It is such a vision that we present in this book.

PART I

The Great Transformation Redux: From Keynesianism to Neoliberalism – and Beyond

1

Broken Paradise:
A Critical Assessment of the
Keynesian 'Full Employment' Era

Looking back on the 30-year-long economic expansion that followed World War II, Adam Przeworski and Michael Wallerstein concluded that 'by most criteria of economic progress the Keynesian era was a success'.[1] It is hard to disagree: throughout the West, from the mid-1940s until the early 1970s, countries enjoyed lower levels of unemployment, greater economic stability and higher levels of economic growth than ever before. That stability, particularly in the US, also rested on a strong financial regulatory framework: on the widespread provision of deposit insurance to stop bank runs; strict regulation of the financial system, including the separation of commercial banking from investment banking; and extensive capital controls to reduce currency volatility. These domestic and international restrictions 'kept financial excesses and bubbles under control for over a quarter of a century'.[2] Wages and living standards rose, and – especially in Europe – a variety of policies and institutions for welfare and social protection (also known as the 'welfare state') were created, including sustained investment in universally available social services such as education and health. Few people would deny that this was, indeed, a 'golden age' for capitalism.

However, when it comes to explaining what made this exceptional period possible and why it came to an end, theories abound. Most contemporary Keynesians subscribe to a quasi-idealist view of history – that is, one that stresses the central role of ideas and ideals in human history. This is perhaps unsurprising, considering that Keynes himself famously noted: 'Practical men who believe themselves to be quite exempt from any intellectual influence, are usually the slaves of some defunct economist. Madmen in authority, who hear voices in the air, are distilling their frenzy from some academic scribbler of a few years back.'[3]

According to this view, the social and economic achievements of the post-war period are largely attributable to the revolution in economic thinking spearheaded by the British economist John Maynard Keynes. Throughout the 1920s and 1930s, Keynes overturned the old classical (neoclassical) paradigm, rooted in the doctrine of *laissez-faire* ('let it be') free-market capitalism, which held that markets are fundamentally self-regulating. The understanding was that the economy, if left to its own devices – that is, with the government intervening as little as possible – would automatically generate stability and full employment, as long as workers were flexible in their wage demands. The Great Depression of the 1930s that followed the stock market crash of 1929 – where minimal financial regulation, little-understood financial products and overindebted households and banks all conspired to create a huge speculative bubble which, when it burst, brought the US financial system crashing down, and with it the entire global economy – clearly challenged traditional *laissez-faire* economic theories.

This bolstered Keynes' argument – spelled out at length in his masterpiece, *The General Theory of Employment, Interest, and Money*, published in 1936 – that aggregate spending determined the overall level of economic activity, and that inadequate aggregate spending could lead to prolonged periods of high unemployment (what he called 'under-employment equilibrium'). Thus, he advocated the use of debt-based expansionary fiscal and monetary measures and a strict regulatory framework to counter capitalism's tendency towards financial crises and disequilibrium, and to mitigate the adverse effects of economic recessions and depressions, first and foremost by creating jobs that the private sector was unable or unwilling to provide. The bottom line of Keynes' argument was that *the government always has the ability to determine the overall level of spending and employment in the economy*. In other words, full employment was a realistic goal that could be pursued at all times.

Yet politicians were slow to catch on. When the speculative bubbles in both Europe and the United States burst in the aftermath of the Wall Street crash of 1929, various countries (to varying degrees, and more or less willingly) turned to austerity as a perceived 'cure' for the excesses of the previous decade. In the United States, president Herbert Hoover, a year after the crash, declared that 'economic depression cannot be cured by legislative action or executive pronouncements' and that 'economic wounds must be healed by the action of the cells of the economic body – the producers and consumers themselves'.[4] At first Hoover and his officials downplayed the stock market crash, claiming that the economic slump would be only temporary. When the situation did not improve, Hoover advocated a strict *laissez-faire* policy, dictating that the federal government should not interfere with the economy but rather let the economy right itself. He counselled that 'every individual should sustain faith and courage' and 'each should maintain self-reliance'.[5] Even though Hoover supported a doubling of government expenditure on public works projects, he also firmly believed in the need for a balanced budget. As Nouriel Roubini and Stephen Mihm observe, Hoover 'wanted to reconcile contradictory aims: to cultivate self-reliance, to provide government help in a time of crisis, and to maintain fiscal discipline. This was impossible.'[6] In fact, it is widely agreed that Hoover's inaction was responsible for the worsening of the Great Depression.

If the United States' reaction under Hoover can be described as 'too little, too late', Europe's reaction in the late 1920s and early 1930s actively contributed to the downward spiral of the Great Depression, setting the stage for World War II. Austerity was the dominant response of European governments during the early years of the Great Depression. The political consequences are well known. Anti-systemic parties gained strength all across the continent, most notably in Germany. While 24 European regimes had been democratic in 1920, the number was down to eleven in 1939.[7] Various historians and economists see the rise of Hitler as a direct consequence of the austerity policies indirectly imposed on Germany by its creditors following the economic crash of the late 1920s. Ewald Nowotny, the current head of Austria's national bank, stated that it was precisely 'the single-minded concentration on austerity policy' in the 1930s that 'led to mass unemployment, a breakdown of democratic systems and, at the end, to the catastrophe of Nazism'.[8] Historian Steven Bryan agrees: 'During the 1920s and 1930s it was precisely the refusal to acknowledge the social and political consequences of austerity that helped bring about not only the depression, but also the authoritarian governments of the 1930s.'[9]

The 1930s were characterised by an opposite trend: the rise of so-called state capitalism, a concept that was first developed by Lenin and Bukharin in relation to the increased state involvement in capitalist accumulation that had begun in the 1880s. Essentially, in response to the failure of private capital to recover from the post-crash slump, all the major European states started extending their control or ownership over key national industries such as coal, steel, transport and electricity generation. The rise of state capitalism was accompanied by a drastic decline in cross-border intra-European trade and transactions, as each national state-industrial complex 'attempted to undertake as wide a range as possible of economic and military functions within its own boundaries'.[10] Military competition increasingly took the place of economic competition: 'The interpenetration of national capitals and the national state finds expression in an important change in the way in which capitalist competition itself takes place. It is increasingly regulated within national boundaries, while assuming the form of military, as well as (or even instead of) market competition internationally'.[11]

As Europe descended into chaos, the United States, under the newly elected president Franklin D. Roosevelt, chose to tackle the Great Depression in a radically different way. By 1933, when Roosevelt was elected president, the crisis had wrought havoc and destruction across the United States. Roosevelt, unlike his predecessor Hoover – whose apathy and inaction had earned him the nickname of 'do-nothing president' – understood the need to act swiftly and decisively. More importantly, he understood the root cause of the Great Depression: out-of-control financial capitalism, which called for radical reforms of the US financial system. In a legislative flurry known as 'the 100 days', Roosevelt forced through more radical reforms in three months that Hoover had done in four years, with some of the laws being proposed, discussed and voted on in a single day. As the French economist Pierre Larrouturou writes, Roosevelt's 'aim was not to "reassure the markets", but to *rein them in*'.[12] The laws and regulative agencies created by Roosevelt to 'rein in the markets' included the Glass–Steagall Act of 1933, which separated commercial and investment banking; the Securities Act of 1933, which regulated the securities market; and the setting-up of the Securities and Exchange Commission. Furthermore, Roosevelt understood that financial reform, although necessary, was not enough: he also did away with Hoover's let-the-markets-sort-themselves-out approach, and implemented a huge government stimulus plan to kick-start the economy, known as the New Deal, during which the government funded countless public projects and social programmes, including Social Security. It included 24,000 miles of sewer lines, 480 airports, 78,000 bridges, 780 hospitals, 572,000 miles of highway, and upwards of 15,000 schools, court houses and other public buildings.[13]

Even though Roosevelt's New Deal was partly inspired by Keynes' writings, the British economist's argument was won not so much by Roosevelt's historical New Deal but by World War II, which was a sharp practical lesson in Keynesianism, as Keynes' colleague at Cambridge, Joan Robinson, wrote.[14] According to the idealist narrative, the military conflict showed the traumatised elites of the Western world, as well as the swelling and increasingly powerful ranks of unionised workers, that large-scale government spending could bring an economy to full employment very quickly when private spending declined, and could thus be used to avoid a repetition of the deadly 1930s mixture of high unemployment, austerity, national aggression and beggar-thy-neighbour policies. Keynesianism (or better, as we shall see, the 'bastardised'[15] version of Keynes' approach that came to be known as neo-Keynesianism) thus emerged from the war as the most popular school of economic theory in the Western world, heralding the so-called Fordist-Keynesian era of macroeconomic policy.

Though the precise institutional forms of the Fordist-Keynesian model differed from one country to another, depending primarily on the political context in which they were introduced, in general terms this period was marked by the heavy use of public spending to supplement private spending – and more generally by the systematic and pervasive involvement of the state in the economy – with the aim of maintaining full employment, on the basis of a class compromise between labour and capital. This included 'the regulation of the reproduction of the working class through the wage [system], social insurance and social security, on the basis of a generalised expectation of rising wages'.[16] On capital's behalf, this meant 'accepting' that '[t]he state could focus on full employment, economic growth and the welfare of its citizens, and that state power should be freely deployed alongside of, or if necessary, intervening in or substituting for market processes to achieve these ends'.[17]

According to the idealist narrative, this model started to crumble in the 1970s under the weight of the so-called neoliberal counter-revolution: an ideological war on Keynesianism waged by a new generation of die-hard free-market economists, led by the anti-Keynesian *par excellence* of the second half of the twentieth century, Milton Friedman. Ultimately, the idealist narrative rests on a fundamental faith in the power of ideas to shape the world, and thus views the shift from the Keynesian to the neoliberal era largely as *the victory of one ideology over another*, rather than the result of changes in the inner functioning of the global economic system. Implicit in such an idea- and agent-centred worldview is the understanding that at any given time there are always, potentially, different varieties of capitalism to choose from.

THE REGULATION VIEW:
KEYNESIANISM AS A CAPITALIST REGIME OF ACCUMULATION

An alternative explanation of the Keynesian era is the one put forward by the so-called regulation theory school, a Marxist-influenced approach to radical political economy that emerged in the late 1960s. The regulation theory school was a reaction to orthodox Marxist theories that offered a simple and direct explanation of historical change in terms of a 'law of accumulation'. Regulationists countered that there is a multiplicity of social forces operating in modern history alongside capital – working-class resistance, environmental change, race, patriarchy, gender, culture, etc. – that cannot be explained simply as functions of capitalism's inner logic. In the founding work of regulation theory, French economist Michel Aglietta set out his goal of giving 'a theoretical foundation to the periodization of capitalism into successive stages of historical evolution'.[18] According to regulation theory, capitalism develops across its history through a series of discontinuous stages. Each distinctive stage of capitalist development is based on an industrial paradigm (mass production, for example), which in turn gives rise to a *regime of accumulation* or pattern of growth (a pattern of production and consumption which allows for capital accumulation). Accumulation regimes are periods of relatively settled economic growth and profit across a nation or region. These periods of capital accumulation are underpinned, or stabilised, by a *mode of regulation*: a plethora of laws, institutions, customs and hegemonies, both national and international, that create the environment for long-run capitalist profit and facilitate the reproduction of a particular accumulation regime. Such regimes eventually become exhausted, falling into crisis, and are torn down as capitalism seeks to remake itself and return to a period of profit. However, the construction of a new regime of accumulation cannot be accomplished solely through the market. As Simon Clarke noted, it is the state, on the basis of the outcome of the inevitable class struggle that ensues during the transition from one phase to another, that 'ultimately secures the functional integration of the regime of accumulation' by 'sponsoring the restructuring of the regime of accumulation and associated forms of regulation, including those that are a part of the state itself', thus imposing order on to chaos.[19]

In regulation terms, Fordist-Keynesianism was a specific stage of capitalism characterised by a stage-specific regime of accumulation. Bob Jessop describes the Fordist accumulation regime as one where a national economy's dynamism

> would be based on intensive accumulation in one or more leading sectors, rising productivity due to economies of scale and/or other sources of relative surplus value, rising wages indexed to rising productivity and profitability, a corresponding growth in mass consumption, rapid domestic expansion in the production of mass consumer goods and/or the various complementary goods and services needed to enjoy them, and, to close the circuit, sufficient export earnings to finance the import of mass consumer goods and other inputs needed to keep the virtuous circle in operation.[20]

The state played a vital role in the promotion of this virtuous circle: it managed aggregate demand, through state consumption as well as through the transfer and redistribution of income, so that firms would have enough confidence to undertake extended and expensive R&D (research and development) as well as the subsequent heavy capital investment involved in complex mass production; it generalised mass consumption norms so that most citizens could share in the prosperity generated by rising economies of scale; it supported firms through financial and investment aid, R&D funds, public procurement, market protection, etc.; it invested heavily in R&D itself, particularly in areas where the private sector was too risk-averse, thus playing a key entrepreneurial role in the development and commercialisation of new growth-enhancing and profit-boosting technologies in areas such as aviation, nuclear energy, computers, the Internet, the biotechnology revolution, etc., as Mariana Mazzucato shows in her book *The Entrepreneurial State*;[21] it created telecommunications and transport networks, a crucial infrastructure for modern economies; it invested in public education, thus supplying firms with an increasingly skilled workforce; and, more generally, it created the national and international regulatory framework needed for the smooth functioning of the system (through the global umbrella of US hegemony, the repression of speculative finance, the stabilisation of exchange rates, the secure provision of energy, etc.).

In other words, as Stuart Hall and others wrote in the seminal 1978 book *Policing the Crisis*, the state ended up 'managing capital where capital could no longer successfully manage itself', which meant '*drawing the economic class struggle increasingly on to its own terrain* [in] a more overt and direct effort by the state to manage the political class struggle'.[22] The state increasingly played the role of striking 'bargains' with the working class, to give it a 'stake' in the system through the mediation of the organised labour movement, whose institutions had 'progressively been incorporated into the management of the economy as one of its major corporate supports'.[23] This meant regulating an uneasy balance between concessions and restraints, oriented towards supporting capital's growth and stability in the long term, and ensuring the 'pacification and harmonisation of the class struggle'.[24]

From a regulationist perspective, the expansion of the state's responsibilities during the Fordist-Keynesian era was not simply something that was begrudgingly accepted by the capitalist class, in the name of a class compromise imposed upon them by powerful unions and enlightened political elites (though that might have certainly been the case for individual capitalists); on the contrary, *state interventionism was an indispensable element of the Fordist mode of regulation*. Of course, one should not take this to mean that class struggle or Keynes' theories played no role whatsoever in the creation of this unique period in human history, as some orthodox Marxists argue. Far from it. It simply means that the Keynesian era cannot be explained solely in terms of working-class strength or the triumph of Keynesian ideology, as argued by the idealists, just as it cannot be explained solely in terms of the challenge posed by the Soviet Union or the trauma caused by the war. Nor can it be explained as the 'inevitable' result of the emergence of Fordist mass production technologies, which had in fact already been available for decades. As already mentioned, regulation theory emerged precisely in response to this kind of extreme historical determinism. Instead, the Fordist-Keynesian regime of accumulation's 30-year-long *pax moneta* should be viewed as the outcome of the fortuitous *confluence*, in the aftermath of World War II, of the 'right' social, ideological, political, economic, technical and institutional conditions. 'In short, the emergence of a new stage capitalism is never a fait accompli', Richard Westra writes. 'Nor can it be explained by economic theory alone.'[25] It is always the result of the complex interaction between different dimensions of the historical process.

It goes without saying that Fordism would hardly have been possible if Keynes had not provided the technical and ideological foundations for class compromise by offering capitalists *and* workers a framework through which to work out their conflicting distributional claims in a mutually beneficial manner (for a while at least). This was nothing less than revolutionary. Until Keynes came along, left politics had been largely dominated by Marxist-inspired socialist economic theory. While Marxism had been hugely useful as a tool for analysing the inner workings of capitalism and for mobilising the working classes, in practical terms – insofar as mass movements of the left in capitalist societies had been concerned – it had proven of little use, if not as a justification for revolutionary goals. As Przeworski and Wallerstein wrote: 'Marx's economics, even its most sophisticated version, is not a helpful tool for addressing workers' distributional claims within capitalism and it is useless as a framework for administering capitalist economies'.[26]

With Keynesianism, on the other hand, 'the distribution bias of the left toward their electoral constituency found a rationalization in a technical economic theory'.[27] This supplied working-class parties with a justification for holding office within capitalist societies without necessarily pushing for all-out socialism: if Keynesianism could resolve the contradictions of the capitalist mode of production, the question of the ownership of the means of production became secondary. At the same time, Keynesianism showed capitalists that workers' demands for increased consumption, higher wages and better social provisions needn't necessarily come at the expense of profits, productivity and growth, as claimed by orthodox economic theories; on the contrary, Keynes argued that consumption (demand) was the *motor force* of production, and therefore that higher consumption and government spending was in the interest of capitalists as well. As Léon Blum put it, 'a better distribution … would revive production at the same time that it would satisfy justice'.[28]

It is equally clear, however, that capital adopted Keynesianism *also* 'because it believed that the various restrictions and regulations would be beneficial to the process of capital accumulation *at that historical moment*, particularly in comparison with the poor record of accumulation presented by its recent experience without those restrictions during the Great Depression'.[29] Essentially, Keynesianism expressed the belief that rising wages and public expenditure would resolve the contradictions inherent in capital accumulation:

> On the one hand, the growth of the mass market would banish the problem of overproduction that had underlain crises, depressions and wars. On the other hand, rising wages, welfare benefits and public services would reconcile the working class to its subordination to the wage form while providing the healthy, educated and contented labour force required to sustain accumulation.[30]

There was some resistance to the new Keynesian orthodoxy: a minority of economists, notably Friedrich Hayek and Milton Friedman, continued to hold on to the old doctrine. Campbell claims that 'most finance capital never accepted the Keynesian compromise', but that it accounted for only 15 per cent of capital.[31] Governments and large corporations, on the other hand, 'accepted Keynesian ideology because increased economic activity by the state was accompanied by much higher levels of profitability in the US and major European states than under the pre-war ideology of economic liberalism'.[32] As Chris Harman notes:

> Keynesianism as an ideology reflected the reality of capitalism in the period after the Second World War. National economies were increasingly dominated by near-monopolies that worked with the state to struggle for global dominance against near-monopolies based in other national economies. The result was a seemingly relentless trend towards increased state involvement in capitalist accumulation.[33]

THE DOMESTICATION – OR HIJACKING – OF KEYNES' THEORIES

The system was able to sustain growth and a relatively equitable distribution of income/wealth in advanced countries for three decades, as real wage growth kept pace with productivity growth. Workers felt they were sharing in the overall gains of the system. This leads to romanticised and nostalgia-ridden accounts of that period by contemporary Keynesians, even though it was also riddled with profound contradictions, at both the national and international level. On 27 December 1971, Joan Robinson delivered a lecture at an American Economic Association meeting.[34] The topic of her paper was what she termed 'the second crisis of economic theory'. The first crisis had been the crisis of neoclassical theory in the wake of the Great Depression, which had paved the way to the rise of Keynesianism. The second crisis, which Robinson saw unfolding at the beginning of the 1970s, was a crisis of Keynesianism itself. 'The second crisis is quite different', she noted. 'The first crisis arose from the breakdown of a theory which could not account for the *level* of employment. The second crisis arises from a theory that cannot account for the *content* of employment.'[35]

What she meant was that, following World War II, Western governments had taken up Keynes' lesson on *how* to achieve full employment and sustained output through government spending, but had conveniently discarded his message about what should be produced, by and for whom, and for what ends, and dismissed questions as to whether the success of standard policy could be sustained. On various occasions Keynes conceded that he did not expect either monetary or fiscal instruments to be powerful enough to maintain stability and guarantee the positive development of human society; that, he argued, would require a general social control over investment ('a somewhat comprehensive socialisation of investment', as he described it)[36] and a certain degree of state planning – a middle way between the extremes of complete state control and leaving decisions entirely in private hands – in response to 'the failure of the unplanned industrial world of Western Europe and America to regulate itself to the best advantage'.[37] In a 1932 radio broadcast, Keynes explained his concept of democratic state planning:

> [I]t is of the essence of state planning to do those things which in the nature of the case lie outside the scope of the individual. It differs from Socialism and from Communism in that it does not seek to aggrandise the province of the state for its own sake. It does not aim at superseding the individual within the field of operations appropriate to the individual, or of transforming the wage system, or of abolishing the profit motive. *Its object is to take hold of the central controls and to govern them with deliberate foresight and thus modify and condition the environment within which the individual freely operates with and against other individuals.*[38]

For Keynes, the purpose of such a policy was about much more than simply maintaining an optimum level of output and abolishing unemployment; its ultimate aim was nothing less than to usher in a new (post-capitalist?) era for humanity, one in which the basic economic needs of men would be satisfied and thus 'for the first time since his creation man will be faced with his real, his permanent problem – how to use his freedom from pressing economic cares, how to occupy the leisure, which science and compound interest will have won for him, to live wisely and agreeably and well'.[39]

Regrettably, all notions of 'socialisation', along with the more radical elements of the *General Theory* – on issues such as the management of interest rates, the interactions between the financial and the 'real' economy, wages and prices, the non-neutrality of money, the international monetary system, etc. – were lost in the formalisation (and normalisation) that his theories underwent in the immediate post-war period. While some economists drew more radical implications from Keynes' theory, the forefathers of mainstream 'Keynesianism', known as neo-Keynesianism (which Joan Robinson would later label 'bastard Keynesianism') attempted – successfully in the end – to reconcile Keynesian macroeconomics with neoclassical microeconomics (rational and optimising households and firms, competitive markets where price movements ensure full employment, etc.), in what came to be known as the 'neoclassical synthesis'. As Robinson wrote, 'the economists took over Keynes and erected the new orthodox'.[40] Within a year of the *General Theory* being published, the British economist John Hicks proposed the so-called IS-LM (Investment Saving-Liquidity Preference) model of 'general equilibrium', which would become one of the centrepieces of the neoclassical synthesis. Even though it represented, at best, a gross simplification of Keynes' original vision – as Lars P. Syll writes, 'almost nothing in the post-*General Theory* writings of Keynes suggests him considering Hicks's IS-LM anywhere near a faithful rendering of his thought'[41] – the model soon became synonymous with 'Keynesianism'.

There were ideological and political, as well as practical, reasons for this. Keynes' biographer, Robert Skidelsky, wrote that in the context of the 'desperate urgency' to cure the mass unemployment arising from the Great Depression,

> it was not surprising that the earliest 'Keynesians' saw his book as a machine for policy, and interpreted it primarily as providing a rationale for public spending. ... [T]he leading constructors of the 'IS-LM' Keynesianism, had a clear motive: to reconcile Keynesians and non-Keynesians, so that the ground for policy could be quickly

cleared. These early theoretical models incorporated features which were not at all evident in the magnum opus, but which conformed more closely to orthodox theory.[42]

This trend towards the 'domestication' of Keynes' theories continued after the war. The political atmosphere of the time, particularly in the United States, discouraged those who might have attempted to explain the implications of Keynes' revolutionary theory fully. The American economist Paul Samuelson is usually credited for saving the textbook pedagogical basis of the Keynesian revolution from the anti-communist hysteria that ravaged American academia in the years immediately following the war.[43] In his effort to reconcile Keynesian economics with neoclassical theory, Samuelson argued that high unemployment is always a temporary phenomenon caused by the fact that wages and prices tend to be rigid in the short term; eventually they will fall, causing the economy to self-correct and unemployment to decline, even if the government takes no corrective action. In Keynes' vision, however, there is no tendency for the economy to self-correct. Left to itself, a market economy may well remain permanently depressed. This sleight of hand 'saved the term "Keynesian" from being excoriated' from the post-war textbooks, Paul Davidson writes. 'But the cost of such a saving was to sever the meaning of Keynes's theory in mainstream economic theory from its *General Theory* analytical roots. ... Samuelson's view of Keynesianism resulted in aborting Keynes' revolutionary analysis from altering the foundation of mainstream macroeconomics.'[44]

Even worse, this hijacking of the *General Theory* ultimately led to the so-called 'Keynesian' approach being discredited during the 1970s, as we shall see, even though this approach was a pale reflection of what Keynes had developed in the 1930s.

FROM UTOPIA TO NIGHTMARE

In policy terms, as far as the theory was concerned, once the more radical layers of Keynes' theories had been stripped away, what was left was little more than the need to accord the state more discretion in its fiscal and monetary policies, which in itself is not particularly radical or even progressive (though most governments went well beyond that, as we have seen). As Joan Robinson wrote:

Now that we all agree that government expenditure can maintain employment we should argue about what the expenditure should be for. Keynes did not *want* anyone to dig holes and fill them. He indulged in a pleasant daydream of a world in which, when investment had been kept at the full employment level for thirty years or so, all needs for capital installations would have been met, property income would have been abolished, poverty would have disappeared and civilized life could begin. But the economists took up the argument at the point where it had broken off before the war. When there is unemployment and low profits the government must spend on something or other – it does not matter what. As we know, for twenty-five years serious recessions were avoided by following this policy. The most convenient thing for a government to spend on is armaments. The military-industrial complex took charge.[45]

This development was the focus of the 1968 modern classic by Paul Baran and Paul Sweezy, *Monopoly Capital*, in which the authors described the American political-economic system as one where the basic needs for human development, such as education and housing, went unmet, while a belligerent militarism – also involving Europe, through NATO – and all the negative cultural traits associated with consumerism were pursued with great effort in the interest of profit (military spending constituted the majority of federal government spending until 1969).[46] Governmental direct expenditure, dominated by armaments and militarism, was mostly non-targeted and unproductive, while the welfare system was based on money transfer payments, not job and resource creation.[47] The reason why the elites favour military spending over other forms of government spending is easily understandable. An informative *Business Week* article published in 1949 recognised that social spending could have the same 'pump-priming' effect as military spending, but pointed out that for businessmen 'there's a tremendous social and economic difference between welfare pump-priming and military pump-priming'.[48] The latter 'doesn't really alter the structure of the economy'. For the businessman, it's just another order. But welfare and public works spending 'does alter the economy. It makes new channels of its own. It creates new institutions. It redistributes income.' And so on. Military spending enhances capitalist interests and scarcely involves the public, but social spending does, and has a democratising effect. For reasons like these, military spending is much preferred.[49] As Robinson noted, this was the toxic legacy of the hijacking of Keynes' theories:

> Whatever were the deeper forces leading into the hypertrophy of military power after the world war was over, certainly they could not have had such free play if the doctrine of sound finance had still been respected. It was the so-called Keynesians who persuaded successive presidents that there is no harm in a budget deficit and left the military-industrial complex to take advantage of it. So it has come about that Keynes' pleasant daydream was turned into a nightmare of terror.[50]

Meanwhile, gross domestic product (GDP) growth became an end in itself. As a result, full employment was indeed achieved, but at a very heavy price (which we are still paying today): for those at the periphery of the United States' informal empire – war, poverty, exploitation and environmental devastation; for the 'lucky few' under the umbrella of the US 'protectorate system'[51] – rampant consumerism, alienation, pollution and degradation of the social and biological environment. In this sense, one could indeed say that the neoliberal era 'came from the womb of the Keynesian era itself', as Riccardo Bellofiore writes.[52] In *A Contribution to the Critique of Hegel's Philosophy of Right*, Marx suggested that humans have the capacity for self-deceit and create religions for that purpose. He wrote: 'Religious suffering is, at one and the same time, the expression of real suffering and a protest against real suffering. Religion is the sigh of the oppressed creature, the heart of a heartless world, and the soul of soulless conditions. It is the opium of the people.'[53]

After World War II, mass consumption became the new 'opium of the people'. In 1950, American sociologist David Riesman published *The Lonely Crowd: A Study of the Changing American Character*, which described middle-class life in the US.[54] It went on to become the bestselling sociology book of all time. Previously, people had what Riesman calls an 'inner-directed' motivation, meaning that they acted according to their own set of behavioural rules. In the mass consumption age, on the other hand, people increasingly understood their 'self' with reference to the way they observed everyone else living.

Consumerism defined visible patterns for others to mimic – the type and size of car in the driveway, the style of house, the clothing worn, etc. One of the consequences of this patterned behaviour was to divert people's attention away from the underlying conflict between labour and capital, which had always been apparent in the pre-Keynesian era, before the consumption possibilities expanded for all. Conformity also allowed capitalists to saturate markets with mass-produced and ever-cheaper products that delivered high margins. As the purchasing power of workers increased, giving them the means to access the ever-growing torrent of goods (and then services) flowing into the shops, their attention increasingly shifted away from the production process towards the shopping centre. And this despite the fact that the rapid accumulation of capital in the post-war boom imposed a heavy burden on workers: structural changes required a high degree of labour mobility, uprooting workers and destroying their communities. Technological changes demanded a high degree of adaptability on the part of workers, and imposed a progressive intensification of labour to meet competitive pressure. Simon Clarke noted that '[t]he working class as a whole was reconciled to such pressures by the generalisation of the collaborative system of industrial relations on the basis of a generalised expectation of a rising standard of living, and by the extension and rationalisation of the welfare apparatus'.[55] Ultimately, one could argue that while the material conditions for workers improved during this period and attenuated their desire for an overt confrontation with capital, it also set in place the complacency, driven by mass consumption, that would allow the neoliberal resurgence in the 1970s.

This also led to an 'end of history' complacency among a large section of the left, stemming in part from a failure to appreciate the extent to which the expansion of the state's responsibilities under the Fordist-Keynesian system was, in fact, a crucial component of that specific regime of accumulation. As Leo Panitch notes, many social democrats convinced themselves 'that they had done much more than they actually had to shift the balance of class power, and the relationship between states and markets'.[56] For example, in his 1956 book *The Future of Socialism*, the British Labour politician Anthony Crosland criticised Marxist notions and Labour Party orthodoxy that public ownership of the means of production was essential to make socialism work, arguing that the developed world (or Britain at least) had already entered a post-capitalist phase, in which all the characteristic features of capitalism had been *permanently* eliminated, thanks to a fundamental shift of power in favour of labour vis-à-vis capital, and of the state vis-à-vis the market.[57] Needless to say, this was not the case.

BRETTON WOODS: JUST ANOTHER GOLD STANDARD?

Meanwhile, at the international level the contradictions inherent in the Bretton Woods arrangements – which had provided an international framework for currency stability in the immediate post-war years – had already started to emerge by the late 1950s. The so-called Bretton Woods system – also known as the dollar exchange standard or gold–dollar (dollar–gold) standard – was essentially a modified gold standard, whereby the central banks of most advanced nations were required to maintain their currencies at agreed fixed rates against the US dollar, which in turn was convertible into gold at US$35 per ounce. It was thought that this would provide a nominal anchor for the exchange rate system, given the stability of the gold price. The system, however, came under pressure from the start because countries with trade deficits always faced downward pressure on their currencies, just like they did under the gold standard. As in the previous system, in order to maintain their exchange rates they had to buy their own currencies in the foreign exchange markets using their foreign currency reserves, push up domestic interest rates to attract capital inflow, and/or constrict government spending to restrain imports. In other words, under the Bretton Woods system, governments faced very real policy constraints – similar to the ones that had led to the breakdown of the gold standard. The nations with weaker currencies were often faced with poor growth rates, higher unemployment and depleted foreign reserves, which fuelled political instability. The effective operation of the system required all the participating nations to have a more or less similar trade strength, which of course was impossible and ultimately proved to be its undoing.

The use of the US dollar as a reserve currency – which effectively bestowed upon the United States the 'exorbitant privilege' of not having to pay for its imports, unlike everyone else, because it could simply help itself to the foreign goods and services it needed by paying foreigners with its own currency, 'printed' (issued) at no cost – further exacerbated the instability of the Bretton Woods system. The Belgian economist Robert Triffin warned in the early 1960s that the system required the US to run permanent balance-of-payments deficits so that other nations, which used the US dollar as the dominant currency in international transactions, would be able to acquire them. By 1959 – due to money flowing out of the US through the Marshall Plan, the military budget and American purchases of foreign goods – the number of US dollars in circulation had exceeded the amount of gold that was backing them up. As a result, other countries started to worry about the value of their growing dollar holdings, and to question whether the US would continue to maintain the gold convertibility indefinitely. This led nations to increasingly exercise their right to convert their dollar holdings into gold, which significantly reduced the stock of US-held gold reserves. The so-called Triffin paradox (or Triffin dilemma) was that the Bretton Woods system required the expansion of US dollars into world markets, which undermined confidence in the dollar's value and led to increased demands for convertibility back into gold. The loss of gold reserves, in turn, further reinforced the view that the US dollar was overvalued. The only way for the United States to resolve the dilemma would have been to cut its budget deficit and raise interest rates to attract dollars back into the country. But this would have pushed the US economy into recession, which was politically unpalatable. It was also inconsistent with the country's policy objectives at home (the so-called 'war on poverty') and abroad (the maintenance and expansion of the global network of semi-permanent US installations and the prosecution of the Vietnam War).

US spending associated with the Vietnam War eventually overheated the domestic economy and expanded US liquidity in the world markets even further. The resulting inflation was then transmitted through the fixed exchange rate system to Europe and beyond, because the increased trade deficit in the US fuelled stimulatory trade surpluses in other nations. Throughout the 1960s, it became increasingly clear that other nations could not run an independent monetary policy as a result of their central banks having to maintain the exchange rate parities under the Bretton Woods agreement: if the exchange rate was under attack (due to a balance-of-payments deficit, for example), the central bank would have to intervene to soak up the local currency with its reserves of foreign currency (principally US dollars). The scope for fiscal policy was also severely restricted: if this was used too aggressively, the central bank would be forced to pursue a restrictive monetary policy to curb the rise in imports engendered by the fiscal expansion, which in turn would cause the domestic economy to contract (as the money supply fell) and unemployment to rise. Although countries could revalue or devalue (one-off realignments), this was frowned upon and not common. Ultimately, it is clear that under the dollar exchange standard, just like under the pure gold standard, governments faced severe constraints on their autonomy. Similarly, the system was politically difficult to maintain because of the social instability arising from unemployment. The tensions continued to build up throughout the 1960s and eventually exploded in August 1971, leading to the collapse of the Bretton Woods system, after US president Nixon suspended the convertibility of US dollars into gold. Meanwhile, contradictions in, and threats to, the post-war Keynesian framework started emerging at the domestic level as well.

2

Destined to Fail: Understanding the Crisis of Keynesianism and the Rise of Neoliberalism

THE IDEALIST VIEW (AGAIN): NEOLIBERALISM AS
THE VICTORY OF ONE IDEOLOGY OVER ANOTHER

In the early 1970s, the capitalist world economy entered a period of instability and crisis. Even though the collective GDP of the advanced economies was expanding (though at a diminished rate compared to previous decades), and the core capitalist countries were far richer than ever before, many of the problems that had plagued the capitalist economies prior to the Keynesian era – poverty, squalor, mass unemployment, inequality, instability (within as well as between nations) – reappeared. As a result, the Keynesian framework, and the institutions and policies associated with it, which until then had sustained an ever-rising tide of economic prosperity and employment in advanced countries (albeit afflicted by serious problems, as we have seen), came increasingly into question. Within two decades, full employment policies were abandoned in virtually all advanced countries, replaced by nominally 'free-market' policies – based upon the privatisation of state enterprises, trade liberalisation, deregulation of the financial sector and fiscal retrenchment, among other things – that today generally fall under the rubric of neoliberalism. To this day, the causes of this seismic ideological, economic and political paradigm shift are still hotly debated.

One school of thought, common to those of an idealist disposition, views the shift from the Keynesian to the neoliberal era largely as the victory of one ideology over another. According to this narrative, the Keynesian model started to crumble in the 1970s under the weight of the so-called neoliberal counter-revolution: an ideological war on Keynesianism (which initially took the form of monetarism) waged by a new generation of die-hard free-market economists, mostly based at the

University of Chicago, led by Milton Friedman. As already mentioned, such a conclusion rests on a fundamental faith in the power of ideas to shape the world. And what better proof of this than Friedman's extraordinary career? Though Friedman's work covered a wide range of topics, his public image was largely defined by his theories on monetary policy. By the late 1960s, Friedman had already achieved star-like status, at least in the realm of the economics profession. In 1967 he was elected president of the influential American Economic Association (AEA). In his 1967 presidential address to the AEA, Friedman laid out the main tenets of monetarism, which rested on the belief in 'the potency of monetary policy', deemed by Friedman to be a much better tool for stabilising the economy than fiscal policy (government spending and taxation).[1] Friedman's entire theoretical edifice rested on the idea that central banks can directly control the money supply. This was somewhat of an obsession for Friedman. 'Everything reminds Milton of the money supply. Well, everything reminds me of sex, but I keep it out of the paper', MIT's Robert Solow wrote in 1966.[2]

The monetarist or quantity theory of money asserts that banks need excess reserves before they can loan out deposits (according to the so-called 'money multiplier') and thus that central banks can directly, or *exogenously*, control the money supply by influencing the minimum reserve requirements of banks or by increasing reserves through so-called open market operations (what today we call quantitative easing). Moreover, it implies that banks and bankers are mere 'intermediaries' between borrowers and savers, thereby requiring pre-existing deposits before they can extend loans to other customers. For centuries, up until the 1930s, this had been the dominant view of 'money'. As Keynes and others (such as Schumpeter) have shown, though, this is not how credit-money works in a modern economy. The causality actually works in reverse: when a bank makes a new loan, it simply makes an entry into a ledger – Keynes called this 'fountain pen money'; nowadays it usually involves tapping some numbers into a computer – and creates brand new money 'out of thin air', which it then deposits into the borrower's account. In other words, instead of deposits leading to loans, it actually works the opposite way: it is the loans that lead to newly created deposits. Banks worry about their reserve positions after the fact. Reserves are only required to ensure all the cross-bank transactions on any day will be reconciled – or, to put it more obviously, that cheques do not bounce. Only if it has insufficient reserves does the commercial bank turn to the central bank, which is obliged to provide reserves on demand. Pre-existing deposits aren't even touched – or needed, for that matter. In short, the money supply is *endogenously* demand-driven and largely controlled by private banks, not central banks. At best, central banks can only hope to influence the money supply indirectly, by adjusting their key interest rates or by influencing the market interest rate through open market operations. The Bank of England summarised this succinctly: 'The quantity of reserves is therefore a consequence, not a cause, of lending and money creation.'[3] It went on to say:

> The bank therefore creates its own funding, deposits, in the act of lending, in a transaction that involves no intermediation whatsoever. … The fact that banks *technically* face no limits to increasing the stocks of loans and deposits instantaneously and discontinuously does not, of course, mean that they do not face other limits to doing so. But the most important limit, especially during the boom periods of financial cycles when all banks simultaneously decide to lend more, is their own assessment of the implications of new lending for their profitability and solvency.[4]

In his early work, Keynes shared the then consensus view that 'unconventional' monetary policies are sufficient to pull an economy out of a slump, by bringing down the long-term market interest rates.[5] By 1936, however, seven years into the Great Depression, Keynes had changed his mind about the 'potency' of monetary policy. In the *General Theory*, he argued that in a recession/depression, when interest rates are very low (close to zero or even negative), the 'transmission mechanism' breaks down, meaning that changes in the money supply have little effect on the economy. In such a context, an expansionary fiscal policy – in particular, an increase in government spending – is necessary to get an economy growing again. This was – and still is – Keynes' greatest lesson, forming the post-war consensus about the primacy of fiscal policy vis-à-vis monetary policy. Since the beginning of his academic career, Friedman had been crusading against this consensus. In 1963 he published *A Monetary History of the United States, 1867–1960*, with Anna Schwartz, in which he argued that the Great Depression had not been caused by excessive deregulation, but, on the contrary, by excessive regulation and government intervention.[6] Friedman almost single-handedly resurrected the pre-Keynesian view that market economies are inherently stable in the absence of major unexpected fluctuations in the money supply, and consequently that governments should intervene in the economy as little as possible and, more specifically, should eschew the use of discretionary fiscal and monetary policies, believed to be inherently inflationary, with the former limited to the pursuit of a balanced (or surplus) budget and the latter concentrated purely on price stability. In more philosophical terms, Friedman's theories chimed with those of early 'neoliberals' such as the Austrian School economists Ludwig von Mises and Friedrich Hayek, who saw the capitalist market as something that is 'natural' and necessary for ensuring freedom, and viewed any form of government intervention that disturbed the (assumed) natural functioning of the market mechanism not only as unnatural and liable to fail, but also as an assault on human freedom – one that ultimately leads to the 'road to serfdom', as Hayek put it in the 1944 book by the same name, arguably the most celebrated publication in the neoliberal canon. Hence Friedman's obsessive use of the word 'freedom' in his writing and proselytising (*Capitalism and Freedom, Free to Choose*, etc.).

Friedman argued that central bankers had to 'prevent money itself from being a major source of economic disturbance' and provide a 'stable background for the economy'.[7] The best way to achieve this, he said, was for the central bank to target 'magnitudes that it can control', and he considered the 'monetary total-currency plus adjusted demand deposits' to be the most desirable of these magnitudes. The policy advice that emerged was the famous 'monetary targeting' approach, whereby the central bank should aim to achieve 'a steady rate of growth' in the money supply (of, say, 3 per cent a year) – and not deviate from that target, no matter what. 'The idea was to put monetary policy on autopilot, removing any discretion on the part of government officials', Paul Krugman notes.[8] Friedman rejected the idea that central banks could use changes in the money supply to target a politically desirable unemployment rate (or any other rate, such as the interest rate or exchange rate, for that matter).

This was related to Friedman's theories about inflation. In 1958, the New Zealand economist A. W. Phillips had shown that there was a historical correlation between unemployment and inflation, with high inflation associated with low unemployment and vice versa (this relationship is known as called the 'Phillips curve'). This meant that there was a trade-off between unemployment and inflation – a discovery that obviously had serious implications for policymaking, because it meant that governments always had the choice of accepting a higher inflation rate in exchange for a lower unemployment rate. In his 1967 speech, however, Friedman argued that 'there is no long-run, stable trade-off between inflation and unemployment'.[9] In other words, if policymakers were to try to keep unemployment low through a policy of higher inflation, they would achieve only temporary success. According to Friedman, unemployment would eventually rise again, even as inflation remained high. The economy would, in other words, suffer the condition that Paul Samuelson would later dub 'stagflation'. Friedman's argument was that after a sustained period of inflation, people would build the history of past inflation and the expectations of future inflation into their decisions. So workers, for example, once they understand that the purchasing power of their wages will be eroded by inflation, will demand higher wage settlements in advance, so that real wages keep up with prices, giving rise to a self-reinforcing feedback loop and ultimately leading to both higher unemployment (as firms will be forced to lay off workers to reduce costs) *and* higher inflation.

Friedman's argument wasn't new: the idea that in a period of sustained expansion inflation may accelerate as a result of workers building the history of inflation into their bargaining behaviour – leading to a so-called 'wage–price spiral' – was well understood by Keynesian economists. However, this misses the fundamental agenda that Friedman was pursuing. In attacking the prevailing view that there was a stable trade-off between inflation and unemployment, Friedman was attempting to reclaim the terrain that neoclassical monetary theory had lost after the Great Depression, by denying the effectiveness of fiscal and monetary interventions by government in sustaining full employment.

Central to this conclusion was the concept of the 'natural rate of unemployment' that Friedman introduced. Put simply, it argued that a free market would deliver a unique unemployment rate that was associated with price stability (implying that whatever the level may be, it was the 'full' employment level, because it was consistent with price stability), and that government attempts to manipulate that rate using fiscal and/or monetary policy would only lead to accelerating inflation. To accept the monetarists' logic was to also realise that there was now a policy lacuna, which required a fundamental reassessment of the way in which the government operated in the economy. The prescription was for policymakers to concentrate on price stability by controlling the rate of monetary growth and to let unemployment settle at this 'natural' rate, ignoring popular concerns that it might be too high. So, by maintaining price stability, central banks would simultaneously fulfil any charter to maintain full employment. It was sleight of hand but it would come to be increasingly accepted by policymakers. Monetarism was born. It was soon discovered by central banks that they could not, indeed, control the growth of the money supply, and attempts to do so were quickly abandoned. But this evidential failure didn't quell the thirst in academic and policymaking circles for the anti-government monetarist doctrine.

LEADING THE WAY: THE UK'S EMBRACE OF MONETARISM

It is largely believed that these ideas gained (once again) a sudden popularity during the oil crisis of the early to mid-1970s, as the stagfla-tionary scenario predicted by Friedman – the simultaneous incidence of high unemployment and accelerating inflation – became a reality, catching most Keynesians off guard and confirming Friedman's status as a prophetic economist. To a certain extent this is true. But what most accounts of the rise of monetarism fail to acknowledge is that monetarist theories had started to percolate into policymaking well before the 1970s oil crisis. Britain is a perfect case in point. In 1968, the British professional magazine *The Banker* published four articles in its December issue that were devoted to the issue of changes in the money supply and the prominence of these changes in determining GDP and inflation.[10] Friedman himself wrote one of the articles – 'Taxes, Money and Stabili-zation' – in which he reiterated his rejection of fiscal policy as a reliable way of stabilising the economy and promoted his monetary targeting idea. It was essentially a dumbed-down version of his 1967 speech to the AEA, targeted at the professional policymaking community rather than the academy. Other articles claimed that Britain was suffering from excessive liquidity and that the central bank should severely restrict the amount of 'spending money' that the non-government sector had access to. One article directly attributed the so-called excessive liquidity to government fiscal deficits.

Up until then, the *Radcliffe Report*, a 339-page study of Britain's monetary system after 1931, published in 1959, had been the major framework for conducting monetary policy in Britain. The report rejected the view that 'the central task of the monetary authorities is to keep a tight control on the supply of money'.[11] It also rejected the view that increases in the money supply would inevitably translate into increasing inflation, a core proposition that Milton Friedman was advancing in his 1967 speech, and reiterated the accepted consensus at the time that it was *spending* that created the inflation risk, not the level of bank reserves or currency in existence. The opening article of the December 1968 edition of *The Banker* explicitly attacked this orthodoxy. It essentially rehearsed Friedman's claim that the Bank of England had to focus on controlling the money supply if Britain was to achieve any sense of economic stability. Aled Davies provides an excellent account of this period in his paper 'The Evolution of British Monetarism: 1968–1979'.[12] As Davies recounts, following Friedman's 1967 speech, influential media outlets such as the *Financial Times* ran stories that promoted his ideas. Davies also notes that Friedman's message was reverberating throughout the financial markets and business sector in Britain; he lists a range of leading firms that were starting to propagate the message about monetary targets. By the end of 1968, the Bank of England was catching the virus. In its December edition of the *Quarterly Bulletin*, a new section was introduced, 'Money Supply: April–September 1968', which discussed movements in the broad aggregate (deposits plus notes and coins) in the previous quarter. Importantly, the Bank explicitly linked the budget deficit to monetary growth (alongside private bank lending) – a relationship that would play a central role in Margaret Thatcher's 1980s slash-and-burn anti-inflationary strategy.

Moreover, as part of the conditionality that the Labour government accepted in relation to two stand-by arrangements that it negotiated with the International Monetary Fund (IMF) in 1967–9 to deal with the country's chronic balance-of-payments deficit, it was agreed that the Bank of England would start controlling the money supply – and in particular domestic credit expansion, which was the aggregate that the IMF wanted governments to control. In *International Monetary Cooperation Since Bretton Woods*, Harold James writes that this decision formalised the 'beginnings of an intellectual conversion' within the British Treasury.[13] This leads to a rather stark conclusion: Britain – and the British Labour Party – effectively succumbed to monetarism in the immediate aftermath of Friedman's 1967 speech, long before Margaret Thatcher came to power.

By the early 1970s, however, the government was forced to acknowledge that controlling the money supply was a practical impossibility: credit controls were abandoned and money supply targets effectively lost all practical significance. This demonstrated that the basic principles of Milton Friedman's monetarist theory were deeply flawed. However, this didn't stop the monetarists in the UK and elsewhere from broadening their offensive from a concern with monetary policy to 'a frontal assault on the fiscal, legal and administrative powers of the state, and on the supposed power of the trades unions, providing the ideological rationale for a fundamental restructuring of the Keynesian political and industrial relations apparatuses'.[14]

Meanwhile, in France, Valéry Giscard d'Estaing was elected president in 1974. In the traditional struggle between the French policymakers in the planning ministry and the technocrats in the ministry of finance (who were increasingly absorbing the monetarist doctrine), Giscard d'Estaing was in the latter camp. He introduced a vicious austerity programme – the Barre Plan, from the name of the finance minister Raymond Barre – which was the world's first real monetarist experiment, one that Margaret Thatcher would more or less copy later on.

THE COLLAPSE OF THE BRETTON WOODS SYSTEM

The context, as mentioned, was that of the global stagflation – stagnation plus inflation – of the early to mid-1970s. In the mid-1960s, inflation began ratcheting upwards in most developed nations, largely as a result of rising commodity prices (particularly food, beverages and metal) and US spending associated with the Vietnam War, which overheated the domestic economy and marked the first significant deficit in the country's balance of payments. As we saw, the resulting inflation was then transmitted through the fixed exchange rate system to Europe and beyond, because the increased trade deficit in the US fuelled stimulatory trade surpluses in other nations. This caused US liquidity to expand in world markets at an unprecedented rate, raising the prospect of a potential run on its stock of gold: as the number of US dollars in circulation rose, other countries started to worry about the value of their growing dollar holdings, and to question whether the US would continue to maintain the gold convertibility indefinitely. This increasingly led nations to exercise their right to convert their dollar holdings into gold, which significantly reduced the stock of US-held gold reserves. General De Gaulle was particularly vocal in his denouncement of America's *privilège exorbitant*, which enabled the country to amass 'tearless deficits' (*déficits sans pleurs*): thereupon, the French demanded the immediate redemption of their liabilities in gold. It is estimated that by the mid-1960s American paper-dollar liabilities to foreign official agencies exceeded the gold cover. The US authorities devised all sorts of methods to soak up the excess liquidity in the hands of foreigners that might otherwise have been tempted to buy gold (T-bills, higher domestic interest rates, the two-tier gold system, etc.), but they all proved futile. As Leo Panitch and Sam Gindin note, '[i]n less than a generation, the contradictions inherent in the Bretton Woods agreement were exposed'.[15] By 1971, during Richard Nixon's first presidential mandate, it had become apparent that the Bretton Woods system had reached breaking point: on 15 August 1971, US president Nixon unilaterally ended the gold–dollar convertibility (that is, ended the ability of foreign central banks to convert their dollar holdings into gold), effectively transforming the dollar into a *non-convertible fiat currency*. He also applied a 10 per cent surcharge on imported goods. Together with wage and price controls to reduce inflation, these surprise actions became known as the 'Nixon shock'. Commentators around the world reported it as a resounding defeat for the United States – it was anything but. Buttressed by the power of the dollar as the world's reserve currency, the US succeeded in creating a new global hegemonic regime based on a so-called 'T-bill standard'. In short, the United States relinquished the imperative of competing with other nations for world market shares and came to accept its role as 'consumer of last resort', by deliberately buying more than it sold abroad and running large, chronic trade deficits; countries with chronic trade surpluses (such as Japan, Germany, subsequently China, etc.), on the other hand, had little choice but to 'finance' this trade deficit via the buying of large quantities of US securities.[16]

An attempt by the world's major powers to revive the previous system of fixed exchange rates (but without the backing of silver or gold), through the so-called Smithsonian Agreement, failed. By 1973, all the major currencies had begun to float against each other, inaugurating the new era of the 'managed float', whereby the central banks regularly intervened in the currency markets to resist fluctuations that were deemed undesirable, by buying/selling domestic and foreign currencies in the foreign exchange market or by adjusting their bank rates (most European currencies, on the other hand, continued to experiment with various forms of currency arrangements all the way up to the creation of the single currency). As we will see, this new system raised new problems but reduced the constraints on domestic policy, because monetary and fiscal policy was no longer defined by the need to defend an agreed parity. Governments were now free to use fiscal and monetary policy

– within limits – to pursue domestic objectives previously unattainable on a sustainable basis. Initially, however, the collapse of the Bretton Woods system was accompanied by significant instability on the foreign exchange markets, which further exacerbated the inflationary pressures in a number of countries, giving renewed impetus to the anti-inflationary mantra of the monetarists.

Then came the oil crisis. In October 1973, the Organization of the Petroleum Exporting Countries (OPEC) announced an oil embargo in response to the outbreak of hostilities in the Middle East (the 1973 Arab-Israeli War, or Yom Kippur War). A few days later, on 16 October, the Arab nations increased the price of oil by 17 per cent and indicated that they would cut production by 25 per cent as part of a leveraged retaliation against the United States' decision to provide arms to Israel. This was a major shock to the world: the price of oil rose by around three times within eight months and the US dollar appreciated by 17 per cent in the six months to February 1974. Financial markets reacted badly and significant instability emerged in world currency markets. The impact on the fixed exchange rate regime in Europe was particularly severe, with European currencies experiencing major depreciations, causing growing pressure on those countries' balance of payments. There were multiple effects of a varied nature across different economies. Suffice to say that real GDP growth fell significantly in many countries, resulting in rising unemployment, at the same time as the imported oil price rises and the depreciating exchange values triggered accelerating inflation. In an attempt to control inflation governments pursued deflationary policies, but this led to higher unemployment and growing industrial unrest and electoral dissatisfaction, while doing little to curb inflation. Thus deflationary policies would be reversed and expansionary policies reintroduced to combat unemployment and raise living standards. But this would simply exacerbate the inflationary pressures, and the cycle would begin again.

'NO ONE KNEW WHAT WAS GOING ON': STAGFLATION AND THE FAILURE OF NEO-KEYNESIAN THEORY

For many neo-Keynesians, this stagflationary scenario represented a major quandary. Up until the 1960s, many neo-Keynesian economists ignored the possibility of stagflation, because historical experience suggested that high unemployment was typically associated with low inflation, and vice versa (the so-called 'Phillips curve'). The conventional neo-Keynesian view was: (i) that inflation could only result if overall spending in the economy outstripped the capacity of firms to produce goods and services, leaving them no option but to increase prices; and (ii) that unemployment could easily be prevented through demand-side stimulus, that is, more spending. In the context of the early to mid-1970s, though, that would have simply exacerbated the rising inflation; in fact, stagflation appeared to point to the need for the simultaneous application of expansionary (anti-recessionary) *and* contractionary (anti-inflationary) policies.

Not everyone was perplexed, though. Various economists of the post-war period – most notably John Kenneth Galbraith, Nicholas Kaldor, John Cornwall and Sydney Weintraub – understood quite well that a full employment regime could generate self-reinforcing inflationary pressures, as organised labour and capital used their wage-setting and price-setting powers, respectively, to claim a greater share of the national income, thus leading to a so-called wage–price or price–wage spiral (depending on who tried to push their price up first, workers or capital), which in turn could be further exacerbated by supply-side factors (such as an increase in oil and commodity prices). This meant that at a time when a major deterioration in a nation's terms of trade occurred (say, due to an oil price rise), there were no mechanisms in place to allow the economy to adjust to the decline in real income that the external input price shock generated: real wage resistance and profit margin push both prevented a non-inflationary resolution to a national real income loss from occurring. In 1970, Galbraith stated that Keynes had 'become obsolete' as a result of the monopoly power exerted by big business and powerful trade unions. The problems that Keynes had addressed related to demand-side (spending) deficiencies, which led to mass unemployment, whereas the contemporary problems related to the supply side – the struggle between labour and capital for greater shares of national income.[17] John Cornwall noted that this problem did not prove 'that the Keynesian emphasis on aggregate demand is incorrect'; it simply showed that 'demand management is a most unsuitable instrument for reducing inflation'.[18] These economists understood the need for a consensual approach to the problem, via wage and price guidelines that would distribute the burden of disinflation equitably among labour and capital. Rather than try to discipline these inflationary tendencies with austerity, which meant using unemployment as a means of quelling wage demands and flat sales as a means of moderating profit margin pushes, a growing chorus of economists, including Galbraith, advocated the use of incomes policies (wage and price guidelines) to deal with the cost push while avoiding mass unemployment.

These insights, however, were lost in the public debate, as most macro-economists – including many Keynesians – grew increasingly sceptical of Keynesian theories, and started to reconsider their ideas in search of an explanation for stagflation. This provided the monetarists with the perfect opportunity to deal the final blow to the post-war Western economic orthodoxy. A perfect case in point is the debate that took place in Italy in the mid-1970s. The Italian government's reaction to the oil crisis and resulting economic slowdown followed the same pattern as that of other countries: restrictive monetary and fiscal policies in order to contain inflation, and repeated currency devaluation to maintain competitiveness in export markets and to keep the balance-of-payments deficit under control. As elsewhere, though, this policy mix failed to prevent the economy from repeatedly falling into recession. The rapid growth of inflation led trade unions to demand the establishment of a 100 per cent indexation of wages to the rate of inflation (the so-called escalator clause), which they obtained in 1975. It is in this context that the so-called 'Modigliani controversy' took place. In a series of articles in the Italian press, the prominent economist Franco Modigliani, one of the forefathers of the neoclassical synthesis, sharply criticised the escalator clause, arguing that it would produce an unnecessary increase in labour costs. From a theoretical standpoint, he offered an extensive criticism of the agreement in his essay 'The Management of an Open Economy with "100% Plus" Wage Indexation', written in collaboration with Tommaso Padoa-Schioppa and first published in 1977 in the journal *Moneta e Credito*.[19] In it, the two economists argued that the escalator clause was inherently inflationary and that a reduction in real wages was necessary in order to bring Italy out of the crisis. Modigliani was also keen to stress that real wage compression was a painful but necessary step to bring down unemployment. The fact that 'Keynesians' like Modigliani were arriving at such distinctly *un*-Keynesian conclusions – Keynes would never have accepted the proposition of a wage cut leading to an increase in the demand for labour, Luigi Pasinetti later noted in a scathing critique of Modigliani's theories[20] – shows the extent to which the neoclassical synthesis, by remaining wedded to the pre-Keynesian orthodoxy, effectively paved the way for monetarism, which easily discredited neo-Keynesianism on the grounds of a logical inconsistency between its microeconomic foundations and the 'Keynesian' macroeconomic policy prescriptions.

'THE FISCAL CRISIS OF THE STATE': THE RISE OF A NEW (FLAWED) LEFT CONSENSUS

To make things worse, in the late 1960s and early 1970s, left-wing academics became besotted with notions that the crisis which accompanied the OPEC oil price hikes was to be found in the lack of taxing capacity of governments. Furthermore, they started incorporating the increasingly global nature of finance and production supply chains into their analysis, concluding that these trends undermined the capacity of states to spend and maintain full employment. This became the perceived wisdom among most left-wing intellectuals throughout the 1970s, lending credibility (unwittingly) to the emerging monetarist/neoliberal anti-statist mantra. One of the most influential texts in this respect was the 1973 book, *The Fiscal Crisis of the State*, by American sociologist and economist James O'Connor.[21] Approaching the problem of budgetary analysis from a Marxist perspective, O'Connor correctly noted that the capitalistic state is in a contradictory position, where it has to keep private profits high and growing, by socialising various costs of production that would otherwise be borne by the private sector, while at the same time providing a redistributive function to ensure that workers enjoy some of the prosperity created by the capitalist production process. Both functions require the government to expand its expenditure shares relentlessly. O'Connor placed the source of the crisis of Keynesianism directly within 'this tendency for government expenditures to outrace revenues', which is further exacerbated by the constant struggle between classes over the composition of state spending.[22] He termed this the 'fiscal crisis of the state'.

Consistent with his Marxist leanings, O'Connor believed that the government would increasingly place the tax burden on the working class, which would heighten the class conflict inherent in American capitalism. O'Connor's analysis contains many worthy insights, but ultimately they are all overshadowed by the macroscopic flaw underpinning his entire theory: his adherence to the mainstream belief that currency-issuing governments are financially constrained because they need to 'finance' their spending through taxes or selling debt to the private sector. While that was certainly true during the 1960s, when O'Connor started writing the book – as we noted, under the Bretton Woods fixed exchange rate system governments had to constrain their expenditures to meet the central bank requirements to sustain the currency parity (and, in the case of the US, avoid a run on its gold reserves) – it was not true after 1971, when president Nixon effectively ended the gold convertibility and floated the US dollar. The floating of exchange rates freed governments, to a large degree, from the balance-of-payments constraint. But it appears that O'Connor didn't grasp the significance of what had happened and proceeded as if nothing significant had changed.

This blunder would have far-reaching consequences. In the period following the publication of *The Fiscal Crisis of the State*, a myriad of left-wing articles, academic papers and books emerged reflecting (and cementing) the new common sense: that the breakdown of the Bretton Woods system had reduced, rather than increased, the ability of national governments to pursue expansionary policies and maintain full employment. This idea gained strength once left academics started incorporating 'globalisation' into their analysis, going on to become a self-evident truth in left circles. Even an insightful thinker like Marxist historian Eric Hobsbawm would later write in his magnum opus, *The Age of Extremes*, that the Keynesian model was 'undermined by the globalisation of the economy after 1970, which put the governments of all states – except perhaps the USA, with in enormous economy – at the mercy of an uncontrollable "world market"'.[23]

Such arguments were not unfounded, but often overemphasised the inflationary effects of currency depreciation or underplayed the role that capital and/or import controls could play in moderating speculative attacks and reducing pressure on the exchange rate (for a more detailed discussion of this topic, see pages 211–14). In this context we can better appreciate the early literature on globalisation and economic sovereignty loss. In his 1971 book, *Sovereignty at Bay: The Multinational Spread of US Enterprises*, the late Raymond Vernon, eulogised as 'the discoverer of globalisation', was one of the earliest proponents of the view that the state had lost its fiscal authority.[24] Vernon argued that 'as far as the advanced countries are concerned, the generalization holds: the pattern of coordination, consultation and commitment has evolved to such a point that freedom of economic action on the part of those nations is materially qualified'.[25]

Vernon was referring to two developments that had taken place in the post-war period: (i) the establishment of various multilateral trade agreements and exchange rate arrangements (he was writing before the Bretton Woods system of fixed exchange rates broke down in 1971); and (ii) the extraordinary growth in world trade, due to technological improvements in transport and communications, which led to a substantial increase in the volume of capital flows between advanced nations (particularly in the form of US foreign direct investment, or FDI) and laid the basis for a new internationalisation of production (exemplified by the growing presence of US corporations in Europe). Vernon noted that the burgeoning power of multinational enterprises raised fears that 'as long as the multinational enterprise has the power, difficult or improbable though its use may sometimes be, to dry up technology or export technicians or drain off capital or reduce production or shift profits or alter prices or allocate export markets, there is a latent or active tension associated with its presence'.[26]

As we discuss in Chapter 5, these tensions persist today and are used as the basis for the claim that states must compromise domestic policy to ensure that they do not trigger a negative response from international capital that is 'parked' within their borders. Vernon also claimed that the advent of multinational enterprises had rendered the nature of international transactions more complex, as many financial flows were now conducted within the same enterprise but across national borders. He concluded that 'any state which senses an inadequacy in its capacity to impose effective restrictions at the border has ample reason for harboring that feeling'.[27] He argued that while governments could block flows for a short time, companies would develop new ways of shifting capital, which would leave 'the regulating sovereign ... increasingly at a disadvantage'.[28]

Over the years, many commentators have used this line of reasoning to suggest that taxation bases are now unstable because transnational corporations can easily move across national borders in search of the most favourable tax regimes, which leads governments to engage in tax competition with each other, lowering corporate taxes as well as taxes on high incomes and assets, in a bid to attract capital. This argument was (and is) used to show that the capacity of the government to spend is undermined by the erosion of the taxation base needed to 'finance' spending (without resorting to large-scale deficit financing, deemed to be inherently unsustainable). This, in turn, has allowed governments of all colours in recent decades to falsely construe rising welfare payments as a threat to the fiscal viability of the state, and to lecture citizens about how governments, like households, have to live within their means. As we argue in Chapter 8, much of this concern about tax shifting is misplaced when considering the options facing a currency-issuing government. It is one of the many myths of mainstream macroeconomics whose origins can (also) be traced back to the left's inability to understand correctly the true implications of the shift from fixed to floating exchange rates.

With this in mind, we can better understand why, over the course of the 1970s, most economists – including many well-known Keynesian and left-wing economists – gradually shunned the Keynesian paradigm (even in its 'bastardised' neo-Keynesian form) in favour of monetarist macroeconomics. As American economist Alan Blinder wrote: 'By about 1980, it was hard to find an American academic macroeconomist under the age of 40 who professed to be a Keynesian. That was an astonishing intellectual turnabout in less than a decade, an intellectual revolution for sure.'[29]

Meanwhile, Friedman's simplistic monetarism gave way to a much broader and more sophisticated anti-statist *pensée unique*, based upon the virtues of supply-side economics, financial and trade liberalisation, privatisation and deregulation, and more generally on the superiority of the market economy over state intervention – what today we generally refer to as neoliberalism. This coincided with the gradual dismantling of the post-war Keynesian framework (though not in the direction officially preached by neoliberal ideology, as we shall see). It is important to note that neoliberal ideology did not spring out of nowhere; it had been waiting in the wings of Keynesianism for over 50 years. As Philip Mirowski and Dieter Plehwe have shown, intellectuals associated with the Mont Pèlerin Society (founded by Friedrich Hayek and others in 1947) had been elaborating and promoting 'a total thought collective of more than one thousand scholars, journalists, (think tank) professionals, and corporate and political leaders around the globe' since the end of World War II – a fact that in itself starkly contradicts the neoliberals' proclaimed confidence in the inherent spontaneity of the market.[30]

THE 'COUNTER-REVOLUTION' VIEW: NEOLIBERALISM AS A RESTORATION OF CLASS POWER

From this perspective, one would be easily tempted to attribute the neoliberal restructuring of society that has occurred from the late 1970s onwards to the *theories* developed by Friedman and other academics (most notably those at the University of Chicago). But, as Simon Clarke noted, to view the shift from the Keynesian to the neoliberal era primarily as the victory of one ideology over another

> is to attribute too much coherence and too much power to theories that serve more to legitimate than to guide political practice. The ideas of monetarism are important, but their importance is ideological, in giving coherence and direction to political forces which have deeper roots. ... The debate between monetarism and Keynesianism was not resolved in the seminar room, but on the political stage.[31]

This gives rise to another explanation for the rise of monetarist theory, which ascribes its success not (only) to its intellectual or analytical clout, but to the fact that it provided a convenient justification for the restoration of the unfettered power of capital. Gérard Duménil and Dominique Lévy, for example, frame the rise of neoliberalism as a 'counter-revolution', or even a 'coup':

> The profitability of capital plunged during the 1960s and 1970s; corporations distributed dividends sparingly, and real interest rates were low, or even negative, during the 1970s. The stock market (also corrected for inflation) had collapsed during the mid-1970s, and was stagnating. It is easy to understand that, under such conditions, the income and wealth of ruling classes was strongly affected. Seen from this angle, this could be read as a dramatic decline in inequality. Neo-liberalism can be interpreted as an attempt by the wealthiest fraction of the population to stem this comparative decline.[32]

Monetarism was thus the ideological mask used to conceal this capitalist counter-offensive. The rise in the acceptance of monetarism was not based on an empirical rejection of the Keynesian orthodoxy; rather, in Alan Blinder's words, it was 'a triumph of *a priori* theorising over empiricism, of intellectual aesthetics over observation and, in some measure, of conservative ideology over liberalism. It was not, in a word, a Kuhnian scientific revolution.'[33] However, the right sought to promote monetarism as a way of undermining the commitment to full employment and various financial and labour market regulations, irrespective of the facts. As Alan Budd, economic advisor to the Thatcher government, would later admit:

> There may have been people making the actual policy decisions ... who never believed for a moment that this was the correct way to bring down inflation. *They did, however, see that [monetarism] would be a very, very good way to raise unemployment, and raising unemployment was an extremely desirable way of reducing the strength of the working classes* – if you like, that what was engineered there in Marxist terms was a crisis of capitalism which re-created a reserve army of labour and has allowed the capitalists to make high profits ever since.[34]

A similar argument is put forward by David Harvey, who claims that the capitalists adopted the neoliberal approach because their class power had been diluted under Keynesianism and was threatened in the mid-1970s. Their response was determined by their need for a 'restoration of class power':

> One condition of the post-war settlement in almost all countries was that the economic power of the upper classes be restrained and that labour be accorded a much larger share of the economic pie. ... While growth was strong this restraint seemed not to matter. To have a stable share of an increasing pie is one thing. But when growth collapsed in the 1970s, when real interest rates went negative and paltry dividends and profits were the norm, then upper classes everywhere felt threatened. In the US the control of wealth (as opposed to income) by the top 1 per cent of the population had remained fairly stable throughout the twentieth century. But in the 1970s it plunged precipitously as asset values (stocks, property, savings) collapsed. The upper classes had to move decisively if they were to protect themselves from political and economic annihilation.[35]

Various documents that appeared throughout the 1970s, which expressed this very concept in no uncertain terms, would appear to validate this thesis. One of the most famous ones is the *Powell Memorandum* (also known as the *Powell Manifesto*), which Harvey considers to be the founding document of US neoliberalism. In 1971, Lewis Powell, then a corporate lawyer and member of the boards of eleven corporations, wrote a memo to his friend Eugene Sydnor, Jr., the director of the US Chamber of Commerce. The memo was written two months prior to Powell's nomination by Nixon to the US Supreme Court, but its contents were not made public prior to his elevation. The memo called for corporate America to become more aggressive in moulding society's thinking about business, government, politics and law in the US. Powell noted that the threat to economic elites and ruling classes was not just economic, but *political* as well. Bolstered by strong unions and low unemployment, the labour movement had begun to advance proposals 'to restrict the prerogatives of capital within its own sphere – private business', Andrew Glyn writes.[36] 'A range of plans emerged in the later 1960s and 1970s going well beyond the customary collective bargaining issues of jobs and working conditions.' These included proposals in Germany to extend co-determination rights (which guaranteed equal representation of employees and shareholders on company boards) to one-half of the country's larger companies; a Swedish scheme requiring companies to issue new stocks to wage-earner funds corresponding to a percentage of annual profits, which effectively amounted to a form of gradual collectivisation; and various planning agreements and nationalisation plans, such as the ones put forward by the British government in the mid-1970s and by the French government in the early 1980s (both of which are analysed in detail further on). Understandably, employers vigorously opposed these plans. This was the realisation of what Polish economist Michał Kalecki had predicted 30 years earlier: that even though business leaders had acquiesced to, if not enthusiastically supported, the use of government intervention after World War II, 'the social and political changes resulting from the *maintenance* of full employment' was bound to engender a reaction from the business community sooner or later. In 1943 he wrote:

Indeed, under a regime of permanent full employment, the 'sack' would cease to play its role as a disciplinary measure. The social position of the boss would be undermined, and the self-assurance and class-consciousness of the working class would grow. Strikes for wage increases and improvements in conditions of work would create political tension.[37]

Kalecki noted that even if a regime of full employment were not to reduce profits, '"discipline in the factories" and "political stability" are more appreciated than profits by business leaders. Their class instinct tells them that lasting full employment is unsound from their point of view, and that unemployment is an integral part of the "normal" capitalist system.[38] From this perspective, we can better understand the Trilateral Commission's oft-cited *Crisis of Democracy* report of 1975, written by Michel Crozier, Samuel Huntington and Joji Watanuki.[39] The report was the first explicit proposal to roll back the democratic format of the compromise with organised labour in production. It stated that: 'In recent years, the operations of the democratic process ... have generated a breakdown of traditional means of social control, a de-legitimation of political and other forms of authority, and *an overload of demands on government*, exceeding its capacity to respond.'[40] The report argued that this required, from the establishment's perspective, a multi-level response, based not only on a reduction of the bargaining power of labour, but also on 'a greater degree of moderation in democracy' and a greater disengagement ('non-involvement') of civil society from the operations of the political system, to be achieved through the diffusion of 'apathy'.[41] Lewis Powell was even more explicit. He argued that businesses should 'assiduously cultivate' the state and when necessary use it 'aggressively and with determination'. He appreciated that ultimately 'the payoff – short of revolution – is what government does'. Powell's appeal to American capitalists to engage in class war represented a major turning point in the way the corporate sector approached the political system. It became the blueprint for the American conservative movement and for the formation of a network of influential right-wing think tanks and lobbying organisations, such as the Heritage Foundation, the American Legislative Exchange Council, the Manhattan Institute, the Cato Institute and other organisations, as well as inspiring the US Chamber of Commerce to become far more politically active. Milton Friedman was obviously deeply involved in the burgeoning American right-wing movement, even producing a ten-part PBS miniseries, *Free to Choose* – underwritten by some of the largest corporations in the world, including Getty Oil, Firestone Tire & Rubber Co., PepsiCo, General Motors, Bechtel and General Mills[42] – to disseminate his views. This corporate counterattack was by no means limited to the United States, however: throughout the 1970s and 1980s, right-wing think tanks and lobbying organisations multiplied across the entire capitalist world. In the UK, for example, the Centre for Policy Studies was founded by Tory MPs Keith Joseph and Margaret Thatcher to develop material that would 'limit the role of the state, to encourage enterprise and to enable the institutions of society – such as families and voluntary organizations – to flourish'. Similarly, the influential Adam Smith Institute was also formed in the 1970s as part of this concerted movement to advance the interests of the corporate sector. In Australia, the formation of the business-funded Centre of Independent Studies and the H. G. Nicholls Society promoted the conservative cause. The latter, in particular, launched a head-on attack on the trade union movement, which would later result in legislative constraints on the unions' ability to extract wage demands.

THE STRUCTURAL VIEW: NEOLIBERALISM AS A RESPONSE TO THE STRUCTURAL FLAWS OF KEYNESIANISM

In light of the above, it is clear that neoliberalisation was in part a conscious effort by ruling elites to achieve a restoration of class power. But the counter-revolution argument, while having the benefit of bringing class into the picture, fails to acknowledge the extent to which these political and ideological developments expressed a deeper crisis, of which they were themselves part. This brings us to the third major school of thought concerning the crisis of Keynesianism. It is one that emphasises the *structural* nature of the crisis.

As mentioned already, a common trait of most advanced economies in the early to mid-1970s was a dramatic decline in the profitability of capital: by the mid-1970s, the gross profit share in manufacturing, for example, had sunk by more than one-quarter in a decade, having been pretty stable until the late 1960s.[43] This reflected a combination of factors: a depreciating capital stock (in part because more of the capital stock was machinery, which depreciates faster than factory building), worsening terms of trade (as a result of increased international competition due to the emergence of new centres of economic power such as Germany and Japan), the rise in imported material costs, weak productivity growth and, perhaps most importantly in terms of its political consequences, militant wage pressure. As we have seen, the post-war decades were characterised by a strengthening of trade unionism and institutional changes supporting labour's bargaining position, which in turn was further strengthened by low rates of unemployment. In this context, labour was able to successfully resist attempts by hard-pressed capitalists to raise profits by pushing real wages down. An important manifestation of labour's strong position was the extraordinarily high level of industrial conflict during this period.[44]

This intense distributional struggle between labour and capital over (shrinking) income shares – characterised by inflationary pressures (further exacerbated by supply-side factors, such as the oil crisis), wage–price (or price–wage) spirals and squeezed profit margins – posed a serious barrier to output and employment growth. In such a context, it was (is) easy to construe trade unions as job killers, selfishly tending to the interests of their members rather than considering the interests of workers and the economy as a whole. This is certainly how the mainstream narrative increasingly portrayed them in the 1970s. By resuscitating the neoclassical view that trade unions are 'imperfections' that interfere with the free market's ability to deliver optimal outcomes for all if left to its own devices, monetarism provided the ideological rationale for cracking down on the unions.

But was (and is) it fair to blame the trade unions for the stagflation of the 1970s? Analysing in detail the role played by trade unions in that historical context is beyond the scope of this text. As Richard Freeman wrote, trade unions 'are probably the most idiosyncratic institutions in modern capitalism'.[45] However, while there are substantial differences in the way unions are structured and operate across nations, the one salient aspect of unions that transcends these 'idiosyncrasies' and provides a common organising framework is that *trade unions are an institutional construct of capitalism*. They obey the logic of capitalism; they are embedded in the class conflict that defines capitalism. This means that the nature of capitalist relations defines what unions are and what they (can) do.

In 1865, Karl Marx responded to those who claimed that wage increases are of no benefit to workers and that for this reason trade unions are to be considered harmful, by outlining the many ways in which unions do in fact work in the interests of workers.[46] This includes pushing for wage increases to defend real wages after prices have been pushed up; gaining wage increases to match productivity increases; and gaining higher wages to compensate for longer working days. He characterised these actions, which define union action in 'ninety-nine out of a hundred' instances, 'as reactions of labour against the previous action of capital'. In other words, the logic of trade unions in capitalism, according to Marx, is to respond to the actions of capital. He reiterated that the underlying nature of capitalism involves disputes over the length of the working day and the wages to be paid, which 'is only settled by the continuous struggle between capital and labour, the capitalist constantly tending to reduce wages to their physical minimum, and to extend the working day to its physical maximum, while the working man constantly presses in the opposite direction.'⁴⁷

In other words, trade unions work 'as centers of resistance against the encroachments of capital': even within the narrow logic of the labour–capital conflict, unions can achieve substantial gains for their members. That is their institutional raison d'être. At the same time, Marx knew better than anyone else that there are limits to what trade unions can achieve. These are defined by the power relations within capitalism: simply put, the owners of capital control the means of production and employment, and their expectations of future returns dictate the rate at which the capital stock accumulates over time. In his essay *Inflation and Crisis*, Robert Rowthorn wrote:

> Capitalists control production and they will not invest unless they receive a certain 'normal' rate of profit. If wages rise too rapidly, either because of extreme labour shortage or because of militant trade unionism, the rate of profit falls below its 'normal' level, capitalists refuse to invest, expansion grinds to a standstill and there is a crisis.⁴⁸

So, when assessing the role of trade unions in any given historical period we must be cognisant of the logic of the union as an institution and the limits to its effectiveness within the conflictual relationships that define capitalism. This is how Rowthorn summed up the issue:

> A strong and militant trade union movement may force up wages and resist wage cuts even in the face of high unemployment. In a boom situation this may squeeze profits and bring expansion to a premature end, whilst there is still a large surplus of labour; and in a depression it may delay recovery by reducing profitability. This may sound like a condemnation of the trade union movement, but it is not. It is simply stating the obvious fact that, so long as capitalists control production, they hold the whip hand, and workers cannot afford to be too successful in the wages struggle. If they are, capitalists respond by refusing to invest, and the result is a premature or longer crisis. To escape from this dilemma workers must go beyond purely economic struggle and must fight at the political level to exert control over production itself.⁴⁹

From this perspective, it doesn't make much sense to attack the unions for being successful at what they do – that is, increase wages and reduce working hours (among other things). That is the logic of capitalism. As Rowthorn notes, however, unions can also be 'too successful' in their struggle, in which case a crisis ensues until a resolution in the form of an abatement in the distributional conflict is found – usually through rising unemployment, but also, in more recent times, through harsh legislative constraints being placed on the capacity of the unions.

In the context of the 1970s, things were further exacerbated by the fact that the entire Fordist-Keynesian 'class compromise' rested on the system's ability to accommodate the popular demand for rising incomes and employment in the private sector, which could only be satisfied by the growth of production, *as well as* the capitalist need to subordinate production to profit. Thus, as the demands and expectations of labour and capital went from being *mutually supportive* (the virtuous wages–demand–profit–investment cycle) – or at least non-exclusive, as they had been throughout most of the 1950s and 1960s – to being *mutually exclusive* (with big business and big labour bound in a 'dysfunctional embrace', or zero-sum game as David Harvey put it),[50] the Keynesian political, institutional and ideological framework came under increased pressure from both sides. On the one hand, workers used the trade unions and left/social-democratic political parties to assert their material and political claims, regardless of the constraints of profitability; on the other hand, 'individual capitals sought the support of the state to maintain profitability in the face of rising costs and more intense international competition'.[51]

3

That Option No Longer Exists: How Britain, and the British Labour Party, Fell Into the Monetarist Trap

1964–74: THE BREAKDOWN OF THE SOCIAL-DEMOCRATIC
CONSENSUS AND THE RE-EMERGENCE OF CLASS STRUGGLE

The UK once again provides an interesting case study, reflecting the wider trend across advanced nations. In the mid-1960s, the Labour government of Harold Wilson (1964–70) attempted to manage the distributional struggle – and more generally the wide range of economic problems facing the country, including high inflation and unemployment, and a serious balance-of-payments deficit – through a consensual approach, aimed at combining wage restraint with measures aimed at stimulating private investment and boosting productivity. The plan had the benefit of acknowledging the responsibilities of British capital in bringing about the 'stagnation' of the late 1960s (relative to the average growth rate of the previous decade). British big capital had always been more outward looking than investors in Europe, Japan or even the US. Thus, as capital became increasingly global, British financial capital started increasingly privileging speculative (short-term, high-return) overseas investments over productive investment in Britain. As a result, throughout the 1960s, real gross fixed capital formation and private capital formation in Britain lagged well behind that of other advanced countries. The result was stagnant productivity growth over the same period, which caused British exports to struggle in international markets and the country to incur a rising trade deficit.

When Wilson was first elected, in 1964, he attempted to bring a new sense of vitality to the domestic economy through his National Plan. This initiative was consistent with the concept of 'indicative economic planning' that was in vogue at the time, consisting of state intervention in the form of 'carrots' to firms (grants, subsidies, tax reliefs, etc.) rather than 'sticks' (quotas, output targets, etc.). It was also accompanied by direct public investment in infrastructure aimed at inducing private investors to leverage further productivity gains. The aim was to modernise British industry, which was lagging behind that of other nations as a result of years of neglect from the British capital owners. Wilson's plan suffered a fundamental flaw, however. Ultimately, its success depended on the response of the capitalists: the government had no means of ensuring that the increased profits would be used to raise domestic investment and productivity.

Moreover, the bias towards capital export meant that British capital was prone to oppose 'the measures for dynamising British capitalism, preferring – if not actually liking – the alternative of stagnation'.[1] Furthermore, the problem with a plan that emphasised strong real GDP growth was that the fixed exchange rate system continually constrained the capacity of the domestic economy to grow; the currency pressures that Wilson had to deal with in the context of an ongoing current account deficit (which he inherited) culminated in the decision to devalue in 1967, which effectively jettisoned the National Plan. By the end of the 1960s, the government was in a shambles. The failure of the state to resolve the crisis led to an intensification of the class struggle, as Asad Haider notes:

> The attempt by a social-democratic government to manage the state through an organised version of consensus is finally exhausted and bankrupted between 1964 and 1970, so, gradually, the class struggle comes more and more into the open, assumes a more manifest presence. This development is electrifying. One of its consequences is to translate a struggle which is emerging at the level of civil society and its superstructural institutions ... directly on to the terrain of capital and labour, and thus – in the era of organised late capitalism – on to the terrain of the state.[2]

The failure of Keynesian interventionism to realise the aspirations of the working class led 'to growing pressure from sections of the organised working class for the state to bring capital directly under social control, to complement the socialisation of consumption with the socialisation of production, to subordinate the accumulation of capital to the aspirations of the working class'.[3] Furthermore, an increasingly militant working class had begun to link up with the new counterculture movements of the late 1960s – community groups, welfare rights groups, black and women's groups, anti-war groups, etc. – 'in struggles that demanded not simply more pay or more government expenditure, but that challenged the bureaucratic and authoritarian forms of capitalist power'.[4] In other words, 'the re-entry to the historical stage of the class struggle in a visible, open, and escalating form'[5] hadn't simply become, from capital's perspective, a barrier to accumulation. On a more fundamental level, 'it threatened to provide the foundations for transcending capitalism' itself.[6] As David Harvey recounts, '[d]iscontent was widespread and the conjoining of labour and urban social movements throughout much of the advanced capitalist world appeared to point towards the emergence of a socialist alternative to the social compromise between capital and labour that had grounded capital accumulation so successfully in the post-war period.'[7]

This, as mentioned, provoked an increasingly desperate and alarmed response on behalf of the ruling elites, which 'led to growing demands on the part of capital ... for the subordination of the working class to the rule of the law of value'.[8] It is against this backdrop that, in the early 1970s, the newly elected Conservative government of Edward Heath (1970–4) attempted to resolve the crisis by directly confronting the power of the unions: the Industrial Relations Act of 1971 was an attempt to dismantle the existing institutional apparatuses of industrial relations and smash the bargaining power of the unions once and for all. But this provoked mass opposition, radicalising the class struggle and bringing the workers into direct confrontation with the state. Following a series of disruptive mining strikes – including a month-long general strike – Heath eventually called an election for February 1974 to obtain a mandate to face down the miners' demands, but lost to Labour by a small margin, leading to Wilson's re-election.

1974–9: HOW LABOUR TOOK IT UPON ITSELF TO MANAGE THE CAPITALIST CRISIS

The new Labour government and the miners reached a deal shortly thereafter and the strike was ended, but this simply exacerbated the ongoing distributional struggle. As already mentioned, in Britain as elsewhere the oil crisis had bolstered the monetarist mantra, even among the ranks of the Labour Party. This had widened the rifts between the various factions within the party, which was becoming increasingly polarised. On the one hand, the Labour left was becoming more powerful and strongly rejected any attempts to curtail the power of the unions. On the other, the number of Labour monetarists, who were closer to the Tories than to their colleagues on the left on macroeconomic policy, was on the rise as well, especially within the parliamentary wing of the party. As Aled Davies notes, it was the new chancellor, Denis Healey, who 'did most to further the "monetarist" cause in British public discourse' once the Wilson government was re-elected in '74'.[9]

Not everyone in the Labour Party shared the chancellor's views, however. At the Labour Party's 1973 annual national conference, an ambitious 123-page policy manifesto was unveiled, *Labour's Programme for Britain*. The document, which was largely the brainchild of Tony Benn, Ian Mikardo and Michael Foot, all staunch left-wing members of the party, outlined a socialist vision for Britain. The programme had two major planks. First, the creation of a National Enterprise Board (NEB), which would buy up private firms in the national interest. The aim was to use these enterprises as vehicles for investment planning to spawn higher productivity and sustained economic growth, and more generally to revitalise an industry that had waned under the poor management of British capital. The plan involved, in the first instance, the acquisition of around 25 companies, including large manufacturing firms, as part of the first five years of a 25-year-odd planning horizon. Second, the drawing up of planning agreements with around 100 of the largest private manufacturing firms, in addition to existing public enterprises, in return for financial assistance. The City would be obliged to comply with the work of the NEB through new capital and credit controls designed to redirect it from speculation towards investment in productive industries. But most striking of all, perhaps, was a commitment to significant industrial democracy, a radical departure from the party's traditional corporatist, top-down approach to board representation. Michael Foot was quoted in the *Guardian* as saying that the programme was 'the finest socialist programme I have seen in my lifetime'.[10]

Three days later the 1973 Arab-Israel War broke out and the OPEC embargos began, triggering a chain of events that would end up steering the Labour Party – and Britain – in a very different direction. But that was to come later. While there was strong resistance within the Labour Party's National Executive Committee to accepting the programme's full agenda, the left faction succeeded in garnering its support at the 1973 national conference. Harold Wilson's campaign launch speech embodied the intent of the programme:

> We shall substantially extend public enterprise by taking mineral rights. We shall also take shipbuilding, ship-repairing and marine engineering, ports, the manufacture of airframes and aeroengines into public ownership and control. But we shall not confine the extension of the public sector to the loss-making and subsidised industries. We shall also take over profitable sections or individual firms in those industries where a public holding is essential to enable the government to control prices, stimulate investment, encourage exports, create employment, protect workers and consumers from the activities of irresponsible multinational companies, and to plan the national economy in the national interest.

When Harold Wilson assumed office, in February 1974, he appointed Tony Benn, a key proponent of the programme, as secretary of state for industry. In his book, *That Option No Longer Exists: Britain 1974–76*, John Medhurst provides a detailed account of what happened in the months that followed, when the left came close to implementing a radical socialist economic strategy.[11] Benn wasted no time in drawing up a White Paper for an Industry Act commensurate with Labour's programme, encompassing the commitment to extending workers' control, but the document was significantly watered down by Wilson, especially with respect to the NEB's proposed right to influence the direction of existing firms and impose a statutory framework for economic growth. Benn tried again by drawing up a paper designed to set the Industry Act in the context of a wider Alternative Economic Strategy, which argued for reflation, price and import controls to protect nascent and struggling British industries, public ownership of major financial institutions, and the tackling of systemic inequalities through progressive taxation and social spending. It too was blocked, Medhurst noting: 'When given the paper Wilson wrote a short note in red ink for his office across the cover "I haven't read it, don't propose to, but I disagree with it".'[12]

By the time the NEB was set up under the 1975 Industry Act, its remit had been modified. Its primary role was now that of providing funds for industrial investment. To the left the NEB was a disappointment. Wyn Grant, in an authoritative study of the Wilson government's industrial policy, noted that the NEB 'as it developed was very different from the original conception of Labour's left-wingers of an organisation which could spearhead the transformation of Britain's industrial economy from capitalism to socialism'.[13] That said, the 1975 Industry Act, 'while not satisfying the left, did go further than any previous legislation in increasing the state's role in industry', Martin Holmes wrote.[14] In many ways, the painstaking legislative action on the creation of the NEB had brought to the fore the fundamentally incompatible visions of the right-wing and left-wing factions of the Labour Party. On the one hand was Wilson (and the rest of the party leadership), increasingly under pressure from an establishment that recognised in Benn's industrial strategy 'an existential threat to its power and privileges'; on the other was Benn himself, 'an eloquent and effective socialist in a vital ministerial position who had support across the extra-parliamentary left and trade union movement'.[15] Clearly, the party – and Britain – were at a crossroads, and ripe for a reckoning. By this point, the British ruling elite was apoplectic. Andrew Glyn recalls that the *Times* ran various articles calling for 'a co-ordinated defence against industrial action or wholesale nationalisation' and discussing scenarios in which the armed forces would be called in to break strikes, which could escalate to a situation where 'normal legal administration is impossible and the only authority left is the military commander'.[16]

By this stage, it was clear that a solution to the crisis within the narrow limits of the social-democratic framework (such as the one attempted by Wilson in the mid-1960s) was not an option. A radical resolution one way or another – either on labour's terms or on capital's terms – was inevitable. From a socialist perspective, as the Labour left argued, this meant: (i) bringing a larger share of production under public ownership; (ii) expanding the government's role of employer of first resort (thus reducing the ability of capital to use unemployment as a blackmail tool); and (iii) implementing capital/import controls to manage the country's balance of payments. The leadership of the Labour Party had no intention of permitting such a development, however. The European Economic Community (EEC) referendum of 1975 provided the opportunity for the leadership to inflict a comprehensive and decisive defeat on the left. The overwhelming victory of the 'yes' vote gave Wilson the perfect opportunity to sideline Benn – who had campaigned against the EEC, fearing (correctly) that Treaty of Rome competition clauses threatened the Industry Act – by moving him to the much less influential Department of Energy.

This all but killed the impetus for radical reform. The Labour leadership, in fact, had come to the conclusion that the only way out of the crisis was to restore the profitability of capital. This required it to use its 'indissoluble link' with the leaderships of the trade unions 'not to advance but to *discipline* the class and organizations it represents'.[17] In other words, Labour took it upon itself to use the apparatus of the state to 'manage the capitalist crisis on behalf of capital'[18] – which, as we will see, is precisely what the neoliberal revolution is all about. However, in doing so it painted itself into a corner: increasingly engulfed in monetarist ideology and at odds with the more radical sections of the working class, and with no alternative strategy for managing the economic crisis, the government desperately needed the support of key sections of capital.

By the mid-1970s, however, capital – in the UK and elsewhere – was firmly committed to overcoming the Keynesian political-institutional framework, which it saw as a barrier to its own reproduction. Thus, even though by early 1976 Britain appeared to have weathered the OPEC storm quite well – despite strong shop-floor resistance, the government's voluntary wage guidelines had managed to slow down earnings significantly; inflation had started to fall; and the political and monetary authorities were slowly coming to terms with the new reality of the floating pound, which they had finally allowed to slide, providing a significant boost to the export sector – the British financial-corporate lobby, supported by powerful free-market think tanks such as the Institute for Economic Affairs, started mounting an increasingly aggressive anti-government campaign. The financial press was relentless in its criticism of the government. In this context, we can better understand the events that led to James Callaghan's infamous 1976 speech, which marked the party's break with Keynesianism and precipitated the collapse of Keynesian legitimacy, paving the way for the rise of the neoliberal right.

SOUNDING THE DEATH KNELL OF KEYNESIANISM: CALLAGHAN AND THE 1976 IMF LOAN

The troubles started in March 1976, when the left wing of the Labour Party defeated a public expenditure White Paper calling for the immediate freezing of public expenditure and setting out plans for cuts over the 1977–9 period. Bitter divisions within the party came to the fore once again. These were exacerbated by the growing influence and pressure exerted by the monetarists on chancellor Healey, who clearly also saw the White Paper as a means to 'reassure the market', in today's parlance, by demonstrating the government's commitment to reducing the deficit. Following the defeat of the White Paper, the markets became hysterical: a large-scale sell-off of sterling began, which rapidly lost value against the dollar. Furthermore, as the *Wall Street Journal* had advocated just a few months earlier, financial markets began refusing to buy British government bonds 'until, in their view, the government had "put its house in order".[19] This became known as the 'gilt strike'.

It is quite clear, in retrospect, that this was not just a technical, 'neutral' decision taken in reaction to Britain's economic fundamentals – which were, in fact, improving – but a deliberate move to put pressure on the government to curtail public spending and retrench the welfare state. As the pound began to slide, despite a massive foreign currency loan from the IMF and foreign central banks, James Callaghan – who replaced Harold Wilson as prime minister in 1976 – portrayed the predicament facing Britain as one where the country had *no alternative* but to introduce harsh spending cuts and to resort to further external funding to 'avoid a continuing slide in the exchange rate'.[20] This was not the case, however: Britain could have chosen to challenge the speculators by letting sterling float cleanly and resorting to capital/import controls and improved planning, which would have largely eliminated the need for foreign capital inflows. By refusing to follow this route – for reasons of ideology or ignorance – Britain effectively created its own foreign currency funding crisis. Callaghan's position was perfectly in line with monetarist ideology, which held that nations with floating exchange rates 'should refrain from introducing restrictions for balance-of-payments purposes on current account transactions or payments', as the new IMF guidelines agreed in June 1974 specified.[21] This opposition to restrictions on trade and financial flows did not represent a rejection of restrictions on grounds that they were ineffective. On the contrary, it reflected an ideological aversion for state regulation that benefited workers.

Against this background, in December 1976 the new chancellor, Denis Healey, sent his infamous 'letter of intent' to the IMF – released to the public only in 2005 – agreeing to a programme of harsh spending cuts and monetary restraint in exchange for another loan. Upon news of the loan-cum-conditionalities, speculation against the pound abated. In the letter, Healey eschewed any notion that Britain would move to restrict capital flows or trade. This was a watershed moment for Labour, reinforcing a change in policy orientation away from full employment and social welfare towards the control of inflation and expenditure. Political commentator Peter Riddell wrote in 1983 that all the elements of what would become Thatcherism were already contained in Healey's letter.[22] The government's official line was that it had no other choice because it had 'exhausted its recourse to potential sources of financing other than the IMF'.[23] In fact, 'these concerns about the lack of foreign reserves were all in the context of their commitment to sustain a given level of the pound. The "funding" concerns would have vanished had the government allowed the currency to fully float.'[24]

There are two dominant interpretations of the event: one that sees it as the moment in which the Labour Party, and Britain as a whole, capitulated to the demands of the Americans, effectively surrendering control of British economic policy to the IMF; and another one that sees it as the moment in which the British left was forced to acknowledge the harsh realities of globalisation. They are both wrong. While it is certainly true that from the 1970s onwards the IMF (and other Washington-based institutions) increasingly morphed into tools of US economic imperialism, and that the US government feared that Britain's ongoing crisis would undermine 'assumptions of political stability' and threaten US interests in the region,[25] the reality is that 'the terms of the loan imposed no constraints on the government that it had not already adopted voluntarily'.[26]

In fact, Callaghan had already explicitly rejected Keynesian full employment policies in his infamous address to the party conference in September 1976 – several months before the IMF application. The speech is said to have 'effectively sounded the death-knell for postwar Keynesian policies', and to have 'served the monetarist cause for years to come'.[27] It is also touted by some as the moment at which the British left finally 'faced up' to the reality of the growing irrelevance of the state in the face of global economic forces. Callaghan said:

> Britain faces its most dangerous crisis since the war. ... The cosy world we were told would go on for ever, where full employment would be guaranteed by a stroke of the chancellor's pen, cutting taxes, deficit spending, that cosy world is gone. ... When we reject unemployment as an economic instrument – as we do – and when we reject also superficial remedies, as socialists must, then we must ask ourselves unflinchingly what is the cause of high unemployment.

Quite simply and unequivocally, it is caused by paying ourselves more than the value of what we produce. ... We used to think that you could spend your way out of a recession, and increase employment by cutting taxes and boosting government spending. I tell you in all candour that that option no longer exists, and that in so far as it ever did exist, it only worked on each occasion since the war by injecting a bigger dose of inflation into the economy, followed by a higher level of unemployment as the next step. Higher inflation followed by higher unemployment.

As we have already seen, the high inflation that Callaghan inherited had not been caused by excessive government spending. This stance simply reflected the growing dominance of monetarist theories within the Labour leadership. In fact, as noted by Steve Ludlum, '[t]he evidence suggests ... that the shift away from the post-war consensus on sustaining full employment through demand management had begun a full two years before Callaghan's proclamation of the death of Keynesianism'.[28]

As a 1977 US Congress briefing acknowledged, Labour's leadership had long wanted to move in the direction now being recommended by the IMF, but had not been able to override the opposition of the party's left wing: 'they therefore secretly welcomed being put in a position of appearing to have no choice but to carry out the deflationary policies being dictated from outside Britain'.[29] That is, the IMF loan, far from imposing harsh conditionalities on a reluctant but powerless government, actually provided the government with the perfect alibi with which to head off mounting political opposition, by presenting austerity as the only way forward. The IMF, of course, was more than happy to be of support. It was, in other words, one of the first examples of depoliticisation – a strategy that in subsequent years and decades would become commonplace across all advanced countries, whereby politicians can 'reduce the political costs of unpopular policies by "scapegoating" international institutions'.[30] Colin Hay constructs the issue in terms of whether the policies implemented by the Healey–Callaghan government (even though he is not discussing the 1976 crisis) were *necessary* (summoned by an inexorable logic of economic globalisation), *conditional* (on the perception that such a logic is at work), or altogether *contingent*.[31] To better understand this distinction, Hay notes that 'the extent to which the parameters of the politically possible are circumscribed not by the "harsh economic realities" and "inexorable logics" of competitiveness and globalisation, but by perceptions of such logics and realities and by what they are held to entail'.[32]

In other words, though alternatives to austerity (such as Benn's proposal) did exist at the time, they were 'no longer perceived to exist'.[33] Hay acknowledges that the global economy was undergoing profound changes at the time, but notes that 'only a distinct absence of political imagination and/or a severe dose of political fatalism would imply that such changes narrow the range of alternatives to those which would subordinate social policy to economic imperatives, consigning the universal and redistributivist welfare state to a somewhat nostalgic rendition of the past'.[34]

This leads to the disquieting conclusion that the Labour-led British government of the mid-1970s was the first government effectively to break with the Keynesian consensus (excluding Germany, which never really subscribed to Keynesianism in the first place) and embrace monetarism-morphing-into-neoliberalism, not due to outside imposition or external constraints, but of its own volition. This, in turn, paved the way for Thatcher. While the aforementioned US Congress briefing concluded that 'this IMF agreement can only be termed "soft"',[35] the reality was that it was severe enough in terms of public spending cuts to further drive up unemployment; meanwhile industrial profits remained depressed and domestic investment kept falling.

As world inflation began to rise at the end of the decade, the 'social contract' that had reconciled the unions to wage restraint in exchange for job growth and redistribution finally broke down, leading to a massive wave of strikes, particularly in the public sector, during the so-called 'winter of discontent'. Having failed to resolve the distributional struggle (either one way or the other), discredited the Keynesian ideology, and legitimised monetarism, Labour effectively set up the conditions for the social-democratic 'austerity lite' to be refined into an all-out attack on the working class by Thatcher, who was able to appeal to the public's mistrust of statism and bureaucracy, and growing frustration with union power, to advance a radical anti-labour and (seemingly) anti-statist agenda.

BRAVE NEW WORLD ORDER: THE 'VOLCKER SHOCK' AND THE RESTRUCTURING OF THE GLOBAL ORDER

In 1979, Margaret Thatcher was elected prime minister of the United Kingdom. Just over a year later, Ronald Reagan was elected president of the United States. This officially marked the beginning of what Gérard Duménil and Dominique Lévy call the 'neoliberal counter-revolution' (though, as we have seen, the legitimacy of the post-war Keynesian regimes had been declining since the late 1960s, in no small part thanks to the left's embrace of monetarism).[36] Throughout the 1980s, Reagan and Thatcher paved the way for a new social and economic order – what today we call neoliberalism – that first took hold in the core countries of the US informal empire, and then was gradually exported to the protectorates (and imposed on the countries of the periphery), according to the diktats of the so-called 'Washington consensus' (though, in fact, throughout the 1970s, neoliberal regimes had already been established in various Latin American countries through military operations and coups d'état, most notably in Chile). This period wasn't simply characterised by a radical restructuring of national economies along lines more favourable to capital, as we will see; it also involved the creation of a new international order aimed at reasserting the United States' waning hegemony.

Interestingly, the event that marked the birth of this new international order took place in 1979, more than a year before Reagan's election, during the administration of Jimmy Carter (1977–81), considered one of the most liberal presidents in US history. As we saw, in 1971 the US had reacted to the country's worsening balance of trade (and to the threat of a run on its gold reserves) by ending the gold–dollar convertibility. The move (and the subsequent devaluation) had restored US economic autonomy but had done little to halt America's steep decline in competitiveness, resulting in record-level trade deficits and continued capital flight (both domestic and foreign) throughout the 1970s. For the first two years of his term, Carter actively sought to increase American exports through orchestrated declines in the value of the dollar, but to no avail. Meanwhile, as elsewhere, inflation had been rising relentlessly since the mid-1970s and had reached double-digit levels by the end of the decade. Inflation was regarded by the US policy establishment as the main factor hindering investment and innovation.

Against this background, in 1979, Paul Volcker, who had played an important role in Nixon's decision to suspend the gold–dollar convertibility during his spell at the Treasury, was appointed chairman of the Federal Reserve. At his confirmation hearing in August 1979, Volcker warned that inflation was eating into profits, indicating the need to use anti-inflation measures to redress the balance of strength with labour. The new chairman did not waste time: over the course of the following three years, Volcker oversaw a radical tightening of US monetary policy, known as the 'Volcker shock', aimed not only at restoring the dynamism of the US economy (by attracting foreign capital to Wall Street) and at disciplining labour–capital relations at home (by driving up unemployment and breaking the bargaining power of the unions), but also at disciplining core–periphery relations internationally.

As Guido Giacomo Preparata and Domenico D'Amico write: 'The idea was to give up on the idea of a trade war … and wager everything instead on making "US securities" America's foremost "export". … If America was going to relinquish the imperative of fighting the vassals for world trade share, this meant that, as a rule, she would deliberately buy more than she sold abroad, and thereby be bound to "finance" a *chronic trade deficit* precisely with these "capital" inflows from abroad'.[37] In other words, with respect to Bretton Woods, 'the process of acquiring resources by printing dollars at no cost presently came to be *embedded* in the grand international traffic of financial exchange'.[38] Volcker thus let interest rates rise to historically unprecedented levels, imposing 'the most severe discipline on the US economy – and the world's – ever attempted in the history of the American central bank'.[39]

The interest rate hike set off the sharpest recession in the United States in 35 years. Meanwhile, between 1979 and 1982, unemployment was driven up from 6 to nearly 11 per cent, nullifying the power of the unions and disabling the cost-push effect of wage increases on the cost of living. When real interests began to abate, from 1982 onward, inflation had been tamed down to 3–4 per cent. Internationally, the impact of the manoeuvre was immediate: foreign capital came pouring in (and has continued doing so ever since). For developing countries, the consequences were catastrophic, as the Volcker shock ushered in debt crises across the entire developing world, where a majority of the debt stock was held in dollars. This was no coincidence: as noted by Kees van der Pijl, ever since the early 1970s, US-based right-wing organisations such as the Heritage Foundation had been attacking Third World advocates of a new international economic order on account of their strategy to use the post-1971 dollar inflation for a grand redistribution of global power and influence under the guise of 'self-determination'.[40]

Throughout the 1980s, these state-reinforced policies set the stage for what became known as globalisation – a process that, like earlier developments, was not the result of some inevitable capitalist dynamic but, on the contrary, was largely the outcome of a US-led policy to restructure the global order in a manner favourable to US corporate and financial interests, with the support of the various national elites of the US protectorate. It is important to note that even though neoliberalism is closely associated with the so-called New Right regimes of Thatcher in Britain, Reagan in the US and Brian Mulroney in Canada, it was equally, and perhaps even more vehemently, practised by political regimes of the centre-left, such as the 'third way' social-democratic governments of Europe (and Australia and New Zealand) in the 1980s and 1990s, and the Clinton presidency in the US. As Leo Panitch and Sam Gindin write:

> The US was of course not the only country to introduce neoliberal policies, but once the American state itself moved in this direction, it had a new status: capitalism now operated under 'a new form of social rule' that promised, and largely delivered, (a) the revival of the productive base for American dominance; (b) a universal model for restoring the conditions for profits in other developed countries; and (c) the economic conditions for integrating global capitalism.[41]

The concern with retaining capital and attracting new capital meant that the US started pushing for the liberalisation of capital flows worldwide. To that end, the US government used its influence to bring about a radical paradigm shift within the various Washington-based institutions – most notably the IMF. Capital controls had been an integral part of the post-war Bretton Woods system, and at the time were endorsed by most mainstream economists and international institutions, including the IMF. Throughout the 1970s, however, the IMF began to take an increasingly critical view of capital controls and 'gradually abandoned the view that persistently high unemployment was due to weak demand and increasingly focused on rigid labor markets and other supply-side issues as the source of the problem'.[42] These views would eventually form the core of what became known as the 'Washington consensus', a term introduced into the public lexicon in 1989 by English economist John Williamson to describe the liberalisation policy agenda prescribed to (imposed on) developing countries by Washington-based institutions such as the IMF, the World Bank and the economic agencies of the US government.[43] This included fiscal austerity, trade liberalisation, deregulation of financial and labour markets, and privatisation of state enterprises. As argued by Joseph E. Stiglitz and Jagdish Bhagwati, among others, from the 1970s onwards the IMF (and other Washington-based institutions) effectively morphed into tools of US economic imperialism.[44] That same year (1989), Francis Fukuyama argued that the end of the Cold War and the subsequent 'embrace' of Western-style capitalist democracy by a growing number of countries signalled the 'end of history': the 'end point of mankind's ideological evolution' and the 'final form of human government'.[45] It was in this context, Panitch and Gindin note, that

> the internationalization of the state became particularly important. In the course of the protracted and often confused renegotiations ... of the terms that had, since the end of World War II, bound Europe and Japan to the American empire, all the nation states involved came to accept a responsibility for creating the necessary *internal* conditions for sustained *international* accumulation, such as stable prices, constraints on labour militancy, national treatment of foreign investment and no restrictions on capital outflows. ... *Nation states were thus not fading away, but adding to their responsibilities.*[46]

This underscores a crucial fact: that neoliberalism has very little to do with classical liberalism or *laissez-faire*, and certainly did not entail a retreat of the state in favour of the market (as we will see in greater detail in Chapter 5). However, during this period (and then continuing into the 1990s), the anti-state narrative spearheaded by the monetarists in the 1970s took on a new twist: government intervention in the economy came to be seen not only as dangerous and ineffective but, increasingly, as outright impossible. A new consensus was setting in: that economic and financial internationalisation – i.e. 'globalisation' – had rendered the state increasingly powerless vis-à-vis 'the forces of the market', and that countries had little choice but to abandon national economic strategies and all the traditional instruments of intervention in the economy, such as tariffs and other trade barriers, capital controls, currency and exchange rate manipulation, and fiscal and central bank policies. The best they could hope for were transnational or supranational forms of economic governance. This process – which was generally (and erroneously, as we shall see) framed as a shift from the state to the market – was accompanied by a ferocious attack on the very idea of national sovereignty, increasingly vilified as a relic of the past. Europe – and in particular the European left – played a crucial role in cementing this ideological shift towards a post-national and post-sovereign view of the world. One of the most consequential turning points in this respect was Mitterrand's 1983 turn to austerity – the so-called *tournant de la rigueur* – just two years after the French Socialists' historic victory in 1981.

4
The Paris Consensus: The French Left and the Creation of Neoliberal Europe

By the early 1980s, the French economy had succumbed to the disastrous austerity imposed by the Barre Plan. Unemployment had risen sharply and the French people were in a mood for a change away from the conflictual politics and poor economic outcomes that had characterised the 1970s. The Socialist François Mitterrand was elected president on 10 May 1981, after more than two decades of the French left being excluded from office (ever since the establishment of the Fifth Republic in 1958). Five weeks later, the left backed up Mitterrand's success by winning a majority of seats in the National Assembly in legislative elections. That set the stage for the formation of a government that (for the first time since 1947) also included Communist ministers. This inspired a widespread belief – as incredible as that may sound to us today – that France was headed for a radical break with capitalism. To appreciate this point, it is important to understand the context of the French left's triumph in 1981. As we have seen, by the late 1970s and early 1980s the monetarists had already won some significant ideological and political battles against the post-war 'Keynesian' consensus – most notably in the US and UK. But the war was far from over, especially in continental Europe.

At that time, the old continent was still very much wedded to the 'old' post-war social-democratic consensus. Socialist/communist parties – notwithstanding a slide to the right among their ranks following a period of increased radicalisation up to the mid-1970s – still yielded significant political and electoral power (to give an idea, in the early 1980s the Italian Communist Party still regularly raked in about 30 per cent of the votes). Even though the balance of power had already started to shift away from labour towards capital, unions were still capable of paralysing economic activity through massive general strikes. Social and protest movements – not to mention various left-wing paramilitary organisation, such as the Red Brigades in Italy and the Rote Armee Fraktion in Germany – were sending shockwaves across the continent (barely over a decade had passed since May 1968, after all).

Most European countries (with the notable exception of Germany and a few others) still firmly believed in the need for capital controls and regulated financial markets. As a matter of fact, the need for capital controls was even 'embedded' in the EEC's directives.[1]

This reflected the fact that in the early 1980s economic policy was still very much defined along national lines. Throughout the 1970s, national rivalries had led to a stagnation of the European integration process known as 'eurosclerosis'. Economic problems, the slow pace of enlargement and a perceived lack of democracy meant that negative and apathetic attitudes to the EEC were high. The French, in particular, were reluctant to agree to any supranational authority – a consistent position that had hampered progress towards economic and monetary union since the inception of the idea. In general, globalisation was not yet seen as something inevitable and inescapable; there was still the belief that individual nations had the power to shape their own economic and political destinies – and even to challenge the capitalist system itself. Nothing exemplifies this better than Mitterrand's victory in the spring of 1981.

The new president's policy agenda embodied an ambitious reform programme, encapsulated in his campaign platform – the famous '110 Propositions for France'. Mitterrand came to power in the midst of a deep crisis of French capitalism. Confronted with rising unemployment (largely as a result of the previous government's austerity policies), growing inflationary pressures, low productivity growth and stagnant business activity, the new president promised to take drastic measures to revive the French economy. As radical as it may seem to us today, Mitterrand's manifesto was, in fact, a pretty straightforward programme of Keynesian economic reflation and redistribution. It proposed to fund research and develop innovative ways to fund small and medium businesses that struggled to gain working capital through conventional means; to create at least 150,000 jobs in the public sector as a vehicle for improving health services, education, the postal service and the efficiency of government; to reduce working hours to 35 hours per week;

and to impose a solidarity tax on wealth to reduce inequality. Income support payments would also be increased.

It also proposed extensive nationalisations of France's increasingly uncompetitive industrial conglomerates, in order to maintain employment levels and aid the process of economic reconstruction. In the context of French politics in the late 1970s, the government's nationalisation plan was not as radical as it might appear in retrospect. Indeed, French capitalism had a long tradition of government planning and state-led economic growth. Essentially, Mitterrand's nationalisation plan represented an attempt to revive and extend the post-war *dirigiste* model that the previous right-wing government had attempted to dismantle. The government also intended to subsidise economic activity through deficit spending, primarily through a major expansion of the welfare state. By implementing this platform, Mitterrand claimed, his government would precipitate a 'rupture' with capitalism, and lay the foundations for a 'French road to socialism'. It's easy to see why this represented a moment of immense hope not just for the French left, but for the entire European left – of the kind that Europe has not witnessed since.

By the end of 1982, overall public expenditure had risen by 11.4 per cent. The retirement age was lowered from 65 to 60. Meanwhile, minimum pensions were increased by 20 per cent and family allowances were raised by 25 per cent. The country's statutory minimum wage (the SMIC) was increased by almost 40 per cent. Furthermore, government employment was expanded, with the government hiring 200,000 new civil servants. Union rights were expanded as well, notably through the 1982 Auroux Law, which required annual negotiations between employers and union representatives. Soon after the Mitterrand experiment began, however, it started to unravel. The president's reflation efforts were hampered by a number of factors. First, capital started fleeing the country almost immediately – a sign that French capitalists and financial markets didn't appreciate the government's plan of economic reform and social redistribution. As Rawi E. Abdelal, professor of business administration at Harvard Business School, writes in his book *Capital Rules*:

> The French government tightened its controls on outflows of capital first in May 1981, then again in March 1982, and by March 1983 the regulations were rewritten as restrictively as possible. Importers and exporters were not allowed forward exchange transactions, foreign travel allowances were further reduced, personal credit cards could

not be used abroad, and the infamous *carnet de change,* a booklet in which the French were to record their foreign exchange transactions, was introduced. According to John Goodman and Louis Pauly, the new regulations amounted to 'draconian capital controls'.[2]

However, the French government was unable to halt the flight of capital. At the same time, French capital also went on strike, refusing to invest in the economy. Meanwhile, France, at the start of the 1980s, was also confronted with a particularly unfavourable global economic environment. The French economy was still reeling from the effects of the second oil crisis (1979) and subsequent global recession, which had hammered France's already-weakened industrial sector, crippling traditionally important industries like steel. Moreover, the effects of the recession were exacerbated by the US Treasury's high interest rate policy. The shakeout from the Volcker shock had not only resulted in a severe decline in the US economy, but also in ripple effects throughout Western Europe. With the value of the dollar at an all-time high, officials in other countries quickly moved to deflate their own economies, in order to prevent their currencies from losing value relative to the dollar. In response to the US Federal Reserve Bank's move, the Bundesbank also hiked interest rates in 1981 in an effort to stabilise the mark against the dollar, in what the press of the time described as 'a punishing interest-rate war with the United States'.[3] The effects of these deflationary policies were felt all over Europe, particularly in France, where Mitterrand's reflationary policies exacerbated the downward pressure on the franc.

The problem was that Mitterrand's domestic policy objectives were incompatible with France's membership in the European Monetary System (EMS), the precursor to the eurozone. The EMS was a currency arrangement comprising most EEC countries (designed by former French president Giscard d'Estaing and the German chancellor Helmut Schmidt) that essentially anchored all participating currencies to the German mark, by means of the Exchange Rate Mechanism (ERM), effectively forcing the central banks of other European economies to shadow the Bundesbank's monetary policy. This meant that a nation facing reduced international competitiveness had to cut costs (for example, by constraining wage rises) to bring its inflation rate down and constrain domestic demand to reduce growth in national income and GDP, which would lead to reduced spending on imports. By tying the French franc to the German mark, through the ERM, the EMS restricted the French government's ability to adjust monetary policy to meet the country's macroeconomic needs. France was always going to face downward pressure on its exchange rate while it tried to maintain the currency peg with the mark; by the same token, domestic policies that sought to expand employment and increase domestic spending were always going to come up against a balance-of-payments constraint. With rising imports and a widening external deficit, especially in the context of Germanys' mercantilist policies, central bank policy was biased towards higher-than-warranted interest rates and domestic recession. The same problem plagued all the members of the EMS.

One could say that the French wanted everything: political popularity associated with lower unemployment and improved living conditions on one hand; a straitjacket on perceived German pretensions to European power and continued German subsidies to the Common Agricultural Policy (CAP) on the other. This proved impossible. Continued speculation against the franc forced the Banque de France to buy the currency in large quantities in international exchange markets to maintain the peg. By the time of the third currency realignment, in March 1983 – the French government had already devalued twice, in 1981 and in 1982, mostly to deal with the strengthening mark and the diverging economic policies between the two nations – the French were at a crossroads and the incompatibility of these competing ambitions was obvious. Mitterrand found himself in a position where a decision had to be made about whether to leave the EMS or abandon his progressive agenda. Regrettably, he chose the latter path.

In the spring of 1983, Mitterrand and the Socialists suddenly and drastically reversed course, in what came to be know as the *tournant de la rigueur* ('turn to austerity'): rather than growth and employment, the emphasis was now to be on price stability and fiscal restraint. Indeed, by this time Mitterrand had become 'obsessed with inflation' (to quote one of his colleagues).[4] Mitterrand was convinced by his finance minister (and future president of the European Commission) Jacques Delors to adopt a 'strong franc' (or *franc fort*) policy, in which the French currency would be purposely overvalued to ensure monetary stability and to counteract inflationary pressures. On 16 May 1983, the European Council extended a large foreign currency bailout to France to stabilise the franc on the condition that it tighten fiscal policy. The French agreed to limit their fiscal deficit to 3 per cent of GDP in 1983 and 1984, restraining social security and unemployment insurance payments and cutting the capacity of state-owned enterprises to borrow. Further, the Banque de France was required to reduce the money growth target to create a marked reduction in the rate of domestic credit expansion. The decision was brazen. For being compliant and abandoning its 'Keynesian' programme, the French government was given some short-term foreign currency funds to bolster the exchange rate – in a manner not dissimilar from the IMF's policy of offering loans to struggling nations in exchange for harsh conditionalities.

After the turn to *rigueur*, the president's economic outlook began to mirror the concerns of the business establishment. By 1984, the government had begun to relax employment regulations and cut subsidies for French industry, forcing uncompetitive firms to reorganise and reduce costs. This resulted in a spate of mass layoffs in the country's once-core industries: among the hardest-hit sectors were steel, where the government announced that it was eliminating 25,000 jobs; ship building, which saw its capacity reduced by 30 per cent, resulting in a loss of 6,000 jobs; and mining, which suffered a reduction of state aid by more than a quarter over just five years, resulting in a loss of 20,000 jobs. As noted by Jonah Birch, '[i]n subsequent years, the government oversaw the wholesale restructuring of French capitalism': removing subsidies for struggling firms, allowing large swaths of industry to go bankrupt and dismantling the core institutions of the post-war *dirigiste* model.[5]

Meanwhile, capital controls and restrictions on financial activities were rolled back. The government began to loosen its 'draconian capital controls' at the end of 1983, continuing in the summer and autumn of 1984. In 1985, the Socialists began to liberalise virtually all transactions. Domestic capital markets also experienced a complete transformation, and the process of deregulation between 1982 and 1985 was just as profound. Oriented around a new banking law in 1984, the French financial reform involved privatisations and, ultimately, the removal of credit controls. 'Essentially, the domestic financial reform ended the state-organised *dirigiste* financial system, which had been the very basis of French policy activism for forty years', Rawi E. Abdelal writes.[6] The Mitterrand government also commenced the long-term process of privatising the French state's large collection of public assets.

The reduction in domestic inflation and shift to a current account surplus that resulted from the government's 'scorched earth' approach were celebrated as a demonstration of the policy's success. And on its own terms – centred on a very narrow set of macroeconomic variables –

it was. Yet the social and economic costs of that success were enormous. Net wages fell by 2.5 per cent in 1984, with the wage share, after peaking in 1982, dropping steadily thereafter. The official unemployment rate rose from 7.4 per cent in 1982 to 10.2 per cent in 1985 and continued to increase after that. Not surprisingly, the savings ratio (household savings out of disposable income) fell from 16.4 per cent in 1982 to 13.5 per cent in 1985 as a result of the declining economic growth and rising unemployment. France's output gap (the difference between actual output and the maximum potential output) nearly trebled between 1982 and 1985.

The sudden shift in policy in March 1983 should be understood in the context of the long-standing intellectual battle between the old-school planners – who supported a policy known, literally, as *l'autre politique*, or 'the other policy' (essentially to close off France's markets, to float the franc and reject the constraints of the EMS) – on one side, and the economists and technocrats in the Trésor (finance ministry) and the Banque de France on the other, who had been advocating price stability, financial austerity (*rigueur*) and 'European solidarity' long before 1983. These included prime minister Pierre Mauroy, Trésor director Michel Camdessus (who subsequently went on to become the über-liberal governor of the Banque de France and then the head of the IMF) and finance minister Jacques Delors. It is they that convinced Mitterrand to accept austerity and the constraints of the EMS because 'allowing the franc to float would bring disaster'.[7]

Analysing in detail *why* the French left came to embrace neoliberalism so enthusiastically is beyond the scope of this book. There were multiple agendas at play. For some, such as Mitterrand, it was probably a way of retaining power; to others, 'it offered an appealing political identity, a "modern", "competent" profile, in contrast to the "archaic" and excessively "ideological" image' of the old-school left;[8] others likely underwent a genuine conversion, as they came to see capital liberalisation and financial integration as the necessary price to pay for the modernisation and 'normalisation' of France. What concerns us here are the *effects* of that pivotal U-turn. These cannot be overestimated. Mitterrand's victory in 1981 had inspired the widespread belief that a radical break with capitalism – at least with the extreme form of capitalism that had recently taken hold in the Anglo-Saxon world – was still possible; by 1983 the French Socialists had succeeded in 'proving' the exact opposite: that neoliberal globalisation was an inescapable and inevitable reality. British economist Will Hutton, like almost everyone else, drew the lesson that 'the old instruments of dirigisme and state direction were plainly outmoded'.[9] 'The *tournant*, the Mitterrand U-turn, was an admission of defeat: capital had won the battle of wills and ideologies. The socialist experiment had failed. Mitterrand had succeeded only in destroying Keynesian reflation and redistribution as a legitimate alternative once and for all, or so it has seemed since then.'[10]

The repercussions of that decision are still being felt today. Mitterrand's about-turn is held out by many left-wing and progressive intellectuals as proof of the fact that globalisation and the internationalisation of finance has ended the era of nation states and their capacity to pursue policies that are not in accord with the diktats of global capital. The claim is that if a government tries autonomously to pursue full employment and a progressive/redistributive agenda, it will (i) be punished by global capital (through capital flight, delocalisation, etc.) and (ii) will inevitably incur a balance-of-payments deficit and eventually a balance-of-payments crisis. The result would be economic crisis. This narrative claims that Mitterrand had no option but to abandon the Keynesian agenda encapsulated in the '110 Propositions'. To most modern-day leftists, Mitterrand thus represents a pragmatist who was cognisant of the international capitalist forces he was up against and responsible enough to do what was best for France. For the left, this has essentially meant giving up on the notion of achieving any form of meaningful change at the national level, and accepting the idea that true change can only come at the supranational (and ideally global) level.

In the second part of this book we show that sovereign, currency-issuing states – such as France in the 1980s – far from being helpless against the power of global capital, still have the capacity to deliver full employment and social justice to their citizens. Before we get to that, though, we first have to understand how the idea of the 'death of the state' came to be so engrained in our collective consciousness. This means looking at how the French Socialists, after having embraced neoliberalism, then proceeded to export their newfound views – on everything from capital movements to monetary integration – to the rest of Europe.

ANOTHER EUROPE WAS POSSIBLE: JACQUES DELORS AND THE RISE OF NEOLIBERAL EUROPE

As we have seen, Mitterrand's finance minister, Jacques Delors, was instrumental in persuading the Socialist Party's hardliners that

Keynesian (let alone *socialist*) national economic strategies were no longer an option in an increasingly globalised world. 'National sovereignty no longer means very much, or has much scope in the modern world economy. ... A high degree of supra-nationality is essential', he told John Ardagh.[11] This was a radical departure from France's traditional *souverainiste* stance. Especially if we consider that, by choosing EMS membership above domestic policy considerations, France (and other EMS member states) had effectively accepted to subjugate its own monetary/fiscal policy independence to the Bundesbank, which had became the *de facto* central bank of the entire EEC.

For all of France's historical concerns about supranational (that is, 'European') encroachment on its national sovereignty on the one hand, and German hegemony on the other, it is somewhat ironic that it took the Socialists to give up that freedom – and then not to Brussels, but to Germany of all nations. It was argued that the growing acceptance of the primacy of 'price stability' among French politicians on both sides of the political divide was a reflection of their desire to regain some semblance of French domination in Europe. De Boissieu and Pisani-Ferry noted that 'only a low-inflation, stable-currency France could pretend to some form of leadership in Europe' and 'maintaining France's status within the EC and within the so-called French-German couple' required them to fall into line.[12] In other words, the French political establishment saw *rigueur* as a way to retain power, and the cost to the citizens in the form of suppressed real wages and rising unemployment was subsidiary, at best. Mitterrand 'made the choice of giving priority to France's European commitments over his own initial economic program in 1983'.[13]

This brought about a distinct shift in attitudes among the Socialists towards Europe. Reflecting on the limitations of the national solution in October 1983, Delors said: 'Our only choice is between a united Europe and decline.'[14] As Rawi E. Abdelal notes: 'To the extent that the French left continued to hope for socialist transformation, its members could see Europe as the only arena in which socialist goals could be achieved.'[15] The problem was that, by that point, the French Socialists had little to offer in terms of a Europe-wide progressive alternative. Not only had they already agreed to forsake their national progressive agenda in favour of austerity, but policymakers throughout Europe interpreted the failure of Mitterrand's experiment as the failure of redistributive Keynesianism, essentially leaving only the Bundesbank's monetarism as a legitimate paradigm.

In 1985, Jacques Delors became president of the European Commission, a post he would hold for a decade. The Delors presidency (1985–95) is understood to be groundbreaking, giving the European integration process a forward momentum that had been lacking in the preceding decade. It is also the period in which the foundations of monetary union, and more generally of neoliberal Europe, were laid down – a development in which Delors played a key role. Although Delors and the Commission cannot take all the credit (or blame, depending on your point of view) for the establishment of monetary union, for much debate was still to come, they 'nonetheless performed a pivotal part as recruiting agents for the cause of EMU', as Nicolas Jabko notes.[16]

The French understood that, within the EMS, the Bundesbank effectively set the interest rates for all EMS nations, irrespective of whether the rates were appropriate for other countries. Further, while the formal EMS understanding placed equal burden on the central banks to maintain currency stability, the reality was that nations facing downward pressure on their currencies had to shoulder the burden of adjustment because the Bundesbank increasingly refused to do its share, given that the mark was the strongest currency. For the Germans, intervention would have meant selling marks in the currency markets, which they feared would have ignited domestic inflation as a result of the expanding money supply (in line with monetarist theories). Horst Ungerer and others concluded that 'the hegemonic role of German economic policy … narrowed the choice of economic strategies for its partner countries, impeded growth-oriented policies on their part, and thus perpetuated unemployment problems' and was 'contrary to the community character of the EMS'.[17]

Thus, the French became increasingly convinced that the only way to preserve a fixed exchange rates system (which they were strongly committed to since the introduction of the CAP and, later, the adoption of the *franc fort* policy) while at the same time regaining a degree of policy independence and wrestling control of monetary policy away from Germany, was to push for a full European monetary union. As Jacques de Larosière, then governor of the Banque de France, explained in 1990: 'Today I am the governor of a central bank who has decided, along with his nation, to follow fully the German monetary policy without voting on it. At least, as part of a European central bank, I'll have a vote.'[18] For Delors, EMU – that is, a single European currency – became a priority, and in his role as president of the Commission he set out to persuade his reluctant fellow European policymakers to embrace it.

UNSHACKLING CAPITAL: THE PUSH FOR THE FULL LIBERALISATION OF CAPITAL FLOWS

The first attempt to nullify German dominance of the EMS, which had effectively become a mark zone, came in the mid-1980s during the debate leading up to the signing of the 1986 Single European Act (SEA), the first major revisions of the 1957 Treaty of Rome. The SEA set the objective of establishing a single market by 31 December 1992. It also aimed at improving the speed of decision making in the EEC (by implementing qualified majorities for certain Council decisions) and empowering the European Parliament. But Delors failed to include a commitment in the SEA towards creating an independent (from Germany) European monetary authority, mostly as a result of Germany's reluctance to give up its policy dominance within the EEC by ceding power to a supranational monetary authority. As president of the Commission, Delors also proceeded to export France's new views on capital movements to the rest of Europe, by pushing for the full liberalisation of capital flows across the continent. As Abdelal notes, Delors came to believe that EMU required capital liberalisation: 'Although I had concerns, I came to the realization that the free movement of capital was essential to the creation of the internal market.'[19] Economist Jacques Melitz describes the significance of the French *tournant* for Europe:

When economic historians look back at this important juncture in European financial history, I believe that they will conclude that the French liberalization program was the single most important forerunner of the [EMU]. With this liberalization program came the French support for an integrated European market for financial services, without which the proposal of a Single Market would never have gotten off the ground.[20]

The Commission's initial proposals – including the failed attempt to include the full liberalisation of capital flows in the SEA – were met with fierce resistance in a number of governments, including France, still in the middle of its own transformation, and Italy. As already mentioned, most European countries (with the notable exception of Germany and a few others) at the time still firmly believed in the need for capital controls and regulated financial markets. The breakthrough for Delors came in 1987, with the signing of the Basel–Nyborg agreement. By playing the French and the Italians against the Germans, Delors got the former to agree to further capital liberalisations (thus paving the way for the codification of the norm of capital mobility in Europe) in exchange for the latter committing to coordinating interest rate changes with the other countries and, more importantly, intervening in foreign exchange markets on behalf of the weaker currencies in the EMS. What was truly unprecedented, though, was Germany's official commitment to the goal of monetary union as contained in the agreement. In an impressive display of political shrewdness, Delors had succeeded in killing off two birds with one stone. According to Nicolas Jabko, the two policy objectives – capital liberalisation and monetary union – were, in fact, strictly linked. Europe's central banks had already essentially relinquished their monetary autonomy to the Bundesbank through the EMS. The Commission thus 'raised the political stakes of EMU, acting decisively to liberalise capital movements while exhorting European governments to embrace EMU as a compensatory instrument for regaining monetary sovereignty'.[21] Abdelal writes that:

> Delors and his team also were able to emphasize to policymakers ... [that] Europe had *already* painted itself into a corner. Having chosen free capital and fixed exchange rates, only one choice remained for them, whether it be de facto or de jure. ... Liberal capital rules, authored by French policymakers in Brussels, played a decisive role in encouraging European policymakers to recognize that with monetary union they were giving up a monetary policy autonomy that already was illusory in favor of a seat at the table.[22]

THE BATTLE FOR MONETARY UNION

It should be noted that various developments played into Delors' hand, first and foremost Germany's concerns about the growing anti-German sentiment in Europe. In this context, the German Foreign Office took the diplomatic decision to push for monetary union to quell the ongoing criticism of the 'ugly German', which threatened to derail the progress that the nation had made in restoring its image in the post-war period. The situation had been reached where the French pushed for monetary union to undermine the dominance of the Bundesbank, despite their historical distaste for ceding domestic policy discretion to supranational bodies, and the Germans supported monetary union as part of their vision of a 'European Germany'. The German willingness to advance the common currency was highly conditional, however, and reflected the dominance of the Bundesbank. Hans-Dietrich Genscher, Germany's foreign minister, understood that he could reduce opposition to EMU within Germany (particularly from the Bundesbank) if he could get the other member states to agree to the creation of a fully independent central bank – that is, fully insulated from what the democratically elected polity, at the national or European level, might desire – with the sole mandate of ensuring price stability.

Genscher's proposal was considered at the European Council meeting in Hannover on 27–8 June 1988, which established a working party headed by Jacques Delors to develop a detailed implementation plan for the creation of an economic and monetary union. The Delors Committee deliberately excluded the economics and finance ministers at the suggestion of Delors himself. He wanted the committee to 'consist of the governors of the central banks, who were more independent than the governments'.[23] Delors knew that the Bundesbank would not budge on the independence of a new European central bank and that it would have been difficult to find an agreement if the countries' finance ministers had been involved. 'National treasury officials from several countries balked at German demands on autonomy and focused a great deal more on the economic side of EMU', Howarth and Loedel wrote.[24] Further, the central bankers had been explicitly excluded from the design of the EMS in 1979, which Delors considered had rendered the system prone to failure. Delors thus constituted his committee to minimise any (legitimate) discussions of member state sovereignty and to push through a homogenised monetarist vision for the new united Europe.

By excluding a diversity of opinion, Europe was setting itself up for monumental failure, which manifested itself in 2008 and continues to this day. Verdun asked how the 'consensus on the creation of EMU in the Community could have been reached so easily'.[25] She concluded that the Delors committee constituted an 'epistemic community', defined by Haas as 'a network of professionals with recognized expertise and competence in a particular domain and an authoritative claim to policy-relevant knowledge within that domain or issue-area'.[26] This network also shared normative and causal beliefs and was engaged in a 'common policy enterprise', which means they agreed on 'common practices associated with a set of problems'. The central bankers met regularly and held a similar worldview about the primacy of monetary policy, and the need for fiscal policy to be a passive support to the deflationary strategy defined by the Bundesbank. The neoliberal groupthink was consolidating. In simple terms, the exclusion of the ECOFIN ministers meant that the monetarist-oriented central bankers would quickly come up with a consensus. All members of the committee were firmly wedded to the abandonment of Keynesian macroeconomic policies in favour of the hard-line pursuit of price stability.

Delors said in a 1999 documentary produced by the European Commission that the 'the overall philosophy behind what we proposed and even the structure of the *Delors Report* were very heavily influenced by the *Werner Report*'.[27] However, the *Werner Report* – drawn up in 1970 by a working group chaired by Pierre Werner, Luxembourg's then prime minister and minister for finance – clearly stressed that, in addition to the creation of a European central bank as the issuer of the new single currency, 'transfers of responsibility from the national to the Community plane will be essential' for the conduct of economic policy.[28] The Werner plan thus saw economic and monetary union 'as a lever for the development of political union, which in the long run it cannot do without'.[29] The later *MacDougall Report* (1977) reinforced the need for a central fiscal authority and the responsibility of a European Parliament for the decisions taken by that authority.[30]

Conversely, the committee's report – known colloquially as the *Delors Report* – constructed the EMU in terms of the continuation 'of individual nations with differing economic, social, cultural and political characteristics', noting that the 'existence and preservation of this plurality would require a degree of autonomy in economic decision-making to remain with the individual member countries'.[31] Delors' plan deviated starkly from Werner's vision for a European-level fiscal capacity. Modern federations align the primary fiscal responsibility at the level of the currency issuer. But the Delors Committee concluded that the primary fiscal policy responsibility would remain at the member state level; that is, at the level of the currency user rather than the currency issuer. The European-level oversight would be limited to imposing arbitrary but binding fiscal rules and, importantly, prohibiting the newly created central bank from directly supporting member state governments in times of need. The so-called Delors plan ignored the conclusion of both the *Werner Report* and the *MacDougall Report* that the European Parliament should take responsibility for economic policy decisions at the Community level.

There were several reasons cited for this shift, one being that the French had rejected Werner's vision, which involved a significant transfer of economic policymaking capacity to the supranational level. Officially, the shift was justified by appealing to changes that had occurred in the world economy in the decade following the release of the *Werner Report*, including the demise of the Bretton Woods system, the introduction of the EMS, the inflation spikes that followed the two oil price hikes in the 1970s and the opening up of global financial markets. But all these 'reasons' simply provided a smokescreen obscuring what had really changed: the monetarist disdain for discretionary fiscal policy being used to smooth out fluctuations in private spending and maintain low levels of unemployment was now dominant. The *Delors Report*'s treatment of fiscal policy reflected this new consensus. It recommended 'binding rules' that would impose upper limits on the budget deficits of individual member countries, exclude access to direct central bank credit and other forms of monetary financing, and limit recourse to external borrowing in other currencies.[32]

In other words, the Delors plan constructed counter-stabilisation policy purely in terms of central banks adjusting interest rates to maintain price stability, with an independent central bank being the macroeconomic policy institution deemed necessary at the federal level. This starkly contradicted basic Keynesian theory, and represented a triumph of Bundesbank-style monetary discipline – and a victory for Germany. The *Delors Report* essentially acted as a blueprint for the construction of the EMU in the coming years. Indeed, the report's outline became, with few modifications, the very text of the Treaty of Maastricht's provisions for the progression towards EMU. On 23 January 1972, the governor of the Danish central bank, Frede Sunesen, wrote in the *Financial Times*: 'I will begin to believe in European economic and monetary union when someone explains how you control nine horses that are all running at different speeds within the same harness.'[33]

What eventually allowed the 'nine horses' to be harnessed together into the monetary union was not a diminution in Franco-German rivalry, but a growing homogenisation of the economic debate. The surge in monetarist thought within macroeconomics in the 1970s – first within the academy, then in policymaking and central banking domains – quickly morphed into an insular groupthink, which trapped policymakers in the thrall of the self-regulating free market myth. The accompanying confirmation bias overwhelmed the debate about monetary integration.

Delors also succeeded in persuading EU member countries to introduce full capital mobility by 1992, effectively making the free movement of capital a central tenet of the emerging European single market. This was a binding obligation not only among EU members but also between EU members and third countries. The consequence of this was a European financial system 'that was in principle the most liberal the world had ever known', according to Rawi E. Abdelal.[34] The global implications of this counter-revolution are well explained by Abdelal: 'This new definition of the European [was] itself the engine of free capital's spread on the world stage. … Global financial markets are *global* primarily because the processes of European financial integration became open and uniformly liberal.'[35] The Delors Commission's strategy of promoting capital liberalisation on the way to monetary union almost backfired when, in September 1992, a series of speculative attacks on several of the currencies in the EMS caused the collapse of the ERM. The 1992–3 crisis demonstrated that a system of fixed (or even tightly linked) exchange rates between economies that were disparate in structure and performance would always fail in the context of mobile capital. But, once again, Delors' gamble paid off. The neoliberal groupthink was so entrenched by that point that most politicians took this as evidence of the need to accelerate the move to the single currency. As one commentator put it at the time:

> The significance of this episode lies in the fact that the international capital markets were effectively able to subvert the policies of democratically elected governments in major European countries, despite all the tools and resources available to national governments and despite the monetary cooperation between European countries that had been developed on an inter-governmental basis and through the EU. This would suggest that *there are severe limits to the economic sovereignty of European nation states in the late twentieth century.*[36]

The notion that the exchange rate instability of the early 1990s, like that of the previous decades, could have happened *because of*, not despite, the flawed view of 'monetary cooperation' that dominated European policymaking – centred around the idea that national monetary and fiscal discretion (that is, economic sovereignty) needed to be subjugated to external discipline, and that all restrictions on capital should be lifted – was lost on most commentators. And so the self-deception continued, leading to the adoption of the euro in 1999. The rest, as they say, is history.

5

The State Never Went Away: Neoliberalism as a State-Driven Project

So far, the term 'neoliberalism' has figured quite heavily throughout the text. It is now time to take a more in-depth look at the term, but before we do that, let us briefly take stock of what we have covered so far, insofar as neoliberalism (in theory and practice) is concerned. In Chapter 2, we saw how neoliberalism as a political philosophy and ideology emerged in the 1930s and can be traced back to the work of economists and political philosophers such as Ludwig von Mises and Friedrich Hayek, who saw the capitalist market as something that is 'natural' and necessary for ensuring freedom, and viewed any form of government intervention that disturbed the (assumed) natural functioning of the market mechanism not only as unnatural and liable to fail but also as an assault on human freedom. It goes without saying that this is a very simplistic and one-dimensional definition of neoliberalism, which doesn't even begin to capture the shifting and contradictory nature of neoliberal theory as it evolved over the course of the twentieth century, as we will see further on. We also saw how the neoliberals, for all their proclaimed confidence in the virtues of *laissez-faire* and the inherent spontaneity of the market, put a lot of effort into the promotion of their ideas, through the Mont Pèlerin Society (founded by Hayek and others in 1947) and other organisations.

Furthermore, we saw how – after being shunned for decades in the aftermath of World War II, when Keynesianism established itself as the most popular school of economic theory –a particular form of neoliberalism re-emerged in the late 1960s as a respectable political ideology under the guise of monetarism: an economic school of thought, popularised by Milton Friedman, which argued that market economies are inherently stable in the absence of major unexpected fluctuations in the money supply, and consequently that governments should intervene in the economy as little as possible. In Chapters 3 and 4, we saw how various governments – most notably the British and French – started to adopt monetarist policies (within a Keynesian ideological and political framework) as early as the late 1960s and early 1970s. We also saw how monetarism, despite its failure as a concrete policy (which demonstrated that the basic principles of Friedman's monetarist theory were deeply flawed), subsequently morphed into a much broader and more sophisticated anti-statist ideology based upon the virtues of supply-side economics, financial and trade liberalisation, privatisation and deregulation, and more generally on the superiority of the market economy over state intervention – what today we generally refer to as neoliberalism.

In Chapter 2, we saw how this ideology was aggressively promoted by a network of influential right-wing think tanks and lobbying organisations, most notably in the English-speaking world. We saw how, from the late 1970s onwards, this coincided with the gradual dismantling of the post-war Keynesian framework (though not in the direction officially preached by neoliberal ideology, as we shall see), but we also noted how this development cannot simply be explained as the victory of one ideology ('neoliberalism') over another ('Keynesianism'), but should be understood as the result of a number of overlapping ideological, economic and political factors: the capitalists' response to the profit squeeze and to the political implications of full employment policies; the structural flaws of 'actually existing Keynesianism'; the left's inability to offer a coherent response to the crisis of the Keynesian framework, let alone a radical alternative, etc.

In Chapter 3, we saw how the 'Volcker shock' of 1979 effectively marked the beginning of a new social and economic order – what we could call 'actually existing neoliberalism' – that first took hold in the core countries of the US informal empire, and was then gradually exported to the protectorates (and imposed on the countries of the periphery), according to the diktats of the so-called 'Washington consensus'. Despite the marked differences between countries (and particularly between core and periphery countries), neoliberalism is generally associated, among other things, with trade liberalisation, deregulation of financial and labour markets, wage rollbacks, attacks on trade unions, privatisation of state enterprises and fiscal retrenchment.

Finally, we noted how the *state-driven* character of the so-called 'neoliberal counter-revolution' would appear to contradict the official policy goals of neoliberalism, not to mention the prevailing interpretations of the neoliberal era, commonly associated with a 'rollback' of the state in favour of the market. We concluded that neoliberalism has very little to do with classical liberalism or *laissez-faire*, and certainly does not entail a retreat of the state in favour of the market. If that is the case, however, then *what is the real character of neoliberalism?* It is this question that we aim to answer in this chapter.

EVERYTHING YOU KNOW ABOUT NEOLIBERALISM IS WRONG

Let us start by looking at some of the oft-heard claims about neoliberalism, and whether they conform to reality or not. As mentioned, there is a widespread belief – particularly among the left – that neoliberalism has involved (and involves) a 'retreat', 'hollowing out' or 'withering away' of the state, which in turn has fuelled the notion that today the state has been 'overpowered' by the market. This is understandable, considering that the political and economic philosophy of vanguard ideologues such as Margaret Thatcher and Ronald Reagan emphasised reduced state intervention, free markets and entrepreneurialism. This was summed up well by Reagan's now-famous phrase: 'Government is not the solution to our problem; government *is* the problem.'[1]

This, however, does not fit the empirical record of the past decades. A quick glance at the rate of state expenditure across the OECD countries, for example, shows that there has been little or no decline in the size of the state as a percentage of GDP; if anything, it has tended to rise (the only real exception being post-2008 Europe, as we will see).[2] Even supposedly neoliberal governments did not reduce their public spending and were associated with relatively high deficits.[3] As noted by Kean Birch, the Thatcher government not only failed dramatically to cut public expenditure (with levels of spending remaining the same in 1990 as 1979), but actually ran deficits in most years except 1988–90.[4] On the other side of the Atlantic, the contrast between theory (or propaganda) and practice was even more striking: despite Reagan's 'small government' rhetoric, the national debt more than tripled during his administration as a consequence of tax cuts and increased expenditures on welfare entitlements and military spending (which caused a significant increase in the national deficit, subsequently reined in by Clinton). Moreover, the US national debt grew significantly in real terms, as a result of the government's anti-inflationary strategy.

Should we therefore conclude that Reagan was a closet Keynesian? Far from it. On the contrary, it has been argued that the expansion of public debt under the Reagan administration effectively functioned as a mechanism of upwards redistribution of wealth from the lower to the upper classes, via public debt, as the government went from *taxing* the wealthiest people to fund government expenditure, to simply *borrowing* money off the wealthiest people and then paying them interest on that debt (from the tax revenues paid by all taxpayers). It also led to the emergence of a new asset-owning middle class 'which tied people closer to a particular form of capitalism, one driven by rising asset values rather than incomes as well as the interest returns on those assets', as Kean Birch writes.[5] The expansion of public debt, in turn, also created a kind of (self-imposed) external constraint on the government, since it amplified the pressure exerted on the monetary and political authorities by the government's creditors to avoid resorting to inflation and/or monetisation to reduce the real value of the debt, effectively 'locking in' Reagan's anti-inflationary and pro-rich policies. The view that Reagan used deficits early in his administration to precipitate a perceived crisis, which he could then use to introduce deeper cuts to public spending than would have been possible had he started down that track immediately, doesn't fit the facts. The reality of the Reagan administration is that it simply altered *who* benefited from state intervention rather than reducing state intervention per se.

As noted by Miguel Centeno and Joseph Cohen, 'available data suggests that the policy and macroeconomic changes realised under the neoliberal policy regime are more complex than is often assumed'.[6] First and foremost, it illustrates the basic point that core capitalist countries have definitely *not* been characterised by a withering away of the state in the neoliberal era. Quite the contrary, in fact. As Susan Strange presciently noted in the mid-1980s:

> The end result of 'monetarist' policies may easily turn out to be the exact opposite of its ideological intentions. Instead of freeing the private sector and the market economy from the toils of state intervention, it may actually end – as in Mussolini's Italy – in involving the state more extensively and more permanently in industry and business than it had ever been before.[7]

Interestingly, when GDP reached record heights in the first years of the Reagan administration, government officials boasted to the public that it was because of the free market. However, they provided a different explanation to the business community. James Baker, then secretary of the Treasury, announced at a business convention that the Reagan administration offered more protection to US manufacturers than any of the preceding post-war administrations.[8] According to Noam Chomsky, however, this is a euphemism: in fact, the administration offered more protection than all other administrations combined.[9]

One may ask: if neoliberalism *as an ideology* springs from a desire to curtail the role of the state in the economy, how is it that neoliberalism *as a political-economic reality* has produced increasingly powerful, interventionist and ever-reaching – even authoritarian – state apparatuses? A first, basic answer is that the system the neoliberals allegedly aspire to – which could be defined, in very broad terms, as a strictly market-based order entailing the extension of the market and market-making mechanism into all areas of life – requires a strong state structure to institute, maintain and enforce 'the market'. Indeed, a closer look at the neoliberal canon reveals that the forefathers of neoliberalism were well aware of this. Even someone as ardently anti-statist as Friedrich Hayek was forced to acknowledge in his classic text, *The Road to Serfdom*, that '[i]n no system that could be rationally defended would the state do nothing. An effective competitive system needs an intelligently designed and continuously adjusted legal framework.'[10]

Milton Friedman voiced a similar opinion many years later in his text *Capitalism and Freedom*, where he wrote that 'the role of the government ... is to do something that the market cannot do for itself, namely, to determine, arbitrate, and enforce the rules of the game'.[11] As Joao Rodrigues notes: 'The neoliberals recognized early on that the creation of new markets is a political process, requiring the intervention of an organized power.'[12] Various authors, most notably Philip Mirowski, have argued that neoliberalism's emphasis on the need to reengineer the state in order to guarantee the creation and the well-oiled functioning of the market is precisely what distinguishes it from classic *laissez-faire* liberalism.

It is self-evident, after all, that the process of neoliberalisation would not have been possible if *governments* – who else? – had not resorted to a wide array of tools to promote it: the liberalisation of goods and capital markets; the privatisation of resources and social services; the deregulation of business, and financial markets in particular; the reduction of workers' rights (first and foremost, the right to collective bargaining), and more generally the repression of labour activism; the lowering of taxes on wealth and capital, at the expense of the middle and working classes; the slashing of social programmes, and so on. These policies were systemically pursued throughout the West (and imposed on developing countries) with unprecedented determination, and with the support of all the major international institutions and political parties. Mario Pianta, professor of economic policy at the University of Urbino, writes:

> The official story is that politics took a 'step back', confiding in the efficiency and transparency of the markets and financial system, and in their ability to generate the best results when unhindered by the complications of democracy. The truth is that politics actively worked to accrue the power of the markets and the financial sector, at the expense of everyone else – small manufacturers, workers, citizens.[13]

STATES *VERSUS* MARKETS: A FALSE DICHOTOMY

Of course, this is not how the neoliberals or the politicians framed (or frame) their argument in public, and it is easy to understand why: a narrative that pits the liberating dynamism of the free market (exemplified by the garage inventor à la Steve Jobs) against the ossification and inefficiency of state bureaucracy (exemplified by the government paper-pusher) is much more powerful than the more nuanced neoliberal narrative that sees states and markets as mutually embedded partners, particularly since the latter risks raising many uncomfortable questions regarding the supposed neutrality of the state. In a sense, one could say that the neoliberals were very skilful at exploiting the widespread notion that there exists a fundamental separation or opposition between states and markets, with the balance of power constantly tilting between one extreme (socialism) and the other (free-market capitalism, the system allegedly in place today).

Underpinning this view is the idea – common to mainstream theories of capitalism and the state – that 'capitalism and the market economy are more or less the same thing, and that state power is antithetical to both'.[14] Accordingly, state–market relations are usually framed in zero-sum terms, where the influence of one can only increase at the expense of the other. Early Marxist theorists such as Kautsky and Lenin, for example, rejected the mainstream state–capitalism dichotomy – arguing instead that the state was an expression of the repressive power of the capitalist class (Karl Marx famously described the capitalist state as 'nothing but a committee for managing the common affairs of the whole bourgeoisie')[15] – but nonetheless accepted that capitalism could transcend the state (and to a large degree had done so).[16] They claimed that the mid-nineteenth-century 'free trade' era reflected a 'pure' capitalism, in which the economic (the market) was no longer bound to the political (the state), allowing capital to expand beyond the borders of any given European nation state (various twentieth-century Marxists would later refute this claim).

Similar claims are common today in the context of neoliberal globalisation and 'free-market' policies – a point we will return to further on. As Leo Panitch and Sam Gindin have argued, however, in both cases there is a failure to appreciate the crucial role of the state in making 'free markets' possible and then making them work, leading to a confusing (and erroneous) juxtaposition of 'states' and 'markets':

> Just as the emergence of so-called *laissez-faire* under mid-nineteenth century industrial capitalism entailed a highly active state to effect the formal separation of the polity and economy, and to define and police the domestic social relations of a fully capitalist order, so did [Britain's] external policy of free trade entail an extension of the imperial role along all of these dimensions on the part of the first state that 'created a form of imperialism driven by the logic of capitalism'.[17]

Laissez-faire is, in other words, a myth. This is one of the core arguments at the heart of Karl Polanyi's 1944 classic, *The Great Transformation*.[18] In it, Polanyi dismantled the orthodox liberal account of the rise of capitalism by arguing that the development of modern market economies was inextricably linked to the development of the modern state, since the state was needed to enforce changes in social structure and human thinking that allowed for a competitive capitalist economy. The proclaimed separation of state and market is an illusion, he said. According to Polanyi, the economy is 'embedded' in society – part of social relations – not apart from them. Markets and trading in commodities are a part of all human societies, but in order to create a 'market society', these commodities have to be subject to a larger, coherent system of market relations. This is something that can only be accomplished through state coercion and regulation.

'There was nothing natural about laissez-faire; [the] free market could never have come into being merely by allowing things to take their course', he wrote. 'Laissez-faire was planned ... [it] was enforced by the state'.[19] In other words, the support of state structures – to protect private property, to police the dealings of different members of the ruling class with each other, to provide services that are essential for the reproduction of the system, etc. – was the political prerequisite for the development of capitalism.[20] Adam Smith himself, while rejecting state intervention in the market, never went as far as suggesting that the state had no role to play. On the contrary, the purpose of Smith's analysis of the economic system was to define the proper role of the state:

> According to the system of natural liberty, the sovereign has only three duties to attend to; three duties of great importance, indeed, but plain and intelligible to common understandings: first, the duty of protecting society from the violence and invasion of other independent societies; secondly, the duty of protecting, as far as possible, every member of the society from the injustice or oppression of every other member of it, or the duty of establishing an exact administration of justice; and, thirdly, the duty of erecting and maintaining certain public works and certain public institutions, which it can never be the interest of any individual, or small number of individuals, to erect and maintain.[21]

For capitalism truly to flourish, though, it needed much more than the external support of a 'night watchman' state. 'Capitalism only triumphs when it becomes identified with the state, *when it is the state*', French historian Fernand Braudel wrote.[22] Braudel saw capitalism 'as being absolutely dependent for its emergence and expansion on state power' – on the *fusion of state and capital* – 'and as constituting the antithesis of the market economy'.[23] Furthermore, according to Braudel, it is precisely the coalescence of these two elements of capitalism – state and capital – in sixteenth-century Europe that transformed Europe into the 'monstrous shaper of world history' and allowed the formation of a truly global capitalist economy.[24] However, the state's role in supporting the rise of (global) capitalism was not limited to establishing the necessary legal and infrastructural framework. As Marx put it, capital is not a thing but a relation – a relation that involves the exploitation of workers, which in turn needs to be underpinned by the political structures of the state. In this regard, Colin Hay writes:

Picture a hypothetical capitalist economy unregulated by the state (the archetypal free market) and comprised inevitably of a multitude of competing capitals. Such an economy is inherently crisis-prone. For no individual capital competing for its very survival will sacrifice its own interest in the general interest. Contradictions of 'steering problems' inevitably arise within such an unregulated economy, yet can never be resolved. Accordingly, they will accumulate until they eventually threaten the very stability of capitalism itself, precip-itating a fully-fledged crisis of the mode of production. *A capitalist economy without regulation, despite the now pervasive rhetoric of the free-marketeers, is inherently unstable.*[25]

In other words, the role of the state is that of upholding the interests of capital-in-general, as opposed to the interests of the individual capitals that are its component parts. Elmar Altvater argued that in this context the state must necessarily intervene to secure conditions conducive to continuing capitalist accumulation, thereby performing what he calls a 'general maintenance function'.[26] This comprises:

(i) the provision of general infrastructure ... ; (ii) the capacity to defend militarily a national economic space regulated by the state and to preserve an administrative boundary within which the state is sovereign; (iii) the provision of a legal system that establishes and enforces the right to possession of private property and which outlaws practices (such as insider-dealing) potentially damaging to the accumulation of capital within the national economy; and (iv) the intervention of the state to ameliorate and/or regulate the class struggle and the inevitable conflict between capital and labour.[27]

These functions were evident during the Keynesian era. Under neoliber-alism, however, they by no means 'withered away'; in fact, some of them became even more pervasive, as we will see.

NEOLIBERALISM AS AN AUTHORITARIAN PROJECT

Fernand Braudel's analysis underscores 'the centrality of "force" in deter-mining the distribution of costs and benefits among participants in the market economy'[28] – a point that was well understood even by Adam Smith. As Giovanni Arrighi noted, Smith considered 'superiority of force' to have been 'the most important factor in enabling the conquering West to appropriate most of the benefits – and to impose on the conquered non-West most of the costs – of the wider market economy established as a result of the so-called Discoveries'.[29]

A more recent example of this – and one that flagrantly contradicts neoliberalism's anti-state rhetoric – is the Latin American experience of the 1970s, where a number of neoliberal regimes were established through military operations and coups d'état. The most infamous example is Chile, where in 1973 the democratically elected president, Salvador Allende, was overthrown by a violent US-backed coup led by the dictator, Augusto Pinochet, who proceeded to crush labour unions and popular movements (by establishing a reign of state terror based on the torture and systematic repression of the regime's opponents), and to impose a rapid-fire transformation of the economy based on tax cuts, privatisation of state assets, massive cuts to social spending, free trade and deregulation.

One of Pinochet's economic advisors was none other than Milton Friedman and his Chilean graduate students, who saw Chile as 'a laboratory for cutting-edge free-market experiments', Naomi Klein writes in *The Shock Doctrine*. 'It was the most extreme capitalist makeover ever attempted anywhere, and it became known as a "Chicago School" revolution, since so many of Pinochet's economists had studied under Friedman at the University of Chicago.'[30] Even Hayek visited Pinochet's Chile several times, remarking on one of these occasions that 'my personal preference leans toward a liberal dictatorship rather than toward a democratic government devoid of liberalism'.[31] While Chile was the first and one of the most extreme examples of neoliberal 'shock treatment' – a phrase coined by Friedman – it was far from unique. From the 1970s onwards, a similar therapy was imposed – through financial blackmail, coercion, violence and even outright military intervention – on several countries, from Latin America to Asia to Eastern Europe to the Middle East. In particular, developing countries seeking finance from the IMF and the World Bank were forced to adopt neoliberal policies that included harsh austerity measures – similar to the ones being imposed today on the periphery countries of the eurozone – as a condition of international support. The programmes of structural adjustment and austerity imposed by the IMF on developing countries in the 1980s and 1990s undermined many of the achievements of the previous growth model, driving living standards down and poverty levels up. By the mid-1990s, no less than 57 developing countries had become poorer in per capita income than 15 years earlier – and in some cases than 25 years earlier.[32] In almost all countries where austerity-driven policies were imposed, poverty and unemployment grew, labour rights deteriorated, inequality soared and financial and economic instability increased.[33]

In 2003, even the IMF's Independent Evaluation Office (IEO), in a study which analysed 133 IMF-supported austerity programmes in 70 (mostly developing) countries, acknowledged that policymakers had consistently underestimated the disastrous effects of rigid spending cuts on economic growth.[34] It is important to note that in all these cases, supposedly pro-market policies did not lead to the emergence of a mythical 'free market' in the concerned countries but, on the contrary, resulted in the concentration of vast amounts of wealth and power into the hands of a small political-corporate elite, often leading to the emergence of monopolies and oligopolies, at the expense even of local business interests (one may argue, of course, that this is precisely what happens in the presence of unfettered markets, as anyone who has played Monopoly knows, but that is another argument). As Naomi Klein writes:

> Friedman framed his movement as an attempt to free the market from the state, but the real-world track record of what happens when his purist vision is realized is rather different. In every country where Chicago School policies have been applied over the past three decades, what has emerged is a powerful ruling alliance between a few very large corporations and a class of mostly wealthy politicians – with hazy and ever-shifting lines between the two groups. ... *Far from freeing the market from the state, these political and corporate elites have simply merged*, trading favors to secure the right to appropriate precious resources previously held in the public domain.[35]

This development was not limited to periphery countries, of course. Even in core countries, neoliberalism has not produced 'free' and highly competitive markets, but highly monopolistic and oligopolistic ones, particularly in the financial sector. Sociologists such as Colin Crouch as well as economists like Joseph Stiglitz have shown that neoliberalism has not delivered the promised separation of state and market, pointing instead at the way in which political institutions are increasingly captured by giant corporations, as well as at the growing collusion between business and politicians. A groundbreaking study by the Swiss Federal Institute of

Technology (ETH) – the first investigation into the complex architecture of international corporate ownership – has revealed that a large part of the global economy is controlled by what the authors call an economic 'super-entity'.[36] This comprises 147 incredibly powerful transnational corporations that control 40 per cent of the entire network. Of the top 50 most powerful companies, 45 are financial firms. The list includes Barclays (the most influential corporation in the world, according to the study), JPMorgan, Merrill Lynch, Goldman Sachs, Deutsche Bank and other familiar and less well-known names. Twenty-four companies are US-based, followed by eight in Britain, five in France, four in Japan, and Germany, Switzerland and the Netherlands with two each. Canada has one. The authors note that although no study has demonstrated that this international 'super-entity' has ever acted as a bloc, 'this is not an unlikely scenario'.

Moreover, neoliberalism has been (and is) associated with various forms of authoritarian statism – that is, the opposite of the minimal state advocated by neoliberals – also in the West, as states have bolstered their security and policing arms as part of a generalised militarisation of civil protest. In particular, the large-scale 'anti-globalisation' and anti-neoliberalism demonstrations of the late 1990s and early 2000s were met with levels of state violence and repression unseen since the 1970s (and in some cases unprecedented), culminating in the killing of a 23-year-old protestor, Carlo Giuliani, during clashes with Italian security forces during the G8 summit in Genoa, Italy, in 2001.

This development went hand in hand with a generalised militarisation of international relations. The United States provides the most obvious example, of course. Particularly after the disintegration of the Soviet Union in the early 1990s and the United States' rise to 'hyperpower' status, the conditions emerged for the US to aggressively reassert its global hegemony, through the creation of 'a new world order', in George H. W. Bush's famous words. The Gulf War of 1991 is regarded as the first test of this new global order. As Panitch and Gindin write:

Just as neoliberalism at home did not mean a smaller or weaker state, but rather one in which coercive apparatuses flourished (as welfare offices emptied out, the prisons filled up), so has neoliberalism led to the enhancement of the coercive apparatus the imperial state needs to police social order around the world. The transformation of the

American military and security apparatus through the 1990s in such a way as to facilitate this can only be understood in this light.[37]

It is interesting to note that this period was also characterised by a profound shift in the mainstream public discourse in America: the American empire was now openly talked about, even celebrated. Nothing exemplifies this better than Thomas Friedman's famous 'Manifesto for the Fast World', published in 1999 in the *New York Times Magazine*, in which the journalist urged the United States to embrace its role as enforcer of the capitalist global order: 'The hidden hand of the market will never work without a hidden fist. ... And the hidden fist that keeps the world safe for Silicon Valley's technologies is called the United States Army, Air Force, Navy and Marine Corps.'[38]

With George W. Bush's election, in 2000, this effectively became the US government's semi-official foreign policy, particularly in the aftermath of 9/11. This is not surprising if we consider that many of the leading figures of the Bush administration were associated with the infamous Project for the New American Century, an influential neoconservative think tank founded on the principle that the United States should 'seek to preserve and extend its position of global leadership' by 'maintaining the preeminence of US military forces'.[39]

It is somewhat ironic that at the same time as the right, particularly in the United States, was reaffirming the centrality of the state – and of the American state in particular – in world affairs, many left thinkers were declaring the state dead. The most obvious example is Michael Hardt and Antonio Negri's much-debated book, *Empire*, published in 2000, which essentially argued that the old forms of national sovereignty and imperialism were surpassed and that the world at the dawn of the twenty-first century was experiencing a new form of imperialism: 'a decentred and deterritorializing apparatus of rule that progressively incorporates the entire global realm'.[40] The book's central theme is that the traditional form of imperialism, centred on individual nation states, had given way to an emergent post-modern global structure called 'Empire': a horizontal, transnational capitalist-dominated structure in which, due to the complete elimination of 'the centre', a new form of exploitation of 'the multitude' had been created.

The authors argued that instead of fighting each other, the various imperialist countries were now engaged in a period in which they would interact with each other within the empire and in its interests, in the quest for peace. Of course, this theory would be blatantly disproven just a few years later, as the United States embarked on a series of imperialist and neocolonial wars that only reaffirmed the centrality of the American imperial state. However, the idea of the waning nation state remained a fixture of the left: the (flawed) notion that neoliberalism entailed a retreat of the state in favour of the market was further compounded by the idea that the state had been (was being) rendered powerless by the forces of globalisation.

We can draw two conclusions from these observations. First, not only does neoliberal economic policy require the presence of a strong state, but it requires the presence of an *authoritarian state* (particularly where extreme forms of neoliberalism are concerned, such as the ones experimented with in periphery countries), at both the domestic and international level. Second, neoliberalism and neoliberalisation is not so much, if at all, about using the state to extend the reach of the market – about 'liberating individual entrepreneurial freedoms skills within an institutional framework characterized by strong private property rights, free markets, and free trade', according to David Harvey's definition of neoliberalism[41] – but rather about restructuring the institutional framework of the state, with the aim of placing the commanding heights of economic policy 'in the hands of capital, and primarily financial interests'.[42] This would appear to validate the conclusion that we reached in Chapter 2: that ideology – neoliberal or otherwise – was (is) not the main driver of the neoliberal process. Or better, that neoliberal ideology, at least in its official anti-state guise (with its emphasis on the state/market dichotomy), was (is) a convenient alibi for what has been and is essentially a *political and state-driven project*. Capital remains as dependent on the state today as it did under 'Keynesianism' – indeed, even more so, insofar as it is faced with more crises needing intervention.

POST-CRISIS POLICIES IN THE EUROZONE: REINTENSIFYING STATE INTERVENTION ON THE SIDE OF CAPITAL

In the months and years that followed the financial crash of 2007–9, capital's – and capitalism's – continued dependency on the state in the age of neoliberalism became glaringly obvious, as the governments of the US and Europe bailed out their respective financial institutions to the tune of trillions of euros/dollars. In Europe, following the outbreak of the so-called 'euro crisis' in 2010, this was accompanied by a multi-level assault on the post-war European social and economic model aimed at restructuring and re-engineering European societies and economies along lines more favourable to capital. As Noam Chomsky said: 'Europe's policies make sense only on one assumption: that the goal is to try and undermine and unravel the welfare state.'[43]

Europe's very own shock doctrine can be summed up as the combination of several mutually reinforcing elements. The first of these has been, of course, the imposition on the great majority of European countries (especially those of the periphery) of unprecedentedly harsh fiscal austerity measures, which, as many authors have argued, were not aimed at making the public finances of European governments more sustainable, but simply at re-establishing their debt-servicing capacity – that is, at ensuring that creditors and bondholders would get paid, whatever the social and economic costs (which, as we know, have been enormous). Moreover, these supposedly 'emergency' measures have been institutionalised and constitutionalised through a complex system of new laws, rules, agreements and even a treaty – the Treaty on Stability, Coordination and Governance in the Economic and Monetary Union, commonly known as the Fiscal Compact – aimed at enforcing a permanent regime of fiscal austerity. To this end, 'automatic correction mechanisms' and quasi-automatic sanctions in the event of non-compliance with the rules have been introduced to remove any element of discussion and/or decision making at either the European or national level, thus accomplishing a lifelong neoliberal dream: the complete separation of the democratic process and economic policies, and the death of active macroeconomic management, in what has been described as 'the politics of depoliticisation'.[44]

A second element has been the implementation (or imposition, depending on your point of view) of structural adjustment programmes (SAPs), consisting of internal devaluation (the reduction of wages), neoliberal structural reforms (the liberalisation/flexibilisation of labour markets and reduction of collective bargaining rights) and the privations of public services and assets – particularly in those countries that signed memorandums of understanding with the EU-ECB-IMF troika or entered into agreements for financial aid within the framework of the European Stability Mechanism.

A third element has been the dramatic curtailment of democracy at both national and EU level. This has included the imposition of unelected technocratic governments in Italy (Mario Monti, 2011–13) and Greece

(Lucas Papademos, 2011–12); and Greece, Ireland and Portugal (and to a lesser extent Spain and Cyprus) effectively putting their finances in the hands of the EU-ECB-IMF troika. No one on this body was directly (or even indirectly) elected. These developments raise serious issues of constitutionalism: namely, the tendency of the EU institutions to restrict the area of democratic decision making by democratically elected governments, focusing instead on technocratic rules imposed by undemocratic decision-making bodies, leading to a deepening of the process of depoliticisation, by which macroeconomic decisions are removed from the realm of representative-democratic deliberation and social choice. The European Union has effectively become a sovereign power with the authority to impose budgetary rules and structural reforms on member states outside democratic procedures and without democratic control.

Moreover, the ECB has been exposed for what is really is: a fully fledged political body with the power to bring a country to its knees (and the willingness to use it), as we saw in the summer of 2015 when it cut off liquidity to the Greek banking system 'in order to destabilize … the Greek payments system and force the SYRIZA government into accepting the harsh austerity measures'.[45] In this respect, the democratic deficit that is inherent in the construction of the executive-led EU – which is examined in greater detail further on – has been amplified by the crisis and the response of the ruling elites to it, with the EU's extensive post-crisis reform of its system of economic governance representing a radicalisation of this new constitutionalism (which has been dubbed 'authoritarian constitutionalism').[46] Finally, another aspect has been the increasingly violent repression of public dissent: the police have made widespread use of violence against anti-austerity demonstrators in Spain, Greece, Italy, Portugal and elsewhere.

Are the politicians imposing these policies motivated solely by ideology, oblivious to the extent to which they are forwarding the interests of what Keynes called 'the dominant social force[s] behind authority'?[47] Or is their deliberate aim to consolidate the power of the economic elites by extracting wealth from those below? Whichever is the case, austerity is effectively creating 'the single biggest transfer of resources from low and middle-income people to the rich and powerful in history', as Seán Healy, director of the think tank Social Justice Ireland, wrote.[48] According to the European Trade Union Institute, between 2009 and 2012, as a result of the European Union's increased influence on national wage policies, the majority of EU countries (15 out of 27) recorded falling real wages.[49] The most dramatic declines took place in those countries that were subject to financial bailout programmes, which also registered steep declines in real hourly minimum wages, as well as a drop in the share of GDP going to salaries, indicating a redistribution of income from labour to capital. Various authors have interpreted this as the sign of a class war waged by Europe's ruling elite against the continent's poor, working and middle classes. 'Fiscal consolidation is not the true end goal', argued Aaron Pacitti, an economist at Siena College:

> The primary objective is power consolidation among the world's economic elite who look to cement their position atop the economic hierarchy by extracting wealth from those beneath. ... [D]eficit reduction functions as political cover for ideologically driven policy changes that would otherwise be extremely unpopular and punitive. Austerity policies are part of a one-sided class war being waged by the wealthy against the elderly, poor, and middle class.[50]

The same argument has also been made by Noam Chomsky: 'The only argument I can see for [reconciling austerity policies with their economic consequences] is class war', he said in an interview.[51] Paul Krugman also reached the conclusion that '[t]he austerity agenda looks a lot like a simple expression of upper-class preferences, wrapped in a facade of academic rigor'; in other words, a 'policy of the 1 percent, by the 1 percent, for the 1 percent'.[52] Behind this stance is the fact that the austerity regime's budget-slashing policies have not only produced a long list of losers: ordinary citizens, workers, young people and so on. They have also delivered a clear set of winners – and not just creditors and bondholders. To give an example, in the midst of the worst economic crisis in Europe's modern history, the number of people in Europe with wealth of more than US$1 million rose from 7.8 million in 2010 to 9.2 million in 2012. Over the 2012–13 period, the eurozone saw a further increase in the number of millionaires: France topped the list in the EMU by adding 287 millionaires, followed by Germany at 221, and Italy at 127. Spain gained 47 new millionaires.[53] This was related to the post-crisis recovery of corporate profits, which by 2011 had returned to pre-crisis levels – or exceeded them – thus continuing the almost uninterrupted rise in profit shares registered in developed economies since 2000.[54]

It has not been a bonanza for everyone, though. As the International Labour Organization (ILO) notes, there is a growing polarisation between small and large firms. The profit margin of small firms in 2011 was more than 40 per cent below the pre-crisis average, but for large firms it has been trending upwards since the crisis (despite a small dip in 2011), and by 2010 had returned to pre-crisis levels.[55] According to Pedersen & Partners, by 2012 the revenues of the 100 largest corporations in Europe and the United States had grown by 22 per cent, and their profits by 18 per cent, compared to pre-crisis levels.[56] Of the 50 corporations worldwide with the fastest-growing profits over the 2010–11 period, ten were European. The five biggest banks in Europe made profits of €34 billion in 2011.[57] Rising profit margins were also reflected in global stock indices, which by mid-2013 had come close to – or exceeded – historical highs in both Europe and the United States.

All this points to the conclusion that the crisis has been (indeed, is being) exploited – and in some cases 'engineered' – by Europe's political-financial elite to finally do away with the last remnants of the welfare state – a long-time target of the European political-economic establishment – and impose a radical neoliberal policy regime, based not on a retreat of the state in favour of the market, but rather on a reintensification of state intervention on the side of capital.[58]

GLOBALISATION AND THE STATE

The information hitherto presented is clearly at odds not only with the idea that neoliberalism involves a withdrawal of the state vis-à-vis the market, but also with the idea, equally popular in left-wing circles, that in recent decades the sovereignty of nation states has been progressively eroded by globalisation, and has today been essentially nullified. As we saw, during the 1980s (and then continuing into the 1990s), the anti-state narrative spearheaded by the monetarists in the 1970s took on a new twist: government intervention in the economy came to be seen not only as dangerous and ineffective but, increasingly, as outright impossible. A new consensus was setting in: that economic and financial internationalisation had essentially undermined the ability of governments to control their own economies, and that countries had little choice but to abandon national economic strategies and all the traditional instruments of intervention in the economy and hope, at best, for transnational or supranational forms of economic governance.

As seen in the previous chapters, the European left, particularly in Britain and France, played a crucial role in cementing this ideological shift towards a post-national and post-sovereign view of the world. In Jacques Delors' words: 'National sovereignty no longer means very much, or has much scope in the modern world economy.'[59] No book epitomises this new consensus better than Susan Strange's famous 1997 book, *The Retreat of the State*, in which the British scholar argues that the rise of global financial networks, multinational corporations, regional trading blocs and expansion of the world economy has rendered the state obsolete.[60] As Strange explains, the argument put forward in the book is that 'the impersonal forces of world markets, integrated over the postwar period more by private enterprise in finance, industry and trade than by the cooperative decisions of governments, are now more powerful than the states to whom ultimate political authority over society and economy is supposed to belong'.[61] It can easily be said, without fear of generalising, that today, 20 years after the publication of the book, this opinion is still conventional wisdom – even more so, arguably, considering it is generally accepted that markets have become even more powerful in the meantime. But is it correct?

First we have to define what we mean by 'globalisation', which is not an easy task. Göran Therborn wrote that: 'Like so many concepts in social science and historiography, "globalization" is a word of lay language and everyday usage with variable shades of meaning and many connotations.'[62] Wikipedia defines globalisation as 'the process of international integration arising from the interchange of world views, products, ideas, and other aspects of culture'.[63] In this sense, by reading this book – written in various locations throughout the world over the course of a more than a year – you are participating in a non-economic globalised social process (regardless of the fact that you may have paid for the book in question – or not).

For the sake of argument, though, let's narrow the term down to 'economic globalisation', meaning the increasing integration of economies around the world, particularly in supply chains which necessitate the movement of goods, services and capital across borders. As Therborn noted, though, this raises the crucial question of whether globalisation is 'a system or a stage'.[64] From a systemic perspective, it is clear that the world economy is not 'fully systemized', but continues to be 'shaped by sub-global forces, be they cultural areas, nations, states or sub-state regions, and so on', as it has been for centuries. Therborn identifies various 'waves' of globalisation (beginning in the fourth century AD) and argues that the world is currently experiencing a sixth wave of globalisation, which has been facilitated by political and economic developments that include a reduction in economic protectionist measures, lower transportation costs, new technologies, etc. In this sense, of course, there is nothing intrinsically 'new' about economic globalisation: in fact, capitalism has been global, in the geographical sense, for at least 200 years, if not longer.

Another question is whether this process is driven primarily by economic and technical changes or by the political developments that accompany them in time. In a way, the question was famously answered by Marx in the *Communist Manifesto*, in which he described how the bourgeoisie's

> need of a constantly expanding market for its products chases the bourgeoisie over the entire surface of the globe. It must nestle everywhere, settle everywhere, establish connexions everywhere. The bourgeoisie has through its exploitation of the world market given a cosmopolitan character to production and consumption in every country. ... [I]t has drawn from under the feet of industry the national ground on which it stood. All old-established national industries have been destroyed or are daily being destroyed. They are dislodged by new industries, whose introduction becomes a life and death question for all civilised nations, by industries that no longer work up indigenous raw material, but raw material drawn from the remotest zones; industries whose products are consumed, not only at home, but in every quarter of the globe. In place of the old wants, satisfied by the production of the country, we find new wants, requiring for their satisfaction the products of distant lands and climes. *In place of the old local and national seclusion and self-sufficiency, we have intercourse in every direction, universal inter-dependence of nations.*[65]

In other words, the search for new markets and new ways of organising production is not new, and neither is the idea that that states are constrained by the existence of forces outside their control. Claims that there was a time in which nation states, unlike today, were 'free' to shape the direction of economic activities more or less autonomously, unhindered by external forces, ignore the extent to which national autonomy was already constrained *before* the advent of neoliberal globalisation. As Chris Brown of the London School of Economics writes in the foreword to the 2007 book, *Politics Without Sovereignty*: 'States have always existed in such a context – only states without an "outside" could be genuinely and purely "self-determining", or, to put it another way, only a genuine world-empire could ignore its external environment, because, of course, it wouldn't have one.'[66]

Claims that globalisation undermines the national state often take as their main reference point the Westphalian notion of state sovereignty. 'Westphalian sovereignty' is the principle that each nation state has absolute sovereignty over its territory and domestic affairs, to the exclusion of all external powers, on the principle of non-interference in another country's domestic affairs. In addition, not only is the state said to be free from external intervention, but also from external influence. The doctrine is named after the Peace of Westphalia, signed in 1648, which ended the Thirty Years' War, in which the major continental European states – the Holy Roman Empire, Spain, France, Sweden and the Dutch Republic – agreed to respect one another's territorial integrity, ending attempts at the imposition of any supranational authority on European states. As European influence spread across the globe, the Westphalian principles, especially the concept of sovereign states, became central to international law and to the prevailing world order – what today we refer to as the Westphalian system.

Even though this system formally collapsed in 1914, in theorists' minds Westphalian sovereignty (that is, unlimited sovereign rights) still exists – or better, it *existed* before it allegedly started to be undermined by the imperatives of globalisation in the 1970s and 1980s. This has been described as the 'neoliberal account of globalisation'.[67] In contrast to this view, other authors have argued that Westphalian sovereignty – understood as the twin principle that (i) states should be free from external influence, and (ii) that there should be no authority operating above the interstate system – ended well before the latest round of neoliberal globalisation. Arrighi associates the (partial) supersession of the Westphalian system with Britain's establishment, in the mid-nineteenth century (the mid-Victorian years), of the first true system of world hegemony, defined as the ability of a state – in this case Britain – 'to exercise functions of leadership and governance over a system of sovereign states'.[68]

Moreover, the current era is often juxtaposed against the post-war 'golden age', in which nation states supposedly enjoyed much greater policy autonomy than today. In fact, for all the talk of NATO being 'an alliance of free, democratic nations', the military-political sovereignty of core capitalist countries (Western Europe and Japan) in the post-war era was severely limited by their subordinate position within the hierarchy of the US protectorate system – a point that is often downplayed in mainstream accounts of this period. Further, a closer look at the post-war period reveals important continuities between that period and the neoliberal era. As Sam Gindin notes, it was during that period that 'the building blocks of neoliberalism first emerged'.[69] Most importantly, global trade has had a relatively linear increase since the end of World War II, and had already reached high levels before the 1970s and the decline of Keynesianism.

However, it could be argued that *neoliberal globalisation*, precisely because it represents an 'extreme' form of globalisation – David Harvey coined the term 'time-space compression' to refer to the way the acceleration of economic activities leads to the destruction of spatial barriers and distances[70] – is not only *quantitatively* but also *qualitatively* different from previous stages of globalisation. Let us take this claim to task.

NEOLIBERAL GLOBALISATION: HAS THE STATE BECOME OBSOLETE?

Claims that the current stage of capitalism fundamentally undermines the viability of the nation state often refer to Harvard economist Dani Rodrik's famous trilemma. Some years ago, Rodrik outlined what he called his 'impossibility theorem', which says that 'democracy, national sovereignty and global economic integration are mutually incompatible: we can combine any two of the three, but never have all three simultaneously and in full'.[71] His argument builds upon the traditional insight that students learn about in macroeconomics, the so-called 'impossible trinity', which states that a nation with links to the rest of the world (that is, an 'open economy') cannot simultaneously maintain an independent monetary policy, fixed exchange rates and an open capital account. For example, if a nation chooses to peg its currency and allow capital flows to enter and exit without restriction, it cannot also independently set its own interest rate.

Rodrik takes this argument a step further, by claiming that true international economic integration requires that we eliminate all transaction costs in cross-border dealings. Since nation states are a fundamental source of such transaction costs, it follows that if you want true international economic integration you must be ready to give up democracy (by making the nation state responsive only to the needs of the international economy) or national sovereignty (by creating a system of regional/ global federalism, to align the scope of democratic politics with the scope of global markets).

Over the years, political forces spanning the entire electoral spectrum have skilfully used Rodrik's trilemma to present neoliberal policies – entailing both a curtailing of participatory democracy *and* of national sovereignty – as 'the inevitable price we pay for globalisation'. Even those on the left that claim to oppose neoliberalism often invoke the impossibility theorem to justify the contention that the nation state is 'finished' and that financial markets will punish governments that pursue policies not in accord with the profit ambitions of global capital. But this is not what Rodrik meant. Contrary to conventional wisdom, Rodrik acknowledges that international economic integration is far from 'true'; in fact, it remains 'remarkably limited'.[72] He notes that even in our supposedly globalised world, despite the flowering of global firms and supply chains, there is still significant exchange rate uncertainty; there are still major cultural and linguistic differences that preclude the full mobilisation of resources across national borders, as demonstrated by the fact that advanced industrial countries typically exhibit large amounts of 'home bias'; there is still a high correlation between national investment rates and national saving rates; there are still severe restrictions to the international mobility of labour; and capital flows between rich and poor nations fall considerably short of what theoretical models predict.[73]

The same points can be made today (almost 20 years after Rodrik's article was published): national borders remain cogent because they 'demarcate political and legal jurisdictions' that impose transaction costs, and hinder 'contract enforcement' rules.[74] This is why the latest range of 'free trade agreements' (the Trans-Pacific Partnership (TPP), the proposed Transatlantic Trade and Investment Partnership (TTIP), etc.) have little to do with lowering tariff barriers (which are already at an historical all-time low) and much more to do with limiting the capacity of governments to regulate in the public interest, by means of so-called investor-state dispute settlement (ISDS) mechanisms – a point we will return to further on.

In other words, Rodrik's trilemma is a tautology: of course, it is a definitional truth that if we want global capital to have no limits whatsoever, then nation states have to disappear as legislative vehicles with enforceable jurisdictions (and confine themselves to being servants of global profit-making) and/or citizens must lose their democratic political rights. But, as noted above, that is not the current state of global capitalism (yet), nor is it one that we should aspire to. Therefore, the trilemma has little bearing on reality, except as a political tool or self-fulfilling prophecy.

To better understand this point, let us now take a more detailed look at two of the core features usually associated with neoliberal globalisation, particularly insofar as its alleged impact on national states is concerned: the rise of transnational corporations and global supply chains; and the internationalisation of capital flows.

MULTINATIONAL CORPORATIONS: THE NEW RULERS OF THE WORLD?

Few ideas enjoy as much bipartisan support as the idea that the tremendous increase in the power and influence of so-called *multinational corporations* (often erroneously referred to as transnational corporations), and of the global supply chains that they manage, 'has become the most critical factor in the withering away of the modern system of territorial states as the primary locus of world power', as Arrighi wrote.[75] It is often claimed that these mega-corporations, by virtue of major advances in modern productive forces, technology, transportation and communication, have now 'escaped' their respective states, leading to the emergence of a *transnational* or even *supranational*, rather than simply multinational, capitalist class 'which [is] subject to no state authority and [has] the power to subject to its own "laws" each and every member of the interstate system, the United States included'.[76]

Thus, management guru Peter Drucker, in a 1997 *Foreign Affairs* article, distinguished between 'multinational' and 'transnational' corporations, arguing that even though most corporations were still organised as traditional multinationals – defined as a 'national company with foreign subsidiaries' – they were fast transforming into transnational companies, to whom 'national boundaries have largely become irrelevant'.[77] Indeed, 'successful transnational companies', he contended, 'see themselves as separate, non-national entities'; they have 'only one economic unit, the world'.[78]

Researchers and commentators often point to the ways in which transnational corporations, by threatening to relocate their profits, investments and plants (or even their products) to another country, can 'blackmail' governments to obtain more favourable employment and tax rules, and regulatory and legislative standards. Moreover, it is argued that the central role of transnational corporations in the global production processes – as producers and sellers, innovators, consumers of others' goods and services, providers of capital and credit, and employers – means that to a large degree transnational corporations, not states or domestic firms, now decide what goods are produced, how, where and by whom, therefore determining the outcome of competition between states, the who-gets-what in the great globalisation game. This is understood to have caused a 'shift from state to markets' that 'has actually made political players' of the multinational corporations, as Susan Strange wrote.[79] This usually leads to the conclusion that individual countries, including core capitalist countries, are more or less powerless in the face of these global behemoths, which can only be dealt with at the supranational (and ideally global) level.

These arguments are not new. Multinational corporations have been the subject of intense debate since the early 1960s. Intan Suwandi and John Bellamy Foster recall that early mainstream and left analyses viewed corporations 'as detached from nation-states, constituting entirely independent economic forces'.[80] In *American Business Abroad*, published in 1969, Charles Kindleberger observed that national firms with foreign operations were 'in [the] process of evolving into multinational firms and showing signs of ultimate evolution to international corporations' divorced from nation states.[81] Kindleberger mistakenly claimed, anticipating later globalisation misconceptions, that 'the nation-state is just about through as an economic unit'.[82] In 1971, neoclassical economist Raymond Vernon argued that these developments overrode national political interests because they reflected market-driven processes, which created 'world efficiency' and maximised 'world welfare' by using all available resources in the most productive way.[83]

Over the years, however, radical economists and theorists have challenged this view of multinational corporations as transnational or supranational entities independent of states.[84] In 1964, Paul Baran and Paul Sweezy wrote an essay entitled *Notes on the Theory of Imperialism*, later reprinted in *Monthly Review*, which offered a very different analysis of multinational corporations.[85] They argued that multinational corporations were not to be analysed merely in terms of the firm *versus* the state, but as components of an imperialist world system, in which firms were bound to state structures and class societies, and stood to gain from the hierarchy of nation states within the world capitalist system and the division between centre and periphery. 'These giant corporations', they wrote, 'are the basic units of monopoly capitalism in its present stage; their (big) owners and functionaries constitute the leading echelon of the ruling class. It is through analyzing these corporate giants and their interests that we can best comprehend the functioning of imperialism today.'[86]

Although multinational corporations operated in numerous countries, primarily to take advantage of global labour price differences, they remained linked to particular states (concentrated in the system's core) and classes, for historical, political and economic reasons that were unlikely to be transcended. The relationship was two-way: on the one hand, states were needed to protect and enforce the rights of corporations both domestically and internationally, for example by fostering and implementing 'political-economic policies which will create an "attractive" investment climate abroad, in particular in the underexploited countries', as James O'Connor argued in *The Corporations and the State* in 1974;[87] on the other hand, multinational corporations were used by the dominant states to siphon huge amounts of surplus from the countries of the periphery and therefore maintain and reinforce the global hierarchy of power.

To a large degree, the same is true today. Most studies show that multinational corporations continue to be rooted in the state, and that the influence of nationality on multinational corporations is still strong. The world's largest multinational corporations continue to exhibit a strong 'home-country bias' in terms of employment, sales, composition of the boards of directors, equity ownership (though the effective nationality of ownership has become hard to determine in an economy increasingly dominated by investment funds and shell companies) and asset ownership. According to the Transnationality Index (TNI) developed by the United Nations Conference on Trade and Development (UNCTAD), which calculates a firm's ratio of foreign assets, sales and employment to total assets, sales, and employment, the world's largest multinational corporations all have low TNI scores.[88] Peter Dicken argues that the TNI data refute the assertions of hyperglobalism and proves false the claim that multinational corporations are 'inexorably, and inevitably, abandoning their ties to their country of origin'.[89] If that were the case, we would expect the largest multinational corporations to have the majority of their assets, sales and employment outside of their countries of origin, and thus the majority of those corporations to have high TNIs.

But that is not the case. Thus, he concludes, there is little evidence that multinational corporations have become truly global firms. As Chris Harman noted:

> [T]he state–business relationship does not disappear with multi-nationalisation. The giant company does not end its link with the state, but rather multiplies the number of states – and national capitalist networks – to which it is linked. The successor to state capitalism is not some non-state capitalism (as is implied by expressions such as 'multinational' or 'transnational capitalism') but rather a capitalism in which capitals rely on the state as much as ever, but try to spread out beyond it to form links with capitals tied to other states.[90]

Importantly, as we saw in the aftermath of the 2007–9 financial crisis, multinational corporations continue to rely on governments to create and maintain the conditions for profit-making and offset the effects of crises, both domestically and internationally, by policing the working classes, bailing out large firms that would otherwise go bankrupt, opening up markets abroad, etc. More generally, to the extent that we have witnessed a strengthening of corporate interests in recent years and decades – as a result of trade liberalisation, deregulation, privatisation of state enterprises, mergers and acquisitions, etc. – clearly this has not been the result of inexorable economic and technological changes, but has largely been the product of legislation (or lack thereof).

Similarly, the relentless trend towards increased consolidation, concentration and centralisation of power in the corporate sector through mergers and acquisitions – Bayer's recent acquisition of Monsanto for a record-breaking US$66 billion is only the latest in a long string of mega-deals that have radically reshaped the agribusiness, hi-tech, media, food and other industries in recent years – has only been possible because governments have allowed anti-trust laws to ossify, to the detriment of competition. There was (is) nothing inevitable about these processes. As Susan Strange wrote: 'The shift from state authority to market authority has been in large part the result of state policies. It was not that the [multinational corporations] stole or purloined power from the government of states. *It was handed to them on a plate*.'[91]

The state–corporation relationship is not symbiotic, of course: by allowing mega-corporations to attain unprecedented power, legislators also created a situation whereby these mega-corporations are now able to exert a massive influence on the policymaking process through lobbying and other activities, and are therefore increasingly able to 'impose' their will on governments. However, this simply underscores the understanding within the corporate sector that their interests require them to reach settlements with national governments in order to advance their interests. As Robert Reich noted, the 'free market' is a myth that prevents us from examining how these lobbying efforts work to advance the interests of the corporate and financial elite, and how '[m]any of the most vocal proponents of the "free market" – including executives of large corporations and their ubiquitous lawyers and lobbyists, denizens of Wall Street and their political lackeys, and numerous millionaires and billionaires – have for many years been actively reorganizing the market for their own benefit'.[92]

By the same logic, it would be a mistake to view all states as the victims of globalisation: to the extent that corporations have indeed 'escaped' individual nation states, they have been able to do so only because core capitalist states have established the institutional frameworks that make globalisation possible. As Sam Gindin writes: 'As part of the making of global capitalism, states have been "internationalized": they have come to take responsibility, within their own jurisdiction, for supporting the accumulation of all capitalists, foreign as well as domestic. And so far from becoming less dependent on the state, corporations have come to depend on many states.'[93]

According to David Harvey, even the emergence of readily available information and communication technologies (ICTs), which have played an important role in facilitating the coordination of international business transactions, cannot be understood exogenously of the commitment of states to expand the global reach of their multinational corporations.[94] In other words, neoliberal globalisation was (is) not an inevitable consequence of economic and technical changes, which would mean admitting to its inexorable or unstoppable nature: it was (is) largely the result of choices made by governments.

It is worth noting that the global free trade architecture in place today is the result of a set of relatively recent developments that took place during the 1990s and early 2000s, such as the new World Trade Organisation (WTO) rules agreed in the context of the Uruguay Round (most notably the Agreement on Trade-Related Aspects of Intellectual Property Rights (TRIPS)); the signing of new bilateral and multilateral free trade agreements such as the infamous North American Free Trade

Agreement (NAFTA) between the United States and Mexico, the Free Trade Area of the Americas (FTAA) and the General Agreement on Trade in Services (GATS); and China's admission to the WTO. It is also worth recalling that these were at the centre of a very heated debate at the time, not to mention the target of a strong anti-globalisation movement. As Herman Daly explained in 1993 in a strikingly prophetic essay:

> The broader the free trade area, the less answerable a large and footloose corporation will be to any local or even national community. Spatial separation of the places that suffer the costs and enjoy the benefits becomes more feasible. The corporation will be able to buy labor in the low-wage markets and sell its products in the remaining high-wage, high-income markets. The larger the market, the longer a corporation will be able to avoid the logic of Henry Ford, who realised that he had to pay his workers enough for them to buy his cars.[95]

This, of course, is exactly what has happened: in the last few decades there has been a massive offshoring of manufacturing (and to a lesser degree service-based) jobs from advanced countries to emerging and developing economies, as corporations have delocalised their production to low-wage regions. Indeed, one of the most disruptive consequences of the global free trade architecture characteristic of neoliberal globalisation has been the emergence of a massive global reserve army of labour, which on the one hand has given multinational corporations access to a seemingly unlimited supply of low-wage, highly exploited workers in developing countries, and on the other has become a lever for increasing the reserve army of labour and the rate of exploitation in advanced countries as well.[96]

According to research by Foster, McChesney and Jonna, in 2011 the global reserve army amounted to some 2.4 billion people, compared to 1.4 billion in the active labour army.[97] As they write: 'It is the existence of a reserve army that in its maximum extent is more than 70 percent larger than the active labor army that serves to restrain wages globally, and particularly in the poorer countries'.[98] As a result of this 'great global job shift', many Western countries have experienced waves of deindustrialisation that have laid entire regions and communities to waste. The share of manufacturing as a percentage of US GDP, for example, has dropped from around 28 per cent in the 1950s to 12 per cent in 2016, accompanied by a dramatic decrease in its share (along with that of the OECD as a whole) in world manufacturing.[99]

Since governments in the West did little or nothing to provide millions of blue-collar workers who thereby lost their jobs the means of getting new ones that paid at least as well, many workers have become permanently unemployed or have been forced into low-paid, precarious jobs in the service sector, causing their wages to stagnate or fall, fuelling social insecurity and inequality, disrupting communities and eroding social cohesion. This shift is often framed as a neutral consequence of globalisation; in fact, it was largely a political choice. Even though this process cannot be understood independently of other factors that have boosted the bargaining power of employers vis-à-vis workers – the adoption of labour-saving technologies, the 'financialisation' of the economy, the rise of the service sector, immigration, the decline of unionism, the casualisation of labour, wage compression, etc. – the data show a clear correlation between globalisation (measured by the sum of exports and imports as a percentage of GDP) and inequality in Western societies.[100]

It is worth noting that the *threat* of delocalisation can be as powerful a weapon for employers as delocalisation itself. A study by Kate Bronfenbrenner found that during the economic upturn of the 1990s American workers felt more insecure about their economic future than during the depths of the 1990–1 recession.[101] 'More than half of all employers made threats to close all or part of the plant' during union organising drives; but afterwards 'employers followed through on the threat and shut down all or part of their facilities in fewer than 3 percent' of cases.[102] Either way, it is important to keep in mind that if corporations have been able to weaken workers by shifting jobs and capital overseas, or threatening to do so, it is only because core states created a global architecture that allows them to do so. In this sense, it is incorrect to say that globalisation has allowed corporations to blackmail states by threatening to delocalise to lower-pay countries; in fact, it has allowed corporations to blackmail workers *in alliance with national political-economic elites* (though this appears to be changing, as we discuss in Chapter 6).

It is a well-established fact that in the past 30 years economic inequality within advanced countries has dramatically increased, both in terms of income and wealth, with disparities in income in some countries returning to levels typical of a century ago. Poverty levels have also been rising steadily in all advanced countries since the mid-1980s.[103] Even though in most advanced countries GDP grew by 60–70 per cent between the early 1990s and the second decade of the 2000s, three-quarters of that growth went to 5 per cent or less of the population.[104] In nearly all OECD countries, the share of national income represented by wages, salaries and benefits – the labour share – has been declining, and that of capital increasing.[105] This trend has not been limited to advanced countries, though: according to the ILO, in recent decades emerging and developing countries have witnessed an even steeper decline in the share of domestic income going to labour than advanced countries.[106]

In all countries, the share of national income going to the highest earners has increased between 1980 and 2010.[107] Today, the average income of the richest 10 per cent of the population in OECD countries is about nine times that of the poorest 10 per cent.[108] With few exceptions, changes in the income share of the richest 1 per cent of the population account for most of the increase in the income share of the top decile (one-tenth) of the distribution – with the income of the top 1 per cent showing increases of 70 per cent or more in some countries.[109] A recent study by Oxfam has suggested that the richest 1 per cent of the world may now own the same wealth as all the other human beings put together.[110]

It is often argued that the deindustrialisation of Western societies (and the consequences this has entailed, such as job loss and wage stagnation) was the price to pay for the development and industrialisation of the developing world. China – which has witnessed a staggering export-led growth in the past two decades, as manufacturers from the US and other Western nations poured into the country to take advantage of low wages and other costs, resulting in millions of people being lifted out of extreme poverty and in the emergence of a rapidly growing middle class – is usually held out by mainstream economists and commentators as a shining example of the benefits of globalisation.

However, there are several problems with this narrative. First, it assumes that higher unemployment and wage stagnation in the West were *inevitable* results of deindustrialisation, which was (is) not the case, as we have seen. Second, it assumes that the only way underdeveloped countries can grow is by exporting goods and services to richer countries; yet, throughout the 1990s, until this policy was reversed after the East Asian financial crisis, much of the developing world, especially Asia, experienced rapid growth rates by following an opposite development path (which happens to be the one espoused in mainstream economics textbooks), based on importing capital (to build up their capital stock and infrastructure without depleting their real resources) and running large trade deficits.[111] Moreover, as noted by Ha-Joon Chang, 'export success does not require free trade': since the late 1970s, China and other developing countries have been characterised by a dualistic trade regime in which a strong export-oriented economy coexists with a highly protected domestic economy.[112] Indeed, to the extent that former developing nations have achieved developed status in recent decades, this has not been due to 'globalisation', 'free trade' or low wages, but to carefully crafted state-led policies, including government ownership of banks and key industries (including ones that operate at a multinational level), capital controls, tariff protection, subsidies and other forms of government support.[113] In other words, it has been due to the same policies on which all advanced nations in the world – beginning with the United States – built their success. As Dean Baker writes, 'there is no truth to the story that the job loss and wage stagnation faced by manufacturing workers in the United States and other wealthy countries was a necessary price for reducing poverty in the developing world'.[114]

Third, it doesn't take into account the fact that the supposed 'winners' of globalisation – the millions of factory workers in China and other emerging countries who have seen their incomes rise enormously as a result of offshoring – were (are) to a large degree former peasants and rural workers that in many cases were (are) forced, through economic restructuring ('depeasantisation'), to leave their land and sell their labour in urban factories. Thus, even though their monetary incomes have risen, this does not necessarily mean that their lives and rights have improved. In fact, as John Smith has shown, it is the 'super-exploitation' of workers in the 'South' that is the foundation of modern imperialism in the twenty-first century.[115] 'The starvation wages, death-trap factories, and fetid slums in Bangladesh', Smith writes, 'are representative of the conditions endured by hundreds of millions of working people throughout the Global South', whose surplus value is captured by multinational corporations and transferred to the countries of the capitalist core.[116] Yet, this 'super-exploitation' is often unaccounted for in official statistics:

> GDP is a measure of the part of the global product that is captured or appropriated by a nation, not a measure of what it has produced domestically. The D in GDP, in other words, is a lie. ... The only part of Apple's profits that appear to originate in China are those resulting from the sale of its products in that country. As in the case of the

T-shirt made in Bangladesh, so with the latest electronic gadget, the flow of wealth from Chinese and other low wage workers sustaining the profits and prosperity of Northern firms and nations is rendered invisible in economic data and in the brains of the economists.[117]

Indeed, a huge percentage of trade accounted for as foreign exports of countries such as China isn't even real trade: UNCTAD estimates that 'about 60 percent of global trade ... consists of trade in intermediate goods and services that are incorporated at various stages in the production process of goods and services for final consumption' – that is, trade internal to multinational corporations.[118] Noam Chomsky described this system as 'corporate mercantilism': 'centrally-managed transactions run by a very visible hand with major market distortions of all kinds'.[119]

In a 1977 essay, Joan Robinson offered a similar appraisal of free trade, which she described as little more than an attempt by the strongest competitors in world markets to obtain mercantilist advantages over their weaker competitors.[120] In this sense, it is crucial to distinguish between the different relations to nation states exercised by multinational corporations, depending on whether these states are in the core or periphery of the capitalist world economy. More importantly, though, it is important to remember that markets are never a given. As Dean Baker writes: 'Neither God nor nature hands us a worked-out set of rules determining the way property relations are defined, contracts are enforced, or macroeconomic policy is implemented. These matters are determined by policy choices. The elites have written these rules to redistribute income upward.'[121] Those rules, as we show in Chapters 8–10, can be rewritten, or at the very least resisted.

FINANCIALISATION: MYTH AND REALITY

The stagnation of middle incomes and the declining purchasing power of labour that befell advanced countries from the late 1970s onwards, chiefly as a result of the neoliberal processes of profit-seeking described in previous chapters, didn't simply lead to an increase in inequality. Along with other factors – the exhaustion of the technological and economic foundations of Fordism, the market saturation of mass consumption goods, the rigidity of productive processes, etc. – it also engendered deep-seated stagnationary tendencies in the economy which threatened the profitability of capital and evoked the threat of an under-consumption/overaccumulation crisis. Profits, after all, can only be made if there is a sufficient demand for goods and services, of which wages are a crucial component; moreover, in the face of falling profits, businesses tend to refrain from carrying out investment, resulting in an underutilisation of labour and capital goods that further exacerbates the underlying stagnationary trend. 'Hence, from the second half of the 1970s on, the primary propulsive force of the world economy was the endless attempt of capitalist companies – under the demands of their owners and investors – to bring the profit rate back up, using various techniques, to the highest levels of twenty years before.'[122]

One such technique was financialisation: that is, a massive increase in the size and importance of the financial sector (often referred to as the FIRE – finance, insurance and real estate – sector) relative to the overall economy. Harry Magdoff and Paul Sweezy were among the first thinkers to focus on the emerging stagnation-financialisation nexus in the 1980s. 'Among the forces countering the tendency to stagnation', they observed in one of their later works, 'none has been more important or less understood by economic analysts than the growth, beginning in the 1960s and rapidly gaining momentum after the severe recession of the mid-1970s, of the country's debt structure (government, corporate, and individual) at a pace far exceeding the sluggish expansion of the underlying "real" economy. The result has been the emergence of an unprecedentedly huge and fragile financial superstructure subject to stresses and strains that increasingly threaten the stability of the economy as a whole.'[123]

The relentless growth of the credit-debt system identified by Magdoff and Sweezy only accelerated over the subsequent decades, leading to the emergence in the 1990s of what has been labelled privatised or bubble-driven Keynesianism.[124] Essentially, while governments in the US and Europe were attempting to reduce their fiscal deficits (in line with the neoliberal fiscal paradigm of the 1990s), or at least to divert net public spending from the lower end to the top end of the income distribution, households, faced with stagnant incomes and declining purchasing power, started to borrow more and more to make up the difference between spending and income, leading to a colossal rise in private debt, particularly in the United States, but also in the United Kingdom, Ireland and some continental European countries like the Netherlands, Denmark, Spain and Greece, and in Eastern Europe.

American mortgage indebtedness, for example, constituted the primary source of increase in consumption since 2000.[125] This 'democratization of credit', as Nouriel Roubini calls it, helped fuel the unsustainable asset and credit bubbles that exploded in 2008.[126]

In other words, for years the economy continued to grow primarily because banks were distributing the purchasing power – through debt – that businesses were not providing in salaries. '[F]inancial innovations seemed to have offered a short-term solution to the crisis of neoliberalism in the 1990s: debt-led consumption growth', writes Özlem Onaran.[127] In short, wage deflation and the increasingly leveraged position of households and financial companies 'were complementary elements of a perverse mechanism where real growth was doped by toxic finance'.[128] As noted by Riccardo Bellofiore and others, these dynamics had devastating consequences in terms of class relations, leading to an effective subsumption of labour to finance: whereas under traditional Keynesianism a government uses its own borrowing to smooth fluctuations in labour income over time by sustaining the level of employment, 'under privatized Keynesianism consumption is sustained by separating purchasing power from labour income among individuals, and with no time horizon. Borrowing is undertaken by individuals themselves on the basis of property mortgages or credit card ratings largely divorced from [the] labour market situation.'[129]

This form of privatised Keynesianism was facilitated – and largely made possible – by the dismantling of the post-Great Depression framework of financial regulation, resulting in the deregulation and liberalisation of national banking systems. The Clinton administration's Gramm–Leach–Bliley Act (GLBA) of 1999, also known as the Financial Services Modernization Act, is probably the most illustrious example of this deregulatory frenzy: this repealed the Glass–Steagall Act of 1933, which separated commercial and investment banking and is widely credited with giving the United States 50 crisis-free years of financial stability. With the passage of the Financial Services Modernization Act, commercial banks, investment banks, securities firms and insurance companies were once again allowed to consolidate. Today, many consider the repeal (followed in 2004 by the lifting of the leverage cap on US investment banks) to be an important cause of the late 2000s financial crisis. By allowing financial institutions to consolidate and to take on ever-bigger risks and debts (through securities and other financial products), the GLBA paved the way to the rise of the so-called too-big-to-fail banks, and to the kinds of structural conflicts of interest that were endemic in the 1920s.

Interestingly, although the US banking sector had been seeking a repeal of the Glass–Steagall Act since the 1980s, the decisive push came from Europe. In 1989 (ten years before the passage of the GLBA), the European Community's Second Banking Directive had effectively provided the legal basis for the extension of Germany's so-called universal banking system – that is, a system where banks are allowed to participate in many kinds of banking activities, and to act both as commercial and investment banks – to the rest of the EEC, and for the liberalisation of banking services across Europe.[130] This meant that the major European banks had, over the years, become significantly larger and more concentrated than their US counterparts. They had bought up many smaller banks across the continent, giving rise to the European megabanks. By the 1990s, these now-internationalised universal megabanks had turned their attention to their smaller American counterparts. In those years, Credit Suisse acquired First Boston, SBC acquired Dillon Read and Deutsche Bank acquired Banker Trust. The US banks blamed Glass–Steagall for preventing them from competing fairly with their European counterparts – and technically they were right. The European banks, in short, provided them with the ideal excuse to demand, and obtain, a repeal of Glass–Steagall. To make things worse, as well as scrapping the existing laws and regulations, governments allowed the financial services industry to create a whole array of new esoteric products (such as mortgage-backed securities and derivatives) that effectively allowed financial institutions, through securitisation, to create a never-ending supply of money.

State support for financialisation and 'privatised Keynesianism', however, was by no means limited to deregulation. 'This new configuration of capitalism', Bellofiore writes, was also 'made possible by a new role of the central bank as lender of first resort to support capital asset price inflation'.[131] The chief architect of this transformation was Alan Greenspan, chairman of the Federal Reserve from 1987 to 2006. The Federal Reserve and other central banks essentially adopted a policy of making liquidity available to banks in unlimited amounts with the objective of sustaining the continuous increase in asset values and 'manipulating indebted consumption as the pillar of autonomous demand'.[132] Central banks were thus relegated to a purely ancillary role in the relation to financial markets: namely, that of 'regulating' the system's solvency conditions. This became clear in 1998, when the hedge fund Long-Term Capital Management was saved with US$3.6 billion of public money – a small taste of things to come ten years later, when the strategy of advanced countries in the aftermath of the financial meltdown of 2008 rapidly evolved from a financial bailout, involving trillions of dollars/euros, 'to a much more concerted attempt, for which there are no real historical analogies, to reinstate financialisation as the motor force of the system', via quantitative easing and other unconventional monetary policies.[133]

Moreover, beginning in the 1970s and then gathering pace in the 1980s, the United States and other Western governments also started lifting all controls on capital flows, which until then had been an integral part of the post-war Bretton Woods system. Even in this case the decisive push came from Europe, as we have seen. As a result of these developments, the financial services sector has grown enormously in the past 30 years. In 1980, financial assets were more or less equal to the world's GDP; by 2007 they had grown to be around 4.4 times larger.[134] Most tellingly perhaps, between 1980 and 2007 the world's GDP grew at an average rate of 3 per cent, while the value of financial assets grew at more than 8 per cent – a gap which can only be explained in one way, as Italian sociologist Luciano Gallino observed: '[M]oney creates itself instead of creating use value'.[135] In ten years the value of the derivatives market jumped from US$92 trillion to US$670 trillion in 2007, about 14 times the size of the world's GDP.[136] The most common form of derivatives is foreign exchange transactions, which consist of the buying and selling of international currencies for a profit. In 2007 the volume of foreign exchange transactions was about US$3.3 trillion per day. One day's exports and imports of all goods and services in the world amount to about 2 per cent of that figure – which means that 98 per cent of transactions on these markets are purely speculative.[137]

It is often argued that financialisation has shifted the centre of gravity of the capitalist economy from production to finance, ushering in a new regime of accumulation primarily based on money-dealing and interest-bearing speculative capital – the realisation of what Hyman P. Minsky described in the 1980s as money-manager capitalism.[138] As argued by the French economist François Chesnais, in this regime of accumulation, interest-bearing capital is at the vortex of economic and social relations, and the most important consequence of this central position is that the externality that characterises this type of capital becomes inserted into the very bosom of productive accumulation, generating what he calls 'patrimonial capitalism'.[139] Thus, through the stock market, institutions that specialise in 'finance-led accumulation' – that is, Minsky's money managers: pension funds, collective investment funds, insurance societies, banks that manage investment partnerships, hedge funds, etc. – have become owners of large and globally important corporate groups, and have imposed upon the accumulation of productive capital itself a dynamic guided by an external agent, namely the maximisation of 'shareholder value'.

This has led many authors to describe financialisation as a parasitic process that has occurred (and occurs) at the expense of industrial capital (that is, manufacturing) and the 'real' economy. Chesnais, for example, describes the advance of neoliberalism as a 'coup d'état' in which industrial capital has been forced to subordinate itself to finance capital.[140] The implication of this argument is that if industrial capital still dominated finance capital, capitalism today would not be experiencing a 'mediocre or poor dynamic of investment' or 'the destruction of industrial employment ... and strong pressures which weigh on those jobs which remain'.[141] A similar argument is made by US economist Michael Hudson. He writes that 'banking and rent extraction are in many ways adverse to industrial capitalism', and describes the modern economy as a form of 'rentier capitalism' in which 'finance capital has achieved dominance over industrial capital': 'Transfers of property from debtors to creditors – even privatizations of public assets and enterprises – are inevitable as the growth of financial claims surpasses the ability of productive power and earnings to keep pace. Foreclosures follow in the wake of crashes, enabling finance to take over industrial companies and even governments.'[142]

Hudson echoes another argument that is very common nowadays, particularly in left-wing circles: that the internationalisation of finance and extraordinary growth in the size and power of global capital – along with advancements in communications technology that allow financial capital to move around the globe at amazing speed – have severely limited (if not eliminated altogether) the capacity of individual nation states to pursue policies that are not in accord with the diktats of global finance. The claim is that if a government were to attempt autonomously to pursue a progressive or redistributive agenda, it would be punished by global capital through capital flight (which would then cause a precipitous decline in the exchange rate), rising interest rates on its government debt and speculative attacks on its currency on the foreign exchange markets. Therefore, through these channels, financial markets are able to impose their 'will' on states, influencing government policies on many issues such as fiscal and tax policy, labour market regulation, the welfare system, liberalisation and privatisation. As Gerald Epstein wrote:

> The old Keynesian view which saw national governments as having sufficient autonomy to pursue national goals is now seen as hopelessly *passé*. The new global view eschews any government interference in this global financial market as unrealistic and unproductive given the new reality. Instead, it calls for tight money, financial deregulation, balanced budgets and 'responsible' wage demands.[143]

According to this narrative, finance's power relationship over states is further compounded by its ability to model and reshape opinions concerning the 'health' of nations, through rating agencies, research departments in business banks, direct or indirect ownership of specialist and general media and direct or indirect financing of universities, research centres and/or individual commentators.[144] This has led various authors to speak of a 'tyranny of global finance' that is responsible for 'an unstoppable deterioration of ... national sovereignty'.[145] Lastly, it is often concluded that the only way to tame the overwhelming power of global financial and corporate leviathans is for countries to pool their sovereignty together and transfer it to supranational institutions (such as the European Union) that are large and powerful enough to have their voices heard, thus regaining at the supranational level the sovereignty that has been allegedly lost at the national level.

The argument that finance – or finance capital – today has evolved into an all-powerful superstructure existing independently of states and dominating the rest of the economy, and which states can do little to oppose, is a compelling story which would appear to be validated by the events of recent years – particularly in Europe, where numerous countries, at the height of the euro crisis (2010–12), found themselves at the mercy of financial speculation – and which is reinforced on a daily basis by our politicians' insistence on the need to 'reassure the markets' and the media's obsessive coverage of the ebb and flow of stock markets, as if the entire economy depended on it. But does it hold up to scrutiny?

A number of elements would appear to run counter to this narrative. First, 'finance capital' is hardly a new thing: the term was coined in the early twentieth century by the Austrian-born Marxist economist Rudolf Hilferding to describe what he viewed as a new stage of capitalist development, beginning from about 1870 onwards (and which we know to have lasted for about half a century, until the breakdown of the international order in the 1930s).[146] Unlike the earlier competitive and pluralistic 'liberal capitalism', finance capitalism, which was made possible by interrelated technological, political and economic developments, was characterised by financial rather than material expansion and by an increasing concentration and centralisation of capital in large corporations, cartels, trusts and banks.

Does this sound familiar? The similarities between the turn of the nineteenth century and the turn of the twentieth are indeed striking. Arrighi noted that even though the novelty of the 'information revolution' that has characterised the last decades is impressive, we must remember that submarine telegraph cables had connected intercontinental markets from the mid-1800s onwards. Since then, day-to-day trading and price-making were possible in almost real time in every financial centre of the world, with global bond markets and large-scale international lending growing rapidly during the period. Indeed, FDI in 1913 amounted to nine times world output – a proportion unsurpassed today.[147] While the dramatic increase in the speed and mobility of short-term financial capital in recent decades cannot be denied, this is by no means the whole story, as Gerald Epstein wrote a few years ago:

> Data on the net mobility of capital measuring the in- minus the outflow of capital in a given period of time (flows), or on an accumulated basis over time (stocks), give a very different picture. Data on net asset positions in the nineteenth and twentieth centuries (relative to GDP or their capital stock), which represent how much capital has been transferred from one country to others on a net basis over a long period of time, clearly show that there was much more capital mobility on a net basis in the late nineteenth century than there is in the late twentieth century.[148]

It is not a coincidence that the forces that gave rise to the various subprime crises of 2007–9 and the subsequent Great Recession – not to mention the euro crisis – were eerily similar to the ones that led to the crash of 1929 and subsequent Great Depression. Authors such as Arrighi and Braudel, however, have taken issue with the idea that finance capital was a newborn child of the 1900s, as Hilferding claimed, arguing instead that all capitalist crises – from the Florentine debt crisis in the fourteenth century to Britain's Edwardian era, through the age of the Genoese and the rise and fall of Dutch hegemony – were connected to an excessive growth in the size and power of finance vis-à-vis the rest of the economy.

Braudel noted that 'systemic cycles of accumulation' – intervals featuring rapid and stable expansion of world trade and production, fuelled by an extraordinary growth of the financial superstructure – invariably resulted in a crisis of overaccumulation and an eventual breakdown of the organisational structures on which the previous expansion of trade and production had been based.[149] Interestingly, these past phases of financialisation were also associated, just like today, with widespread processes of 'deindustrialisation' and with a contraction in working-class incomes. The current phase of financial expansion – which, just like its historical predecessors, is based 'on massive, system-wide redistributions of income and wealth from all kinds of communities to capitalist agencies'[150] – is therefore neither new nor unprecedented.

Second, the claim that finance is at odds with industrial capital is also disputable. If that were the case, why have other capitalists – in the manufacturing and other 'real' sectors of the economy – not joined forces to oppose finance in the aftermath of the financial crisis? And why was the turn to neoliberalism and financialisation from the 1970s onwards supported by big business in general, and not just the financial sector? The answer lies in the fact that the search for higher profits after the period of profit margin decreases led to a revolution in management practices and culture within big business in which traditional manufacturing firms increasingly turned to financial services – as providers as well as consumers – to boost their profits; in other words, *they became financial firms themselves*. Thus it was that manufacturing giants such as General Motors opened up financial divisions specialising in consumer credit (instalments, leasing, etc.), nowadays indispensable for selling their products to consumers, and eventually became giants of the financial sector as well. As Christian Marazzi writes, 'the financialization of the economy has been a process ... to enhance capital's profitability *outside* immediately productive processes. ... This means that we are in a historical period in which finance is *cosubstantial* with the very production of goods and services.'[151]

One of the most significant outcomes of this transformation has been a long-term decline in the proportion of surplus value going into new productive investment. Greta Krippner has shown that:

> not only had the share of total US corporate profits accounted for by FIRE in the 1980s nearly caught up with and, in 1990, surpassed the share accounted for by manufacturing; more important, in the 1970s and 1980s, *non-financial firms themselves* sharply increased their investment in financial assets relative to that in plants and equipment, and became increasingly dependent on financial sources of revenue and profit relative to that earned from productive activities. Particularly significant is Krippner's finding that manufacturing not only dominates but *leads* this trend towards the 'financialisation' of the non-financial economy.[152]

In other words, the post-Fordist system is not one in which finance capital has taken control of industrial capital, or has become 'detached' from the real economy; on the contrary, and more worryingly, it is one in which industrial capital and the real economy themselves have become thoroughly financialised.

In light of the above, it is quite clear that the driving force behind the growth in the size and power of finance has been political rather than technological. Few people would deny this insofar as the deregulation of financial firms and financialisation of non-financial firms is concerned. When it comes to the issue of international financial integration, however, the case is less clear-cut. Various authors, for example, cite the Eurodollar market – that is, deposits denominated in US dollars at banks outside the United States, usually in London and Paris – as proof of the fact that as early as the 1960s, when the Eurodollar market experienced a sudden upward jump, capital had already found a means to get around the national capital controls embedded in the Bretton Woods regime. According to Arrighi, the Eurodollar market effectively became an 'offshore' international financial system in which national regulatory oversight was absent, as a result of which 'world liquidity' ended up outside the control of national governments; furthermore, it also meant that governments found themselves under increasing pressure 'to manipulate the exchange rates of their currencies and interest rates in order to attract or repel liquidity held in offshore markets'.[153] According to this narrative, one may conclude that the decision by governments to deregulate capital controls was simply an acknowledgement on their behalf that these had, *de facto*, already become largely ineffective; and that financial integration is the (somewhat inevitable and irreversible) outcome of exogenous dynamics driven primarily by financial institutions and largely outside the control of states.

In fact, as Michael C. Webb showed, the Eurodollar market 'could not have grown without supportive government policies'.[154] If the UK promoted it as an attempt to recapture its past imperial glory and the US as a way for US corporations to internationalise without suffering from capital controls on the repatriation of their international profits or financing of overseas activities, other states encouraged (or tolerated) it because it allowed them to accommodate their need for different currencies, both for trade and investment, and 'to achieve balance-of-payments objectives without undesirable changes in national policies'.[155] Thus, Webb concludes, 'the emergence of large international capital flows in the form of Euromarket transactions can be traced directly to state decisions, which created incentives for private economic actors to increase their international financial transactions'.[156]

As noted in Chapter 3, after the US's abandonment of the fixed exchange rate system in 1971, the United States government started aggressively opposing any form of international cooperation in the administration of inflow and outflow controls, largely as a means to 'finance' its chronic trade deficit with capital inflows from abroad, as well as to promote the interests of its own financial firms. Even though most advanced countries began slowly to liberalise after that point, it is important to note that restrictions on short-term speculative flows remained in place almost everywhere. The decisive push towards a world of total capital mobility would arrive only a decade and a half later, when EU countries accepted that the free movement of capital should become a central tenet of the emerging European single market.

This decision had much more to do with political rather than financial considerations; nonetheless, it underscores the fact that 'international capital mobility can only be mobile to the extent that there is political and government intervention into financial markets', as Gerald Epstein noted.[157] Epstein isn't just referring to the obvious (though oft-forgotten) fact that financial integration can only exist if states consent to cross-border capital flows. Integrated financial markets also 'require asymmetric power relations and institutional structures of enforcement to operate', to guarantee creditors that their debts/credits will be paid back and to enforce debt repayment (by economic, political or military pressure).[158] These include: independent central banks; so-called 'free trade' agreements, which prohibit governments from discriminating against foreign capital; financial deregulation, which makes the problems of macroeconomic management raised by the already high levels of capital mobility even more acute; and transfer of power from democratically elected legislatures to non-elected technocratic bodies. All this in turn requires state power.

In light of the above, we can conclude that the notion of finance as an amorphous power that exists independently of states is largely unfounded. To the extent that finance rules, it is because political institutions have created a regulatory system compatible with the process of capitalist reproduction under its command. As a result, financial corporations remain as (if not more) dependent on the state for their survival as any other corporations. More generally, we have seen how globalisation, even in its neoliberal form, was (is) not the result of some intrinsic capitalist or technology-driven dynamic that inevitably entails a reduction of state power, as is often claimed.

On the contrary, it was (is) a process that was (is) actively shaped and promoted by states (and by the US state in particular, though this appears to be changing), which continue to play a crucial role in promoting capitalist accumulation on a global scale. This includes promoting, enforcing and sustaining a (neo)liberal international framework as well as establishing the domestic conditions for allowing global accumulation to flourish. Moreover, as we have seen, '[e]ven neoliberal forms of economic globalisation continue to depend on political institutions and policy initiatives to roll out neoliberalism and to maintain it in the face of market failures, crisis tendencies, and resistance', as was made clear by the response of governments to the financial crisis of 2007–9.[159] This, Bob Jessop argues, 'exclude[s] a zero-sum approach to world market integration and state power'.[160]

At the same time, it cannot be denied that in many respects – the capacity to promote local industries vis-à-vis foreign ones; to run fiscal deficits; to manage the money supply; to impose duties and taxation; to regulate the import and export of goods and capital, etc. – the economic sovereignty of most states, including advanced capitalist economies, *is* more constrained now than in the past. To what extent, however, is this the result of a *deliberate and voluntary reduction of sovereignty by nation states themselves* rather than external factors over which states allegedly have little control?

We have already seen how two of the main factors that curtail the ability of governments to exercise control over economic policy – financial deregulation and capital mobility – were willingly pursued by national governments. But the same can be said of other factors as well. As noted by Leonid E. Grinin, the 'change and reduction of volume and scope (as well as nomenclature) of state sovereign powers is a bilateral process: on the one hand, the factors fairly undermining the countries' sovereignty are strengthening, on the other ... since the end of World War II, increasingly more states have been willingly and consciously limiting their sovereign rights.'[161]

This has principally taken two forms, in addition to the ones already mentioned: the voluntary surrender of national prerogatives to supra-national organisations and so-called 'superstates' – the most obvious example being the European Union and monetary union, whose member states have gone as far as giving up their currency, probably the most defining element of economic sovereignty – and the self-limitation of such prerogatives through the signing of bilateral investment treaties (of which there are more than 4,000 in operation in the world at present) and increasingly regional trade agreements (such as the FTAA and TPP), which severely limit the capacity of governments to regulate in the public interest, by means of so-called ISDS mechanisms. At their most extreme, these allow corporations to sue governments in private courts for alleged expropriatory or discriminatory practices – not just national-isation of assets but any rule or regulation (including environmental and employment protection laws) that may harm the corporation's expecta-tion of gain or profit.

Clearly, these supranational organisations and international treaties are only possible if there is agreement between states and if these are willing to enforce them locally. This raises an important question, however: why would states willingly choose to curtail their national sov-ereignty? This is the question we turn to in the following section.

THE POLITICS OF DEPOLITICISATION

As we saw in Chapter 2, by the mid-1970s the Keynesian full employment regime hadn't simply become, from capital's perspective, a barrier to accumulation. On a more fundamental level, 'it threatened to provide the foundations for transcending capitalism' itself, Hugo Radice writes.[162] That is to say, the failure of Keynesian interventionism to realise the aspirations of the working class led 'to growing pressure from sections of the organised working class for the state to bring capital directly under social control, to complement the socialisation of consumption with the socialisation of production, to subordinate the accumulation of capital to the aspirations of the working class'.[163] Furthermore, an increasingly militant working class had begun to link up with the new counterculture movements of the late 1960s – community groups, welfare rights groups, black and women's groups, anti-war groups, etc. – 'in struggles that demanded not simply more pay or more government expenditure, but that challenged the bureaucratic and authoritarian forms of capitalist power'.[164]

This led to what the *Financial Times* called 'a revolt of rising expectations'.[165] In other words, as Kalecki had anticipated, full employment hadn't become simply an *economic* threat to the ruling classes but a *political* one as well, which preoccupied elites throughout the 1970s and 1980s. The Trilateral Commission's oft-cited *Crisis of Democracy* report of 1975 argued that this required, from the establishment's perspective, a multi-level response, based not only on a reduction of the bargaining power of labour, but also on 'a greater degree of moderation in democracy' and a greater disengagement ('noninvolvement') of civil society from the operations of the political system, to be achieved through the diffusion of 'apathy'.[166]

This second objective – which the Trilateral judged to be 'a central precondition' for the attainment of the first objective: the transition to a new economic order (that is, neoliberalism) – was achieved primarily through a gradual *depoliticisation* of economic policy: that is, through the removal of macroeconomic policy from democratic (parliamentary) control and the separation of the 'economic' from the 'political', thereby effectively insulating the neoliberal transition from popular contestation.

The various policies adopted by Western governments from the 1970s onwards to promote depoliticisation include: (i) reducing the power of parliaments vis-à-vis that of governments and making the former increasingly less representative (for instance, by moving from proportional parliamentary systems to majoritarian ones); (ii) making central banks formally independent of governments, with the explicit aim of subjugating the latter to 'market-based discipline'; (iii) adopting 'inflation targeting' – an approach which stresses low inflation as the primary objective of monetary policy, to the exclusion of other policy objectives such as full employment – as the dominant approach to central bank policymaking; (iv) adopting rules-bound policies – on public spending, debt as a proportion of GDP, competition, etc. – thereby limiting what politicians can do at the behest of their electorates; (v) subordinating spending departments to treasury control; (vi) readopting fixed exchange rates systems, which, as we have seen, severely limit the ability of governments to exercise control over economic policy; and, most importantly perhaps, (vii) surrendering national prerogatives to supranational institutions and super-state bureaucracies.

The reason why governments chose willingly to 'tie their hands' is all too clear: as the European case epitomises, the creation of self-imposed 'external constraints' allowed national politicians to reduce the politics costs of the neoliberal transition – which clearly involved unpopular policies – by 'scapegoating' institutionalised rules and 'independent' or international institutions, which in turn were presented as an inevitable outcome of the new, harsh realities of globalisation. Recall Callaghan's recourse to the IMF, in 1976, as the external vehicle to divide and conquer the Labour left.

Moreover, as Thomas Friedman wrote, the policies themselves that were adopted in the context of the neoliberal transition – which included maintaining a low rate of inflation and price stability; maintaining as close to a balanced budget as possible, if not a surplus; eliminating and lowering tariffs on imported goods; removing restrictions on foreign investment; getting rid of quotas and domestic monopolies; deregulating capital markets; making one's currency fully convertible; opening one's industries, stock and bond markets to direct foreign ownership and investment, etc. – further reduced the scope of governments by 'narrow[ing] the political and economic choices of those in power' such that 'policy choices get reduced to Pepsi or Coke – to slight nuances of taste, slight nuances of policy, slight alterations in design to account for local traditions, but never any major deviations from the core golden rules'.[167]

In this sense, the 'hollowing out' of substantive democracy and curtailment of democratic controlling rights that has accompanied the neoliberal transition in recent decades – leading to what Colin Crouch has famously termed post-democracy, defined as a society that continues to have and to use all the institutions of democracy, but in which they increasingly become a formal shell[168] – should not be viewed as a separate development, possibly resulting from the pressures of economic and political internationalisation, but as an essential element of the neoliberal project. Stephen Gill's notions of 'new constitutionalism' and 'disciplinary neoliberalism' are particularly relevant: according to Gill, an important aspect of the neoliberal era has been to lock in 'a more limited but still powerful neo-liberal state form insulated from popular-democracy accountability', in which challenges to the dominant political-economic order in the political sphere are rendered more difficult or even illegal, thus exposing populations to the supposedly apolitical 'discipline' of market forces.[169] This 'requires not simply suppressing, but attenuating, coopting and channelling democratic forces, so that they do not coalesce to create a political backlash against economic liberalism and build alternatives to this type of socio-economic order ... [thus] restraining the democratisation process that has involved centuries of struggle for representation'.[170]

Western Europe – unsurprisingly perhaps, considering that Western European states had come to symbolise the 'ungovernability' of Western societies – is where this 'struggle to contain popular expectations, and demobilize popular movements'[171] was brought to its most extreme conclusions. As we saw in Chapter 2, the breakdown of the Bretton Woods system in 1971 was followed by significant instability on the European foreign exchange markets. On one hand, the German mark strongly appreciated against the US dollar and French franc, imposing heavy costs on the German export industries; on the other, the weaker-currency nations (France, Italy, the United Kingdom) experienced major depreciations, triggering accelerating inflation (further exacerbated by US domestic policy and by the OPEC oil price hikes) and causing growing pressures on those countries' balance of payments. This meant that all parties had incentives, for various reasons, for moving towards a system of exchange rate management.

This eventually led to the creation, in 1979, of the EMS, which essentially anchored all participating currencies to the German mark and, consequently, to the inherently 'anti-Keynesian' and anti-inflationary stance of the Bundesbank. This strategy succeeded in fostering greater exchange rate cohesion, but the adjustment fell entirely on the shoulders of the high-inflation, weaker-currency countries, causing their currencies to revalue in real terms and transmitting a disinflationary impulse throughout the EMS. This cumulative process of 'competitive disinflation' led to the low levels of economic growth and high rates of unemployment that characterised the European economy in the 1980s and caused the appearance of structural current account deficits in countries like Italy and France.

In light of this, the decision of the weaker-currency nations to join the EMS, given the loss of competitiveness (and of export shares) engendered by the revaluation of their respective currencies, might appear largely self-defeating (while hugely benefiting Germany). However, such a decision cannot be understood solely in terms of nationally framed interests. Rather, as James Heartfield pointed out, it should be viewed as the way in which one part of the 'national community' was able to constrain another part.[172] The distributional struggle of the 1970s led to increasingly vocal demands on behalf of European capital for the state to discipline the working classes and their organisations, in order – first and foremost – to restore the profitability of capital through wage compression. In this sense, the logic of 'competitive disinflation' hardwired into the EMS allowed national politicians, now 'deprived' of the tool of competitive devaluation, to present wage compression and fiscal austerity as the only means through which to restore a country's competitiveness. In this sense, the EMS was a means to 'institutionalize disinflation'.[173]

Heartfield notes how in Italy, for example, Giuliano Amato succeeded, where previous governments had failed, to persuade the CGIL union to agree to end the inflation indexing of wages in 1992. He did this not by confronting labour directly, via a national referendum, as Giulio Andreotti had when reforming the agreement in 1984, but by reference to the 'external constraint' of the EMS.[174] According to Guido Carli, who at the time was the country's economics minister, 'the European Union represented an alternative path for the solution of problems which we were not managing to handle through the normal channels of government and parliament'.[175] Similarly, Raymond Barre's government of the late 1970s committed France to 'microeconomic austerity and macroeconomic discipline', with the aim of equilibrating the balance of payments that represents 'the external constraint which no country participating … in international trade can escape'.[176] Nigel Lawson, the British chancellor from 1983 to 1989, justified subordinating exchange rates to the European system as an economic policy based on formal rules rather than political discretion.[177] In his words, 'externally imposed exchange rate discipline' would help avoid the 'political pressures for relaxation … as the election approaches'.[178]

Through the prism of depoliticisation we can better understand all the subsequent phases of the European integration process. As seen in Chapter 4, a major breakthrough came in 1986 with the Single European Act, which imposed the mandatory abolition of all capital controls throughout the EEC. This was followed by the *Delors Report*, in 1989, which acted as a blueprint for the Maastricht Treaty of 1992. The treaty established a formal timeline for the establishment of a European Monetary Union, with most participating states agreeing to adopt the euro as their official currency – and to transfer control over monetary policy from their respective central banks to the ECB – by 1999. It was by far the most ambitious monetary experiment in history: even if the central banks of Europe (along with those of most advanced economies) were already formally independent to varying degrees by that time, the Maastricht Treaty brought the concept of independent central banking to a new and historically unprecedented level. It is one thing to put an individual country's monetary policy into the hands of an independent entity charged – officially at least – with acting in that country's best economic interest. It is quite another to put its monetary policy into the hands of a body that acts on behalf of a number of different countries with different economies and, as a result, different requirements in terms of economic policy.

Moreover, a condition made by Germany was that the sole objective of the ECB should be to keep inflation down. In other words, its main, if not its only, criterion for acting would be to ensure price stability. Furthermore, Articles 123 to 135 of the updated form of the Maastricht Treaty, known as the Treaty on the Functioning of the European Union (TFEU), clearly prohibited the financing of public deficits by the ECB. In hindsight, the aim seems clear: to force 'the public sector with a balance of budget deficits into the mechanism of a free market and thereby activating its disciplinary effect', as we saw in the aftermath of the 2007–9 financial crisis.[179] The Maastricht Treaty also famously set out strict deficit- and debt-to-GDP limits for member states – subsequently tightened – essentially depriving countries of their fiscal autonomy (without transferring this spending power to a higher authority) as well as their monetary independence (though the two, of course, go hand in hand). As Heartfield writes, monetary union can thus essentially be considered 'a process of depoliticizing a central plank of economic and fiscal administration, the currency'.[180]

The scope of the Maastricht Treaty, however, extends well beyond the realm of fiscal and monetary policy: as noted by Lukas Oberndorfer, the text effectively sets down the primary legal structure of the economic policy of the European Union.[181] This has since essentially remained unchanged. The EU's guiding principles are clearly espoused in the prefix to the chapter on economic policy, where it states that the EU and its member states are obliged to conduct their economic policy 'in accordance with the principle of an open market economy with free competition' and to comply 'with the following guiding principles: stable prices, sound public finances and monetary conditions and a sustainable balance of payments'. Other relevant articles of the TFEU include: Article 81, which prohibits any form of government intervention in the economy 'which may affect trade between Member States'; Article 121, which gives the European Council and European Commission – both unelected bodies – the right to 'formulate ... the broad guidelines of the economic policies of the Member States and of the Union'; Article 126, which regulates the disciplinary measures to be adopted in case of excessive deficit; Article 151, which states that the EU's labour and social policy shall take account of the need to 'maintain the competitiveness of the Union economy'; and Article 107, which prohibits state aid to strategic national industries.

As this brief overview makes clear, *the Maastricht Treaty embedded neoliberalism into the very fabric of the European Union*, effectively outlawing the 'Keynesian' polices that had been commonplace in the previous decades: not just currency devaluation and direct central bank purchases of government debt (for those countries that adopted the euro) but also demand-management policies, strategic use of public procurement, generous welfare provisions and the creation of employment via public spending. As Ulrich Häde notes, the European treaties are close to the neoliberal concept of 'economic constitution', understood as an anti-interventionist legal framework immune to democratic challenge, capable of constitutionally anchoring neoliberal economic ideologemes and binding economic policy on a European level.[182] In this sense, the current EU treaties represent a paradigmatic break from the 1957 Treaty of Rome, which was founded on a Keynesian view of the state. The current treaties, on the other hand, use the state as an instrument to advance neoliberalism and repress social-democratic leanings.

Interestingly, the concept of 'economic constitution' dates back to the 1930s, when ordoliberal intellectuals – most notably Friedrich Hayek – developed it as a response to the increasing demands for democratisation of the economy. In 1939, Hayek argued that 'interstate federalism' at the European level would be desirable because it would ensure that economic policy would be bound by pre-established rules and as far removed as possible from the democratic decision-making process.[183] Before Hayek, Marx himself had observed that the various bourgeois constitutions of the French republics, and their imitations in other continental states, were deliberately designed to obstruct any fundamental challenge to the dominant capitalist order.[184] This confirms Gill's thesis of the EU as an extreme form of new constitutionalism, the mechanisms of which are well explained by Oberndorfer:

> Even when there is no *direct control*, economic policies are 'surveilled' by European and international financial institutions and thus are subject to a neoliberal 'self-rule'. … Like the establishment of the EMU, these instruments are aimed at securing the neoliberal mode of integration 'by means of political and legal mechanisms that can be altered only with difficulty.[185] … Popular-democratic powers still have the chance to problematise the respective policies of their state apparatus, because they are, at least formally, responsible for them and have decision-making powers. Nevertheless, the fairly effective limitation and/or partitioning of these powers functions entirely in accordance with the governmental pattern of 'surveillance and normalisation' described by Gill: neoliberal path dependency is created by rule-based economic policy, competitive evaluation and self-evaluation and a discursive separation of member states into model students and sinners, although this cannot be imposed unconditionally.[186]

Moreover, as we saw in Chapter 5, in recent years the European Union's new authoritarian constitutionalism has evolved into an even more anti-democratic form that is breaking away from elements of formal democracy (for example through the imposition of unelected technocratic governments), leading some observers to suggest that the EU 'may easily become the postdemocratic prototype and even a pre-dictatorial governance structure against national sovereignty and democracies'.[187]

As already mentioned, however, it would be a mistake to understand the EU's new/authoritarian constitutionalism as an infringement upon the autonomy of nation states by an ill-defined supranational 'European establishment'. Rather, as Oberndorfer writes, 'such encroachments are intended to place the European ensemble of state apparatuses, with its neoliberal configuration, *of which the national executives are part*, in a position to chip away at the social rights that are still anchored in the national legal systems'.[188] This is consistent with our analysis of depoliti-cisation as a process of self-imposed reduction of sovereignty by national elites aimed at constraining the ability of popular-democratic powers to influence economic policy, thus enabling the imposition of neoliberal policies that would not have otherwise been politically feasible. In this sense, the EU's 'economic constitution' – and the single currency in particular – can be said to embody what Edgar Grande defined as the 'paradox of weakness': national elites transfer some power to a supra-national policymaker (thereby *appearing* weaker) in order to allow themselves to better withstand pressure from societal actors – first and foremost labour – by testifying that 'this is Europe's will' (thereby becoming *stronger*).[189] As Kevin Featherstone, a strong supporter of European integration, put it: 'Binding EU commitments enable gov-ernments to implement unpopular reforms at home whilst engaging in "blameshift" towards the "EU", *even if they themselves had desired such policies*.'[190]

This is the essence of depoliticisation. Ultimately, there is no denying that the European economic and monetary integration process was, to a large degree, a class-based and inherently neoliberal project (which in turn was shaped by the geopolitical-economic tensions and conflicts between leading capitalist states and regional blocs, and the conflict-ing interests between the different financial/industrial capital fractions located in those states, which have always characterised the European economy). In this regard, the crisis of the European Union can only be understood within the framework of the wider crisis of neoliberalism.

FROM POST-MODERNISM TO PROGRESSIVE NEOLIBERALISM

Why did the Western left – not only the political left, but also the cultural and intellectual left, and new social movements – passively accept, or even enthusiastically support to a large degree, many of these developments, particularly in Europe? This is partly related to the left falling prey to a series of misconceptions about the capacity of states to implement progressive policies in the face of globalisation, as we have argued. However, this can also be traced back to the left's love affair with post-modernism. Having internalised the impossibility of achieving meaningful systemic change in an increasingly complex and globalised world, the left enthusiastically embraced the post-modernist craze that engulfed social sciences from the 1970s onwards. This was in no small part because it offered a convenient theoretical justification for the left's abandonment of the terrain of the class struggle. This can be said to have set back the left as much as its embrace of monetarism and neoliberalism more generally.

The Marxist tradition developed during the Enlightenment, which had concerned itself with trying to understand the fundamental nature of reality. Marx challenged the dominant belief systems of his age by advancing the notion of historical materialism, which, in short, emphasised that human agency, organised into conflicting classes – the capitalists who owned the material means of production and the workers who didn't – was at the centre of historical development. Marx's conceptualisation of the world conforms to the structuralist idea that reality can be understood through inquiry into the objects that form that reality. For Marx, these objects are defined by the social relations embedded in the organisation of production. Constructing a 'grand narrative' for revolutionary change meant revealing the essence of this reality, and the Marxist political tradition reflected this view.

Post-modernism and its close relative post-structuralism – represented by Jean-François Lyotard, Gilles Deleuze, Jacques Derrida, Michel Foucault and Jacques Lacan, among others – emerged in the late 1960s as a response to the disenchantment with the radicalism of the time, which had been engendered by attempts to apply the ideas of Marx. It was a period when the oppression of the Soviet and Chinese states was becoming increasingly unacceptable to Marxist-oriented thinkers in the West. Radical political movements that had resulted in the failed French revolt of May 1968, and similar failed radical efforts in Japan, Mexico, Germany, Spain, Italy and elsewhere, were in a state of disillusionment. Student protest groups splintered into violent factions. The idea that we can understand history as a grand narrative progressing through time was largely rejected. In particular, the post-structuralists rejected the notion that coherent knowledge (about, for example, the existence of surplus value) could be inferred by analysing the structure of ownership within a production system. They argued that we are incapable of understanding the entirety of human society and we must therefore concentrate on individual pieces of the puzzle rather than drawing generalisations based on the mode of production. It was argued that information is generated by a pluralism of countering interests that are not restricted by the desire to be consistent with any grand narrative based on class. Michel Foucault added the notion, in very crude terms, that everything is relative – that is, that there is no discernible and truthful narrative running through history that is open to objective interpretation. An objective reality may very well exist, but we can never know it.

The intellectual and political left was waylaid by these diverse ideas. It slowly abandoned Marxian class categories to focus, instead, on elements of political power and the use of language and narratives as a way of establishing meaning. This also defined new arenas of political struggle that were diametrically opposed to those defined by Marx. Over the past three decades, the left focus on 'capitalism' has given way to a focus on issues such as racism, gender, homophobia, multiculturalism, etc. Marginality is no longer described in terms of class but rather in terms of identity. Marxian exploitation has been replaced by individual oppression as the fundamental expression of struggle. The struggle against the illegitimate hegemony of the capitalist class has given way to the struggles of a variety of (more or less) oppressed and marginalised groups and minorities: women, ethnic minorities, the LGBTQ community, etc. As a result, class struggle has ceased to be seen as the path to liberation; rather, laws designed to overturn the various 'glass ceilings', for example, have become the desired end. In this new post-modernist world, only categories that transcend Marxian class boundaries are considered meaningful. Moreover, the institutions that evolved to defend workers against capital – such as trade unions and social-democratic political parties – have become subjugated to these non-class struggle foci. Issues such as racism and xenophobia are important, of course. But we need to be cognisant of the way in which the establishment has used these to divide and conquer the working class, and to divert our attention from the antagonistic class relations that lie at the heart of capitalism. Ellen Meisksins-Wood wrote:

> Intellectuals of the left ... have been trying to define new ways, other than contestation, of relating to capitalism. The typical mode, at best, is to seek out the interstices of capitalism, to make space within it for alternative 'discourses', activities and identities. Much is made of the *fragmentary* character of advanced capitalism – whether that fragmentation is characterized by the culture of post-modernism or by the political economy of post-Fordism; and this is supposed to multiply the spaces in which a culture of the left can operate. But underlying all of these seems to be a conviction that capitalism is here to stay,

at least in any foreseeable historical perspective. ... In a fragmented world composed of 'de-centred subjects', where totalizing knowledges are impossible and undesirable, what other kind of politics is there than a sort of de-centred and intellectualized radicalization of liberal pluralism? What better escape, in theory, from a confrontation with capitalism, the most totalizing system the world has ever known, than a rejection of totalizing knowledge? What greater obstacle, in practice, to anything more than the most local and particularistic resistances to the global, totalizing power of capitalism than the de-centred and fragmented subject? What better excuse for submitting to the *force majeure* of capitalism than the conviction that its power, while pervasive, has no systemic origin, no unified logic, no identifiable social roots?[191]

As Meiksins-Wood observes, the embrace of this post-modernist agenda by the 1960s Marxist radicals has meant that the left's traditional focus on class has been replaced by a diversity of struggles, none of which challenge the basis of capitalism. This is one of the main reasons why the left has passively accepted – or even enthusiastically supported – the neoliberalisation of society: as the reconfiguring of global capitalism channelled increasing shares of income and wealth to the top end of the social pyramid, left-wing intellectuals were lost in fierce battles about cultural identity and gender power relations. Worse even, what has emerged in practically all Western countries, as Nancy Fraser notes, is a perverse political alignment between 'mainstream currents of new social movements (feminism, anti-racism, multiculturalism, and LGBTQ rights), on the one side, and high-end "symbolic" and service-based business sectors (Wall Street, Silicon Valley, and Hollywood), on the other' – what Fraser calls 'progressive neoliberalism'.[192] With regard to the specific experience of the United States, she writes:

In this alliance, progressive forces are effectively joined with the forces of cognitive capitalism, especially financialization. However unwittingly, the former lend their charisma to the latter. Ideals like diversity and empowerment, which could in principle serve different ends, now gloss policies that have devastated manufacturing and what were once middle-class lives. ... As that last point suggests, the assault on social security was glossed by a veneer of emancipatory charisma, borrowed from the new social movements. Throughout the years when manufacturing cratered, the country buzzed with talk of 'diversity', 'empowerment', and 'non-discrimination'. Identifying 'progress' with meritocracy instead of equality, these terms equated 'emancipation' with the rise of a small elite of 'talented' women, minorities, and gays in the winner-takes-all corporate hierarchy instead of with the latter's abolition. These liberal-individualist understandings of 'progress' gradually replaced the more expansive, anti-hierarchical, egalitarian, class-sensitive, anti-capitalist understandings of emancipation that had flourished in the 1960s and 1970s. As the New Left waned, its structural critique of capitalist society faded, and the country's characteristic liberal-individualist mindset reasserted itself, imperceptibly shrinking the aspirations of 'progressives' and self-proclaimed leftists.[193]

'Third way' social-democratic parties further cemented this alignment by forging 'a new alliance of entrepreneurs, suburbanites, new social movements, and youth, all proclaiming their modern, progressive bona fides by embracing diversity, multiculturalism, and women's rights'. The result was a progressive neoliberalism 'that mixed together truncated ideals of emancipation and lethal forms of financialization'.[194] This has contributed significantly to the demise of the left as a progressive political force. Indeed, as Fraser argues, the recent surge of right-wing populist parties – which we discuss in Chapter 6 – should not be seen simply as a rejection of neoliberalism *tout court*, but of *progressive neoliberalism* in particular. Therefore, an alternative left strategy must necessarily be grounded not only in an appreciation of the operational reality of fiat monetary systems but also on an understanding of the underlying class relations that define capitalism as an historically specific system of productive organisation. This is not in contradiction with the struggle against racism, patriarchy, xenophobia and other forms of oppression and discrimination.

6

Après Elle, Le Déluge:
Are We Entering a Post-Neoliberal Age?

In Chapter 5, we saw how the stagnationary effects of the post-1970s neoliberal policies of profit maximisation pursued throughout the West were temporarily offset, from the 1980s onwards, through financialisation and debt-based consumption. The inherent contradictions of this new finance-led regime of accumulation exploded in 2007–9, as the mountain of debt accumulated in the previous decades came crashing to the ground, threatening a meltdown of the global economy. Even though Western governments were able to avoid the worst-case scenario and contain (for a while) the economic and political fallout from the financial crisis by reinstating – with even greater emphasis – financialisation as the main motor of the economy, via quantitative easing and other unconventional monetary policies, this did not halt the overall stagnationary trend of advanced economies. On the contrary, despite a relatively rapid 'recovery' throughout 2010–11, the medium- and long-term economic prospects of advanced countries have severely worsened since the financial crisis, with output, investment, employment and all other major economic and social indicators remaining well below pre-crisis levels in most countries, particularly in Europe.

In recent years, economists have struggled to pinpoint the causes of this so-called 'secular stagnation' – a term (first coined during the Great Depression) that has been reintroduced in the economics lexicon as a way of explaining the lack of growth in advanced nations, despite near-zero interest rates and hyper-expansionary monetary policies. Most commonly accepted theories of secular stagnation correctly identify aggregate spending – or better, the lack thereof – as the main source of the problem. However, this structural lack of demand is largely attributed to demography – namely, the decline in the working-age population, which allegedly undermines spending and leaves the economy 'facing persistent shortfalls of demand'.[1] Such theories have the benefit of emphasising the structural nature of the current downturn, but fail to recognise that the lack of aggregate spending is principally the result of structurally enforced policy decisions, not demography: namely, the wage stagnation and declining wage share caused by neoliberalism's 40-year-long war on labour.

The bursting of the subprime bubbles effectively laid bare the scorched earth left behind by neoliberalism, which the elites had gone to great lengths to conceal, in both material (financialisation) and ideological ('the end of history') terms. To paraphrase Warren Buffett, the receding tide of the debt-fuelled boom revealed that most people were, in fact, swimming naked. With debt-based private consumption no longer available as a source of autonomous demand, due to the post-crisis 'liquidity trap' and private sector deleveraging process, the inability of wage-based private consumption to sustain adequate levels of aggregate demand – due to labour's loss of purchasing power in recent decades (further exacerbated by the post-1990s drop in public spending) – became apparent. In this sense, the current stagnation should be viewed as the tail end of the long crisis that began in the 1970s. The situation was (is) further exacerbated by the post-crisis policies of fiscal austerity and wage deflation pursued by a number of Western governments, particularly in Europe, which saw the financial crisis as an opportunity to impose an even more radical neoliberal regime.

Amid growing popular dissatisfaction, social unrest and mass unemployment (in a number of European countries), political elites on both sides of the Atlantic responded with business-as-usual policies and discourses. As a result, the social contract binding citizens to traditional ruling parties is more strained today than at any other time since World War II – and in some countries has arguably already been broken. The Brexit vote (and before that, Jeremy Corbyn's election as leader of the Labour Party) in the United Kingdom, the election of Donald Trump (and the Bernie Sanders campaign for the Democratic Party nomination) in the United States, the rejection of Matteo Renzi's neoliberal constitutional reform in Italy, rising support for the National Front in France and for other populist parties in Germany and elsewhere, the EU's unprecedented crisis of legitimation – although these interrelated phenomena differ in ideology and goals, they all share a common target: they are all rejections of corporate globalisation, neoliberalism and the political establishments that have promoted them.

Many view this neo-nationalist, anti-globalisation and anti-establishment backlash as heralding the end of the (neo)liberal era and the ushering in of a new global order. As *Financial Times* columnist Philip Stephens put it, 'the present global order – the liberal rules-based system established in 1945 and expanded after the end of the Cold War – is under unprecedented strain. Globalization is in retreat.'[2] Trump has especially alarmed politicians and commentators worldwide by announcing a series of protectionist measures: as of mid-2017, the new American president had decided to remove the US from the TPP, had expressed misgivings about the TTIP with the European Union and other free trade deals, and had already started enacting measures to relocalise production to the US, as promised during his electoral campaign, by threatening to impose tariffs on American cars and auto parts made in Mexico and other low-wage countries, resulting in Ford's stunning decision to cancel its plans for a new assembly plant in Mexico and expand a Michigan plant instead.

Without minimising the symbolic and ideological value of these decisions – as Bolivian vice-president Álvaro García Linera wrote, Trump's post-elections moves have 'shattered into a million pieces … the near-religious conviction that all societies were bound to coalesce into a single economic, financial and cultural whole'[3] – the truth of the matter is that globalisation was already in trouble well before Trump's election. Since 2011, world trade has grown significantly less rapidly than global GDP, and has now begun to shrink even as the global economy grows, albeit sluggishly. World financial flows are down 60 per cent since the pre-crash peak. International capital flows today are equivalent to 1.6 per cent of global GDP, down from 16 per cent of GDP in 2007.[4] Capital flows to so-called emerging economies in particular have plummeted. The 'home bias' of investments has hugely increased, and the links between banks and their respective governments have intensified, as evidenced by the eurozone's 'sovereign-bank nexus'. This has led various commentators to conclude that we have reached – and surpassed – the era of 'peak globalisation'.[5] In this sense, protectionist policies – which were also already on the rise before Trump's election – should be seen as a *consequence* rather than a *cause* of the trade slowdown: simply put, as world trade has shifted to a decidedly lower trajectory, and the (real or perceived) social and economic costs of free trade have started to outweigh the (real or perceived) benefits, particularly in advanced countries, political resistance to globalisation has intensified. Bjørn Lomborg, director of the Copenhagen Consensus Center, notes that the use of protectionist policies was up 50 per cent in 2015, outnumbering trade liberalisation measures by three to one.[6] Even though G20 leaders, shortly before Trump's victory, publicly reaffirmed their commitment to free trade and opposition to trade protectionism 'in all its forms', G20 countries accounted for 81 per cent of the recent wave of trade restrictions.[7]

So *why* is trade slowing down (and protectionism on the rise)? In straightforward cause–effect terms, it is largely the result of slow economic growth – that is, the deep post-crash stagnation afflicting advanced capitalist economies, due to the reasons outlined above. However, some observers see a wider trend at play. As we saw in Chapter 2, following the collapse of the Bretton Woods system, the United States, buttressed by the power of the dollar as the world's reserve currency, succeeded in creating a new global hegemonic regime based on a so-called 'T-bill standard'. In short, the United States relinquished the imperative of competing with other nations for world market shares and came to accept its role as 'consumer of last resort', by deliberately buying more than it sold abroad and running large, chronic trade deficits; countries with chronic trade surpluses (such as Japan, Germany, China, etc.), on the other hand, had little choice but to 'finance' this trade deficit via the buying of large quantities of US securities. This introduced the world to an unprecedentedly unstable – and unsustainable – international monetary system. As Vassilis K. Fouskas and Bulent Gokay write:

All real, long-term, 'organic' indicators, as Gramsci would have put it, worsened in this period, if compared with the so-called 'golden age of capitalism' (1950–1970). Thus, unemployment, albeit manageable, became endemic; consumption was buttressed by borrowing rather than real wages; and technological innovation was used by export-led states to cannibalise markets rather than induce real and sustainable development (typical, in this respect, is the example of Germany within the eurozone). Profits in the financial sector soared, but they were consumed among the rich and the speculative arbitragers, magnifying inequality and undermining growth and job creation. Pointedly, China's domestic reforms and its coming onto the global stage through the WTO, coupled with its export drive, cheap manufacturing products and purchasing of assets across the world, signalled a dramatic shift in global political economy, a shift in the centre of gravity from the Atlantic shores to Asia.[8]

The structural, 'organic' decline of Western economies (and in particular of the US as the global hegemonic power), in other words, is not simply a collateral effect of neoliberal financialisation; it is also directly related to China's ascent to superpower status in recent years, itself part of a wider global powershift to the East. Strikingly, China and other emerging market economies accounted for more than 80 per cent of world GDP growth over the 2008–16 period.[9] China has undertaken massive trade and investment deals with other Asian countries as well as with Africa and Latin America, and is on course to displace the US and other Western countries as those regions' main trading partner. This partly explains the huge rise of protectionist measures directed at China in recent years (again, well before Trump's election) by the EU, US and Japan. Some authors have also emphasised that the slowdown of global economic growth might be resulting from ecological factors – that is, constraints on the supply of energy and other biophysical resources that feed into the economic process and impact its functioning.[10]

In this sense, Trump's victory, Brexit and the rise of populist parties 'are but epiphenomena of momentous shifts in global political economy and international geo-political alignments that have been taking place since the 1970s'.[11] Namely: (i) the crisis of the neoliberal economic model and ideology, which is no longer able to overcome its intrinsic stagnationary and polarising tendencies and to generate societal consensus or hegemony (in material or ideological terms), and is increasingly unable to deliver benefits even to its core supporters; (ii) the crisis of globalisation, which is no longer able to offer an escape from the inexorable pressures of overaccumulation and overproduction, largely due to increased competition from countries like China (which in turn are facing crises of overaccumulation of their own); (iii) the ecological crisis; and (iv) the crisis of US hegemony, which is no longer able unilaterally to enforce the global neoliberal order, neither through *soft power* (that is, through pro-Western multilateral institutions such as the IMF and World Bank), as it did during the 1990s, nor through *hard power* (that is, through brute military force), as it did throughout the early 2000s, as demonstrated by the West's fumbling in Syria. Trump's tough stance on China and other surplus countries (such as Germany) accused of currency manipulation, and his plans for 'renationalising' US economic policy, should thus be understood in the context of an unfolding collapse of the neoliberal order.

What we are witnessing is not the end of globalisation – which will continue, although it will likely be characterised by increased tensions between the various fractions of international capital, particularly between the US, Germany, Japan and China, and by a combination of protectionism and internationalisation – but rather the birth of a *post-neoliberal order*. From a historical perspective, there was no reason to believe that neoliberalism would go on indefinitely. As we saw in Chapter 2, each distinctive stage of capitalist development is based on a specific accumulation strategy or hegemonic project, which derives its strength from its ability to guarantee economic growth and profit across a nation or region, while at the same time satisfying different social groups. Such regimes eventually become exhausted, falling into crisis. In this sense, just like Keynesianism fell into crisis in the 1970s and was supplanted by neoliberalism as the dominant accumulation regime, we can expect neoliberalism – now facing a crisis of its own – to give way to a new configuration of capitalism. The difference between then and now is that there is no new coherent ideology or accumulation regime waiting in the wings to replace neoliberalism. But we can be sure that it will involve the currency-issuing state as a central player (for example, the Chinese state is driving massive changes in global capitalism through its use of fiscal deficits and planned development).

The vague neo-protectionist and neo-nationalist rhetoric of 'global Trumpism', to use Mark Blyth's apt definition,[12] does not yet represent a new hegemonic force – as testified by the huge rift that it has opened within established political, economic and cultural elites. In other words, it is too early to say what this post-neoliberal order will look like. Antonio Gramsci famously described organic crises such as the one that we are currently going through as situations in which 'the old is dying and the new cannot yet be born'. 'In this *interregnum*', he wrote, 'a great variety of morbid symptoms' – such as the ones that we have described above – tend to appear.[13] If the future looks bleak, however, it is not because neoliberalism is inexorably destined to be supplanted by some form of twentieth-century fascism, as most mainstream and – alas – left analyses would have us believe, which inevitably leads to the conclusion that 'reforming the status quo' is the only viable alternative. No: what has allowed these 'morbid symptoms' to emerge as the dominant reaction to neoliberalism and globalisation is simply the fact that right-wing forces have been much more effective than left-wing or progressive forces at tapping into the legitimate grievances of the masses that have been disenfranchised, marginalised, impoverished and dispossessed by the 40-year-long neoliberal class war waged from above.

In particular, they are the only forces that have been able to provide a (more or less) coherent response to the widespread – and growing – yearning for greater territorial or national sovereignty, increasingly seen as the only way to 'take back' some degree of collective control over politics and society. Given neoliberalism's war against sovereignty, it should come as no surprise that 'sovereignty has become the master-frame of contemporary politics', as Paolo Gerbaudo notes.[14] As we have already seen, the hollowing out of national sovereignty and curtailment of popular-democratic mechanisms – what has been termed depoliticisation – has been an essential element of the neoliberal project, aimed at insulating macroeconomic policies from popular contestation and removing any obstacles put in the way of economic exchanges and financial flows. Given the nefarious effects of depoliticisation, it is only natural that the revolt against neoliberalism should first and foremost take the form of demands for a *repoliticisation* of national decision-making processes – that is, for a greater degree of democratic control over politics (and particularly over the destructive global flows unleashed by neoliberalism), which necessarily can only be exercised at the national level, in the absence of effective supranational mechanisms of representation. The European Union is obviously no exception: in fact, it is (correctly) seen by many as the embodiment of technocratic rule and elite estrangement from the masses, as demonstrated by the Brexit vote and the widespread euroscepticism engulfing the continent.

The fact that the vision of national sovereignty that was at the centre of the Trump and Brexit campaigns, and that currently dominates the public discourse, is a reactionary, quasi-fascist one – mostly defined along ethnic, exclusivist and isolationist lines, aimed at ensuring the security and protection of the 'national community' against the threat posed by a variety of internal and external enemies (minorities, migrants, Muslims, foreigners in general) and based on an even more exploitative and authoritarian form of capitalism – should not be seen as an indictment of national sovereignty as such. History attests to the fact that national sovereignty and national self-determination are not intrinsically reactionary or jingoistic concepts – in fact, they constituted foundational notions in the development of the modern left, seen in the work of Jean-Jacques Rousseau and its influence on the Jacobins and the French revolution, and were the rallying cries of countless nineteenth-

and twentieth-century socialist and left-wing liberation movements. Even if we limit our analysis to core capitalist countries, it is patently obvious that virtually all the major social, economic and political advancements of the past centuries were achieved *through the institutions of the democratic nation state*, not through international, multilateral or supranational institutions, which in a number of ways have, in fact, been used to *roll back* those very achievements, as seen throughout this book. The problem, in short, is not national sovereignty as such, but the fact that the concept in recent years has been largely monopolised by the right and extreme right, which understandably sees it as a way to push through its xenophobic and identitarian agenda.

So why has the contemporary left not been able to develop an alternative, *progressive view of national sovereignty* in response to neoliberal globalisation? The answer should be clear by now: over the course of the past 30 years, most strands of left-wing or progressive thought have accepted the notion that national states have essentially been rendered obsolete by neoliberalism and/or globalisation and thus that meaningful change can only be achieved at the international/supranational level or – even worse – have come to view national sovereignty as an inherently reactionary construct, synonymous with international conflict and repressive control over migration.[15] Furthermore, as we discuss in detail in the second part of the book, most leftists have also bought into the macroeconomic myths that the establishment uses to discourage any alternative use of state fiscal capacities. For example, they have accepted without question the so-called household budget analogy, which suggests that currency-issuing governments, like households, face financial constraints and thus must limit their spending or face sanctions from private bond markets. The latter are claimed to be able to starve governments of funds and force them to run out of money. The idea that a currency-issuing government can run out of money is, of course, non-sensical, but through careful framing and use of language, it has become a widely held belief in the general public debate – and among the left.

This is particularly evident in the European debate, where, despite the disastrous effects of the EU and monetary union, the left to a large extent continues to cling on to these institutions and to the belief that they can be reformed in a progressive direction, despite all evidence to the contrary, and to dismiss any talk of restoring a progressive agenda on the foundation of retrieved national sovereignty as a 'retreat into nationalist positions', inevitably bound to plunge the continent into 1930s-style fascism.[16] This, however, is tantamount to relinquishing the discursive and political battleground for a post-neoliberal hegemony – which, as we have seen, is inextricably linked to the question of national sovereignty – to the right and extreme right. It is not hard to see that if progressive change can only be implemented at the global or even European level – in other words, if the alternative to the status quo offered to electorates is one between *reactionary nationalism* and *progressive globalism* – then the left has already lost the battle.

It needn't be this way, however. A vision of national sovereignty which offers a radical alternative to that of both the right and the neoliberals – one based on popular sovereignty, democratic control over the economy, full employment, social justice, redistribution from the rich to the poor, inclusivity, and more generally the socio-ecological transformation of production and society – is not only necessary, it is possible. The fiscal capacity of the currency-issuing state remains intact and can be used to advance these objectives just as it has been used to 'fund' neoliberalism. This alternative is also the necessary prerequisite for the construction of a new international(ist) world order, based on interdependent but independent sovereign states. It is such a vision that we present in the second part of this book.

PART II

A Progressive Strategy for the Twenty-First Century

7

Towards a Progressive Vision of Sovereignty

Times of organic crisis can be frightening, but they can also be incredibly fertile. They throw dominant paradigms into doubt, expose the false claims made by elites and open up new horizons. They set the wheels of history – of which elites always claim to represent the end point – in motion once again. In doing so, they create huge opportunities for change – including progressive change, of course. The current crisis is no different. Jim Stanford provides a poignant example of how the crisis is bringing about an important paradigm shift:

> For a quarter-century we were told that monetary policy was a technocratic, rules-driven process, best governed by so-called 'independent' central banks, immune from political pressures. Of course, those central banks were never independent: their role, and the policy edifice they oversaw, was always profoundly biased in order to elevate the interests of financial wealth (through strict inflation control) over other economic and social priorities. The global financial crisis and its aftermath, however, laid bare that those supposedly untouchable 'rules' were arbitrary, temporary, and discretionary. The advent of quantitative easing policies, in particular, proved what lefty critics had been saying all along: namely that money is created out of thin air every day (by commercial banks and central banks alike); the big issue is who controls that process, and what is the money used for? Now the genie is out of the bottle, and there is new space for progressive visions of unconventional monetary policies to address persistent stagnation and unemployment – like using the central bank's money-creating powers, for instance, to underwrite useful investments in public, physical and social infrastructure. The idea that monetary policy rules and inflation targets are binding, natural, and permanent has been destroyed.[1]

The concept of central bank independence – one of the main tenets of neoliberalism – is today openly challenged even by mainstream politicians. During his presidential campaign, Trump claimed that the Federal Reserve had been 'doing political things', with reference to its low interest rate policy, and as a result had created a 'false economy'. More recently, Patrick McHenry, the vice-chairman of the US House of Representatives Financial Services Committee, questioned the right of the chair of the Federal Reserve to negotiate financial stability rules 'among global bureaucrats in foreign lands without ... the authority to do so'.[2] The British prime minister, Theresa May, made an almost identical argument with her criticisms of the Bank of England when she warned of the 'bad side effects' of the Bank's monetary policies.[3] In all of these cases, politicians are seeking a change in the fiscal-monetary mix: looser fiscal policy, harder monetary policy. This has led *Financial Times* commentator, Wolfgang Münchau, to claim that the era of central bank independence may be coming to 'an end'.[4] Even though the assumption that central bank independence effectively exists at present is contestable, as we will see later on, and the ideology underlying this shift in public dialogue is essentially reactionary in nature, the fact that the *concept* is now being openly contested is good news for progressives: as seen in previous chapters, the theory and (to a lesser degree) practice of central bank independence has been one of the most powerful fronts in the fight against discretionary macroeconomic policy interventions by elected governments, by *de facto* reducing the scope of active fiscal policy (as demonstrated most manifestly in the EMU). Its 'end', if that is indeed what we are witnessing, should thus be welcomed by progressives.

The same is true of the neoliberal tenets of fiscal policy: in the wake of the financial crisis, large government deficits – eschewed for decades – became legitimate again, even though that rediscovered flexibility was applied in a biased manner and only insofar as it was necessary to keep the system afloat, as we have seen. The ideology of deficit- and debt-phobia still wields considerable power, of course, but the notion that large government deficits inevitably mean the end of the world as we know it has become untenable. If anything, we have seen that the opposite is true: temporary economic stimulus was 'probably the most important reason we didn't have a full replay of the Great Depression', Paul Krugman wrote.[5] On the other hand, various studies have unequivocally shown that the policies of fiscal austerity have led to lower output and higher debt-to-GDP, unemployment, poverty and inequality levels, particularly in Europe, plunging the continent – and especially the countries of the periphery – into the worst social and economic crisis in modern times.[6] Indeed, the swelling ranks of mainstream economists, policymakers and commentators that are openly calling for more expansionary fiscal policies indicate that there is a paradigm shift underway in this arena as well, though this has yet to translate into a policy shift in most countries, largely due to the resistance of capitalists (and the political elites that they command).

The most striking recognition has come from the IMF, which in a series of recent works has reversed several of its standard policy recommendations, on the basis of the evidence provided by its own research. In a summary of policy suggestions unexpectedly titled *Neoliberalism: Oversold?*, IMF authors euphemistically argue that 'the benefits of some policies that are an important part of the neoliberal agenda' – first and foremost fiscal consolidation – 'appear to have been somewhat overplayed'.[7] Trump's approach to trade deals also represents a lesson for progressives:

If there is one crucial lesson from the extraordinary developments … in the North American auto industry (including Trump's threats against Ford, GM, and Toyota, and Ford's stunning decision to completely cancel its new assembly plant in Mexico), it's that politics matter. Nothing about the economy is ever natural or permanent – and the immense resources invested in convincing us they are, are actually trying to disempower and silence the potential power of those being hurt by the current system of globalization. We've now seen that when it suits powerful forces, global rules can be rewritten in an instant; decisions of global megacorps overturned swiftly and effectively; provisions of trade deals simply ignored. … [T]he stunning way in which [Trump] is wading into the private investment decisions of enormous corporations, overruling their established global strategies, and simply ignoring the supposedly sacrosanct rules of trade deals, is an important reminder for all of society that the 'economy' is nothing more or less than the conscious decisions which human beings make about how to work, produce, and distribute. Those conscious decisions always reflect power and competing interests, they are never 'natural' or 'automatic' or 'omnipresent'. If Trump can rewrite international economic treaties on the strength of a few tweets, before even taking office, then we can do the same thing – but only if we build a political movement with the same confidence and power.[8]

The success of Bernie Sanders' campaign, which overlapped with Trump's platform on a number of key issues affecting the economic security of working families – most notably on trade deals such as the TPP, which Sanders argued would 'undermine US sovereignty'[9] – while differing widely on issues such as taxes, immigration and social rights, testifies to the fallacy of the zero-sum approach of the mainstream left and to the possibility of articulating and garnering mass support around a progressive vision of sovereignty and opposition to financialisation and neoliberal globalisation without foregoing 'an anti-racist, anti-sexist, and anti-hierarchical vision of emancipation', as Nancy Fraser writes.[10]

A similar shift in public discourse can be observed in Europe as well. The European elites' response to the crisis, and the decade-long stagnation/depression that it has engendered, have exposed the brutal, undemocratic and class-based logic of power underpinning the European Union and monetary union in particular, making Europe unpopular as never before – as documented by the Eurobarometer surveys – and shattering many illusions regarding the possibility of achieving democratic reform and economic/employment growth within the boundaries of the current European institutional (and constitutional) architecture. Moreover, there is a growing awareness, even among elites, of the fact that the EU/EMU appears to be set on an irreversible trajectory of fragmentation and balkanisation – symbolised by Brexit – that is bound to lead to its inevitable disintegration. Furthermore, the EU's crisis of legitimation has been exploited by right-wing forces (such as the National Front in France) to peddle a reactionary vision of national sovereignty, which in turn is exacerbating Europe's centrifugal tendencies. The mainstream left, on the other hand, continues to see it as its mission to *save Europe from itself*, by defending the European economic and integration process against the threat of neo-nationalism, in the belief that the European Union, as much as the eurozone, is compatible with a return of social-democratic policies, a Keynesian-style relaunching of the economy and the creation of a fully fledged supranational democracy.

This position, however, presents numerous problems, which are ultimately rooted in a failure to understand the true nature of the EU and monetary union. First of all, it effectively reduces the left to the role of defender of the status quo, thus allowing the political right to hegemonise the legitimate anti-systemic – and specifically anti-EU – grievances of citizens. More crucially, however, it ignores the fact that the EU's economic and political constitution, analysed in Chapter 5, is *structured* to produce the results that we are seeing – the erosion of popular sovereignty, the massive transfer of wealth from the middle and lower classes to the upper classes, the weakening of labour, and more generally the rollback of the democratic and social/economic gains that had previously been achieved by subordinate classes – and is designed precisely to impede the kind of radical reforms to which progressive integrationists or federalists aspire to.

Certainly, there are many measures that could be undertaken at the European level to stimulate the economy, reduce social injustice, make debt sustainable, etc., even within the current treaties, as demonstrated by countless proposals put forward in recent years.[11] However, these measures – let alone a more wide-ranging reform of the treaties in a more solidaristic and Keynesian direction, which would require the ability of EMU itself to run budget deficits with the support of the ECB (which itself should be subject to sweeping institutional reform), a full mutu-alisation of the debt, permanent fiscal transfers from richer to poorer countries, etc. – are simply not politically viable in light of the current balance of power, among countries as much as among classes. As Richard Tusk, Frank G. Thomson professor of government at Harvard, writes:

> Even if Europe's left parties do succeed in forging a common program, the EU is not the kind of political entity whose approach to the world can be altered by popular politics. Popular politics is precisely what the EU was designed to obstruct. Like independent central banks and constitutional courts, its institutions are essentially technocratic. Tech-nocracy is not (as some like to pretend) a neutral or rational system of government. Instead, it confers immense power on culturally select bodies whose prejudices will be those of the class their members are drawn from. [Progressive integrationists such as Yanis Varoufakis believe] that the EU may change. ... But the kind of shift in European politics that Varoufakis and others want to see is simply not possible within the present structures of the EU: it would require sweeping institutional change of a kind nowhere on the agenda. Without that ... the left in Europe is reliant purely on an article of faith – a conviction that the left *must* prevail, even in the face of all the constraints imposed on popular sovereignty by the EU.[12]

As Elias Ioakimoglou, economic adviser to the Greek Institute of Labour, sums up the issue: 'The eurozone is not just a currency area, it is a capital accumulation regime in which certain tendencies prevail – including the tendencies to remove social protections, to decrease wages, and to abolish the social and political rights that are the core of citizenship. These effects are embedded in the architecture and the operation mode of the eurozone. It was built that way. So you can't fix it.'[13] Moreover, even in the unlikely event that an alignment of left movements/governments should emerge simultaneously at the international level, there is little reason to believe that Germany and the other countries of the 'ordoliberal bloc' would ever be part of such an alliance, considering that anti-Keynesianism is deeply engrained in Germany's monetary and political establishment and that 'it is … hard to see Germany ever giving up on this', as Wolfgang Münchau wrote.[14] In fact, if such an improbable alliance were indeed to arise, the most likely outcome would be a German exit from the monetary union, leading to a likely collapse of the entire currency system (precisely the outcome that such a strategy aims to avoid). This is a reminder of the fact that capital accumulation regimes such as the eurozone only last insofar as they are beneficial to capitalist elites; once they stop being so, they tend to be swiftly abandoned.

Furthermore, the notion that the EU can be transformed into a fully fledged supranational democracy ignores the fact that for the great majority of ordinary European citizens, linguistic barriers and cultural differences impair the opportunity for political participation at a supranational level. This became apparent in the debate over the *Spitzenkandidat* system, used for the first time in the 2014 European elections to select the Commission president. Following the elections, many argued that Jean-Claude's Juncker's appointment was democratically legitimated by the fact that he was the candidate of the parliamentary group with the largest number of MEPs, the European People's Party (EPP). Jürgen Habermas and other prominent intellectuals wrote in support of Juncker's appointment, suggesting that European citizens have the right to choose who leads the European Commission and that the election results showed that Juncker was 'the people's choice'.[15] From a purely formal standpoint, they were right. But most of those who voted for the national parties that are members of the EPP did not even know what the EPP or who Juncker was. This episode shows that there is a very real risk of EU-level democracy resulting in a form of *supranational depoliticised post-democracy*.

More generally, any debate about the 'parliamentarisation' of the EU needs to take into account the crucial difference between the formal electoral-representative process and true popular control. As argued by Lorenzo Del Savio and Matteo Mameli, further integration, even if accompanied by a strengthening of the electoral-representative component of the EU, is not necessarily equivalent to more popular control. It is assumed that an enhanced version of the EU parliament would suffice for proper democratic control over the EU's major decisions. But this ignores the question of oligarchic capture, Del Savio and Mameli note:

> Oligarchic capture does not just affect regulatory bodies and unelected officials. It also affects elected representatives. Augmenting the powers of elected officials that are vulnerable to oligarchic capture means augmenting the power of economic oligarchies. It means weakening popular control. Elected national parliaments and executives are highly imperfect tools for achieving popular control over decisions that affect people's freedom and well-being. Supranational parliaments and executives are even more inefficient in this respect.[16]

The problems relating to lobbying and to the revolving doors issue – not just between big businesses and regulatory agencies but also between big businesses and elected offices – are in fact exacerbated at the supranational level.

> It is for this reason that, in general, the transfer of sovereignty to international loci of political decision-making contributes to the weakening of popular control. International loci are in general physically, psychologically, and linguistically more distant from ordinary people than national ones are. This distance means more room for oligarchic capture. International loci of political decision-making are usually designed in such a way as to make it extremely difficult for ordinary citizens to understand how decisions are taken and to be able to influence and contest such decisions in an effective manner. This enhances the effectiveness of the mechanisms of oligarchic capture.[17]

The bottom line is that a progressive reform of the EU/EMU is not only impossible in practical terms – as acknowledged by a growing number of mainstream economists such as Joseph Stiglitz, Paul De Grauwe and others – but also undesirable in popular-democratic terms. Reality would appear to be slowly dawning on Europe's radical left as well, which has traditionally been supportive of European integration. In this regard, the rise and fall of the Greek left-wing party SYRIZA was a watershed moment for many European progressives. SYRIZA's election, in January 2015, reawakened hopes of the possibility of a different Europe, one of solidarity and democracy instead of competition and top-down decisions – 'another Europe' of social justice and popular participation. These hopes were soon dashed, as the Greek government was made to accept, by means of blackmail and coercion (such as forcing the Greek banks to close for five days preceding the referendum), the onerous terms of yet another loan agreement conditional on further austerity and deregulation measures. In particular, the experience of SYRIZA proved that the ECB can easily paralyse a country's banking system by cutting off its banks' access to central bank liquidity, thus effectively bringing a defiant government to its knees without actually expelling that country from the monetary union. Many, even on the left, took this as the confirmation of the fundamental impossibility of reforming the EU. As a result, we are witnessing more voices, movements and political parties and events calling for a dismantling of the eurozone and a return to national currencies, seen as a necessary precondition for achieving meaningful progressive change in any given country.

Opinions differ (wildly) as to the best way for countries to regain their monetary (and thus fiscal) sovereignty. Some favour an *orderly and coordinated dismantling of the single currency*. This would arguably be the most painless solution, but it appears implausible for the very same reasons that a progressive reform of the eurozone is implausible: because it would require a level of solidarity and coordination that is nowhere to be seen at the moment and is not likely to emerge in the near future. Others propose a *unilateral exit* from the monetary union and possibly even from the European Union. Politically, this would be easier to achieve, requiring only the will of the exiting government. The mainstream viewpoint commonly associates the prospect of a unilateral exit of one or more nations with predictions of devastation, catastrophe, hyperinflation, financial market lockout, etc. Even though such catastrophic prospects are largely overblown, based as they are on mainstream assumptions about the economy and particularly about the ability of governments to determine the outcome of the exit process and the opportunities provided to countries that were to regain their full monetary and fiscal sovereignty, there is no denying that the transition to a new, state-controlled currency would present serious economic and technical challenges and involve significant costs, especially in the short term.

Several models have been put forward to describe how a nation such as Italy or Greece might unilaterally exit the monetary union. Any exit scheme has to address the same issues: how to handle the euro-denominated public and private debt that is outstanding; how to handle bank deposits denominated in euros within the exiting nation; how to ensure financial stability is maintained; how to introduce the new currency (for example, unilaterally or as an interim dual currency); how to manage the inevitable large currency depreciation and to minimise the resulting inflation risk and protect real living standards; how to reduce speculative capital flows (for example, by using capital controls); how to deal with any changes to the legal framework governing cross-border trade if the nation is also expelled from the EU, among other issues. The estimated likely overall consequences that have been put forward crucially depend on the economic framework that underpins them. Neoliberal macroeconomics, which downgrades the importance of fiscal policy and currency sovereignty, not surprisingly provides the basis for catastrophic predictions. These economists project massive and ongoing currency depreciation leading to an uncontrollable surge in inflation, which debases the currency. They predict that the nation's banking system would collapse in the face of large capital outflows, debt delinquency and the state's incapacity to defend the capital base of its banking system. They predict that there would be massive outflows of skilled labour, which would undermine the future productivity of the nation. They predict that the nation would have to default on its debt obligations, which would not only force the country into a costly, drawn-out legal morass, but would also see it being shunned by international capital markets. As a consequence, they claim that the government would not be able to fund itself and would run out of money. Further, they predict that credit would also become unavailable to the private sector, and businesses and the housing market would collapse. This catastrophic scenario sees the nation mired in depression, poverty, social disintegration and isolation. Civil anarchy would erupt and give way to authoritarian regimes. This future, it is argued, would surely be many times worse than a future within the eurozone. All of these predictions have been rehearsed in the recent literature. Almost every day someone writes something along those lines.

Conversely, adopting a heterodox macroeconomic framework as the basis for analysis leads to dramatically different projections. It should be made clear that no one really knows for sure what would happen. It is hard to project the costs of an exit. But we can deduce several things based on historical experience. It is highly likely that the benefits of exit would outweigh the costs, if the exit decision is simultaneously accompanied by a decision to reject the current flawed neoliberal approach in favour of a fiscally active policy stance that seeks to maximise the well-being of the citizenry. If the exiting government refuses to free itself of the various self-imposed external constraints characteristic of neoliberal regimes and continues on the path of austerity, privatisation and wage restraint, then the exit is likely to be even more costly than continued euro membership. If, on the other hand, the government chooses to use its regained currency and fiscal sovereignty to bring idle resources (including the unemployed) back into productive use – while at the same time re-establishing a degree of control over capital, trade and labour flows as well as over the national financial sector and other key sectors of the economy – full employment and economic growth could be achieved relatively swiftly, without the country in question necessarily incurring disastrous balance-of-payments or inflationary problems.

Analysing in detail the minutiae of a progressive euro exit is clearly beyond the scope of this book (though it has been described at length in previous works by the authors, such as the book *Eurozone Dystopia* by William Mitchell).[18] The point that we wish to make here is that the current crisis of the EU and monetary union should not be seen as a cause for despair but rather as an opportunity for the left to embrace (once again) a progressive, emancipatory vision of national sovereignty. This needn't necessarily come at the expense of European cooperation. On the contrary, there is ample evidence that the vice-like grip of the single currency, by exacerbating intra-European divergences, causing widespread social devastation and fuelling national resentments on a scale unseen in the post-war era, is now endangering European multilateral cooperation on crucial matters such as immigration and other issues. Abandoning the euro would not undermine that sort of cooperation. On the contrary, by allowing governments to maximise the well-being of their citizens, it could and should provide the basis for a renewed European project, based on multilateral cooperation between sovereign states.

The fact that many taboos are falling as a result of the crisis of the neoliberal order – on issues such as central bank independence, fiscal deficits and free trade – provides a further opportunity in this respect. Many false myths, however, persist. These continue to prevent many progressives – even those that are ideologically in favour of enhancing national sovereignty – from fully embracing a progressive vision of sovereignty, in the eurozone as much as in those countries that already possess their own currency. It is these false myths that we analyse in the following chapters, by relying on the insights provided by modern monetary theory (MMT), a macroeconomic theory that describes and analyses the way in which 'money' works in monetarily sovereign countries.

8

A Government is Not Like a Household: An Introduction to Modern Monetary Theory

THE FAILURE OF MAINSTREAM MACROECONOMICS: POST-TRUTH BEFORE IT WAS COOL

There has been a lot of talk regarding 'post-truth' in recent years. We are increasingly being told that we have entered a new era of politics: the post-truth era. But what does the term mean exactly? The *Oxford English Dictionary* – which chose the term as its 2016 word of the year – defines post-truth politics (or post-factual politics) as a political culture 'in which objective facts are less influential in shaping public opinion than appeals to emotion and personal belief'. According to this commonly accepted definition, however, it hard to see what is so novel about the so-called post-truth era: using biased or misleading information – or 'alternative facts', to use another fashionable term – to influence public opinion is a tactic as old as politics itself. It's called propaganda. So how should we explain the post-truth hysteria that is currently engulfing the West? Are we to believe that the same political-media establishment that blatantly lied about Iraq's possession of weapons of mass destruction to justify the aggression and occupation of the country, to cite the most flagrant example of establishment-sponsored propaganda in recent years, has taken up a sudden interest in 'the truth', however loosely we define the concept? Such an answer is clearly laughable.

A more sensible explanation is that Western elites are increasingly losing their ability to control the flow of information to the general public – and thus to determine the outcome of electoral disputes, as seen in the 2016 British referendum and US presidential election – due to the rise of social media and (mostly) Internet-based alternative information platforms (as well as the counter-propaganda of non-Western countries such as Russia and China). This represents a clear threat to the ruling classes. In such a context, the political and corporates elites can only hope *indirectly* to control the flow of information that is beyond their sphere of influence, by using the mainstream media and other channels (such as academia) that they do effectively control to fix the premises of discourse by circumscribing the terms of acceptable debate – the 'real news' of the established media vis-à-vis the 'fake news' of social media and the alternative media more generally – thus excluding the viability of alternative viewpoints, whether fact-based or not. The aim of this form of 'soft propaganda' is not to uphold the truth against post-truth, but rather to uphold the establishment's account of *the way things are*, which often has very little to do with the truth or reality, against alternative accounts of reality that may threaten the dominant order. There is nothing particularly new about this form of propaganda either. It has been going on for decades.

Nowhere is this more evident than in the realm of macroeconomics, and particularly the narrative that has been spun about the capacities (or alleged lack thereof) of national governments that issue their own currency (which encompasses almost all nations). In essence, the dominant narrative in macroeconomics is based on what we might call 'fake knowledge'. Mainstream macroeconomists, who profess an abiding faith in the ability of the self-regulated market to deliver optimal outcomes, declared some years before the crisis, with an arrogance characteristic of the profession, that the business cycle was dead. They claimed that large swings in macroeconomic performance (recessions and mass unemployment, and booms and busts), which had dominated the attention of economic policymakers in the post-war period, were now a thing of the past. University of Chicago professor and Nobel Prize in Economics winner Robert Lucas Jr (in)famously declared in 2003 that 'macroeconomics in this original sense has succeeded: its central problem of depression-prevention has been solved, for all practical purposes, and has in fact been solved for many decades'.[1] The former US Federal Reserve Bank governor, Ben Bernanke, followed that up with the claim that the world was enjoying an unprecedented period of 'great moderation' because governments had prioritised monetary policy to concentrate purely on price stability and the pursuit of fiscal surpluses.[2]

Just before the financial crisis revealed its worst, Olivier Blanchard, then chief economist at the IMF, claimed that 'the state of macro is good'.[3] He asserted that a 'largely common vision has emerged' in macroeconomics, with a 'convergence in methodology'. He also noted that the dominant approach in macroeconomics had 'become a workhorse for policy and welfare analysis' because it is 'simple, analytically convenient [and] reduces a complex reality to a few simple equations'. It didn't seem to matter to these economists that in mainstream models 'there is no unemployment' because according to the mainstream paradigm all fluctuations in unemployment are the result of workers making the optimal choice between work and leisure. The public was led to believe that these mainstream economists had triumphed over the old Keynesian interventionists who had overregulated the economy, sucked the spirit out of private entrepreneurs, allowed trade unions to become too powerful and bred generations of indolent and unmotivated individuals who only aspired to live on income support payments. The dominant narrative was that with the economic cycle now under control, economic policy should concentrate on deregulating labour and financial markets and reducing income support payments to the unemployed, so that the market could work more efficiently.

Recently, Paul Romer, who earned his PhD in economics in the 1980s at the University of Chicago, the temple of neoliberal economics, provided a scathing attack of his own profession in a paper titled 'The Trouble With Macroeconomics'.[4] Romer describes mainstream macroeconomics as having been in a state of 'intellectual regress ... for more than three decades', culminating in the obsession for so-called Dynamic Stochastic General Equilibrium (DSGE) New Keynesian models – which Romer describes as 'post-real' – that lie at the heart of mainstream economics. These are highly complex and abstract mathematical models that attempt to explain aggregate economic phenomena, such as economic growth, business cycles and the effects of monetary and fiscal policy, on the basis of microeconomic principles that have no bearing on macroeconomic reality, which the models erroneously assume to be governed by stable causal mechanisms. That is because the models in question rely on assumptions about human behaviour that belie the knowledge adduced by social scientists that actually study such behaviour (such as psychologists, sociologists, etc.).

It should come as no surprise that mainstream economists first failed to predict the financial crisis, and then proposed 'remedies' (i.e. austerity and wage repression) that dramatically worsened it. In 2011, the IMF's IEO released a caustic assessment of the institution's performance in the lead-up to the financial crisis.[5] The IEO identified neoliberal ideological biases within the IMF, and determined that it had failed to give adequate warning of the impending financial crisis because it was 'hindered by a high degree of groupthink', which, among other things, suppressed 'contrarian views'. The report stated:

> The prevailing view among IMF staff – a cohesive group of macro-economists – was that market discipline and self-regulation would be sufficient to stave off serious problems in financial institutions. They also believed that crises were unlikely to happen in advanced economies, where 'sophisticated' financial markets could thrive safely with minimal regulation of a large and growing portion of the financial system.[6]

The report also says that 'IMF economists tended to hold in highest regard' DSGE New Keynesian economic models proven to be inadequate.[7] Willem Buiter, hardly a radical economist, described DSGE models as useless 'self-referential, inward-looking distractions at best', which 'exclude everything relevant to the pursuit of financial stability'.[8] Paul Krugman noted that mainstream economists were blind 'to the very possibility of catastrophic failures in a market economy' and that their policy prescriptions, based on an unjustified belief in the efficiency of markets, had created the circumstances that would lead to the crisis.[9] As the worst economic crisis in 80 years was building, most economists were waxing lyrical in their own world of self-aggrandisement and self-congratulation.

Simply put, the entire edifice of mainstream macroeconomics is built on a sequence of interrelated lies and myths that have no connection to reality, but reinforce the erroneous view that a self-regulating private market with minimal government interference will deliver maximum wealth for all. To address criticism that mainstream economists play around with 'models' that have little correspondence to reality, Milton Friedman famously stated that it is not how 'real' the models are but how well they predict real outcomes that should guide their credibility. Even on that flawed premise, mainstream macroeconomics has proven to be a disastrous failure. The financial crisis led to rather extreme policy responses from governments and central banks. All the mainstream predictions of the outcomes of these policies (for example, that the large bond-buying exercises conducted by central banks would be inflationary, or that the significant increase in fiscal deficits would drive up interest rates) have been proven to be completely wrong.

It is easy to conclude that those who hang on to these failed mainstream approaches are little more than cult worshippers who have lost all scientific credibility. Yet they maintain their hegemony in several ways. Economics students are forced to use textbooks that give false accounts of how the financial sector works; they are brainwashed with mythical accounts about the impact of the government on private markets; and, above all, they are taught that if markets are left to their own devices, the outcomes will be superior to those that involve regulation or government oversight. They also control hiring processes in our universities, access to the 'high status' publication outlets and major research funding bodies, and, importantly, create networks that allow for transition between the academy, business and government. These networks are a pervasive and powerful force for discipline. Advantages (publications, research grants, promotions, consulting opportunities, influence, etc.) accrue to those who conform to the rules. Socialisation begins in one's student days and persists as one progresses through a career.

In this sense, mainstream economics, with its reliance on blind belief rather than empirical evidence, is more akin to a religion – with economists playing the role of high priests, custodians of a body of knowledge too complex to be understood by common people – than a science. In recent decades, this has led to the emergence of what Joe Earle and others call an 'econocracy': 'a society in which political goals are defined in terms of their effect on the economy, which is believed to be a distinct system with its own logic that requires experts to manage it'.[10] That expertise – which has allowed policymakers throughout the neoliberal era to (mis)represent to the public unpopular political decisions as being neutral *technical* decisions, separate from politics and class interests, in yet another form of depoliticisation – is now being increasingly challenged. To understand why there is so much resistance to abandoning failed economic theories, we need to understand that the mainstream economics paradigm is much more than a set of theories that economics professors indoctrinate their students with. Mark Blyth notes that mainstream economic theories 'enshrine different distributions of wealth and power and are power resources for actors whose claims to authority and income depend upon their credibility', which explains, in part, why there is such resistance to abandoning them, even though it is clear that they are bereft of any evidential standing.[11]

Considering all this, it is hardly surprising that these models completely and utterly failed to predict the financial crisis and subsequent

Great Recession. Neither is it surprising that citizens are losing faith in the economics profession. In this respect, the outcome of the British referendum on the country's membership of the European Union was a watershed moment: despite months of incessant fear-mongering by virtually all parties of the British and European political spectrum, all major international organisations and media outlets, and (almost) the entire economics profession – which unanimously claimed that an 'exit' victory would have apocalyptic consequences for the UK, instantly causing a financial meltdown and plunging the country into a deep recession – the majority of voters opted for Brexit anyway. In doing so, they proved economists wrong once again, since none of the day-after catastrophic scenarios predicted in the run-up to the referendum occurred. In this sense, the Brexit vote was not simply a rejection of the political establishment; it was also a rejection of the dominant economic narrative peddled by the self-appointed experts of the academic and economic establishment. The reasons are easily explained. As Ann Pettifor wrote, the hardship experienced by a growing number of citizens – in the form of low wages, insecure low-skilled jobs, bad housing, high rents and public sector austerity – 'is indirectly a consequence of the economics profession':

> Economists led the way to financial liberalisation of the past forty years, which led to soaring levels of debt, crises and financial ruin. Economists dictated the terms for austerity that has so harmed the economy and society over the past years. As the policies have failed, the vast majority of economists have refused to concede wrongdoing.[12]

As we have seen, many of the myths of mainstream economics – such as those regarding the alleged virtues of 'free trade' and the 'free market' – concern concepts that find no correspondence in actually existing capitalism, which relies heavily on measures designed and promoted by the state on behalf of capital, and thus can be easily dismissed as simple ideological veils designed to shield from our view the true nature of capitalist exploitation and regimentation, which we have analysed at length in previous chapters.

Other myths and 'alternative facts', however, continue to inform policymaking and are therefore much more dangerous. Most of these relate to the impact of monetary and fiscal policy, the principle tools available to national governments. These claims include: that fiscal deficits inevitably lead to inflation and impose crippling debt burdens on future generations; that fiscal deficits do not influence aggregate demand because consumers and firms will factor into their spending decisions the future tax burden (needed, the argument goes, to 'pay off' the deficit/ debt) and thus will increase their savings today to meet their future tax obligations – the 'Ricardian equivalence hypothesis'; that government borrowing (allegedly needed to 'fund' the deficit) competes with the private sector for scarce available funds and thus drives up interest rates, which reduces private investment – the 'crowding out' hypothesis; that an excessive debt will make the government insolvent; that if govern-ments cut their spending, the private sector will 'crowd in' to fill the gap – another version of the 'Ricardian equivalence' myth, and many more.

Why do these myths continue to hold so much sway – among economists and policymakers alike – despite the lack of empirical evidence and the growing body of theoretical research (even from mainstream sources, as we have seen) that disproves them? The reasons suggested are numerous and often overlapping: ideology, lobbying and vested interests are among the main ones. This is how John Maynard Keynes, reflecting on the 'victory' of the neoclassical model – the precursor to neoliberalism – in the early twentieth century, explained its success:

It must have been due to a complex of suitabilities in the doctrine to the environment into which it was projected. That it reached con-clusions quite different from what the ordinary uninstructed person would expect, added, I suppose, to its intellectual prestige. That its teaching, translated into practice, was austere and often unpalat-able, lent it virtue. That it was adapted to carry a vast and consistent logical superstructure, gave it beauty. That it could explain much social injustice and apparent cruelty as an inevitable incident in the scheme of progress, and the attempt to change such things as likely on the whole to do more harm than good, commended it to authority. That it afforded a measure of justification to the free activities of the individual capitalist, attracted to it the support of the dominant social force behind authority.[13]

Paraphrasing Keynes, we could thus posit that the power of mainstream economics resides in the fact that it explains much social injustice as the inevitable consequence of the objective constraints faced by policymak-ers and state apparatuses, which obviously attracts to it the support of the dominant social forces (and of policymakers themselves). The fact that the policies arising from modern mainstream economics benefit only the richest – the so-called '1 per cent' – would appear to validate this hypothesis. In other words, if these theories and policies continue to prove themselves incapable of restoring prosperity it is not only because their fundamental macroeconomic assumptions are not grounded in reality – it is because *they were never intended to do so*. More troubling, however, is the fact that these myths also hold considerable sway among progressive and radical thinkers and politicians. These myths represent a huge obstacle to the conceptualisation of a radical alternative to neoliberal (or post-neoliberal) capitalism. It is to these to that we will now turn our attention.

MONETARY SOVEREIGNTY: A PRIMER

One of the most pervasive and persistent myths – which undergirds many of the myths outlined above – is the assumption that governments are revenue-constrained, that is, that they need to 'fund' their expenses through taxes or, if they register a fiscal deficit (i.e. if expenses exceed revenues), through debt. This leads to the corollary that governments have to 'live within their means', since ongoing deficits will inevitably result in an 'excessive' accumulation of debt, which in turn is assumed to be 'unsustainable' in the long run. Former US president, Barack Obama, reiterated this myth when he announced, in December 2009, that the country '[does not] have enough public dollars to fill the hole of private dollars that was created as a consequence of the crisis'.[14] The problem with Obama's assertion is that it is simply not true. As we will see, monetarily sovereign (or currency-issuing) governments – which nowadays include most governments – are *never* revenue-constrained because they issue their own currency by legislative fiat.

It wasn't always this way. Under the Bretton Woods system of fixed exchange rates and gold convertibility that was in place prior to 1971, governments were indeed limited in their spending capacity by the value of the gold held by the central bank. This was because the outstanding stock of money that the central bank would issue was proportional to its gold reserves; if a government wanted to spend more, it had to reduce the money held by the non-government sector using taxation and/or bond sales. Clearly, the decision to enter this type of monetary system was voluntary, but once the decision had been taken, the government was bound to operate in that manner. Institutional machinery was then established to facilitate the issuing of bonds to the private markets, although central banks could still purchase government debt. In some periods, central banks purchased significant amounts of government debt. That system came to an end in August 1971, when US President Nixon abandoned gold convertibility and ended the system of fixed exchange rates. Once governments started to adopt so-called fiat currency monetary systems and flexible exchange rates in the 1970s, all the spending caps and debt limits that had some operational significance under the Bretton Woods system became irrelevant.

Modern currencies are often called fiat currencies – from the Latin word *fiat* ('it shall be') – because there is no promise made by the government to redeem them for precious metal. Their value is proclaimed by 'fiat': the government merely announces that a coin is worth, let's say, a half dollar without holding a reserve of precious metal equal in value to a half dollar. A consequence of this is that governments that issue their own currencies no longer have to 'fund' their spending: technically, they can simply create the necessary money 'out of thin air'. They never need to 'finance' their spending through taxes or selling debt to the private sector, since the level of liquidity in the system is not limited by gold stocks, or anything else. In other words, governments are free from the revenue constraints that existed under the Bretton Woods system. The reality is that currency-issuing governments such as those of Australia, Britain, Japan and the US can never 'run out of money' or become insolvent. These governments always have an unlimited capacity to spend in their own currencies: that is, they can purchase whatever they like, as long as there are goods and services for sale in the currency they issue. At the very least, they can purchase all idle labour and put it back to productive use. This 'fundamental principle' was spelled out even in a recent Deutsche Bank report: 'Unlike any corporate, government or household, a central bank has no reason to be bound by its balance sheet or income statement. It can simply create money out of thin air (a liability) and buy an asset or give the liability (money) out for free.'[15]

Moreover, a flexible exchange rate means that governments no longer have to constrain their expenditures to meet the central bank requirements to sustain a fixed parity against a foreign currency. This, of course, does not apply to countries that are part of the EMU: they effectively use a foreign currency, much like a state government in, say, the US or Australia and thus they *do* face the risk of insolvency. The ECB, which issues the currency in the eurozone, however, like any other central bank, can never run out of euros nor become insolvent.

However, most of the analysis appearing in mainstream macro-economics textbooks, which filters into the public debate and underpins the cult of austerity (and, alas, most left responses to it), continues to ignore the post-1971 shift and to rely on gold standard logic, which does not apply to modern fiat monetary systems. This is evident in the flawed analogy often made between the household budget and the sovereign government budget. When former British prime minister, David Cameron, said in June 2011 that 'if you have maxed out your credit card, if you put off dealing with the problem, the problem gets worse',[16] he was inferring that the government deficit is just like credit card debt and that Britain was facing bankruptcy. He was misleading susceptible voters by invoking the false neoliberal analogy between national government budgets and household budgets. This analogy resonates strongly with voters because it attempts to relate the more amorphous finances of a government with our daily household finances. We know that we cannot run up our household debt forever and that we have to tighten our belts when our credit cards are maxed out. We can borrow to enhance current spending, but eventually we have to sacrifice spending to pay the debts back. We intuitively understand that we cannot indefinitely live beyond our means. We can quite literally 'run out of money'.

Neoliberal ideologues draw an analogy between the two because it implies that government deficits – just like 'household deficits' – are intrinsically reckless. This analogy, however, is false at the most elemental level: households are *users* of the currencies, meaning that they have to seek funds before they can spend; sovereign governments, on the other hand, *issue* the currency that the households use. Thus, they can consistently spend more than their revenues because they can, technically speaking, create the currency out of thin air if necessary. They face no solvency constraint precisely because they face no revenue constraint. This is the exact opposite of what most students learn in mainstream macroeconomic textbooks, which typically use the flawed analogy between the household budget and the sovereign government budget to argue that the same principles that constrain the former apply to the government. Stephanie Bell noted that that the erroneous understanding that a student will gain from a typical macroeconomics course is that 'the role of taxation and bond sales is to transfer financial resources from households and businesses (as if transferring actual dollar bills or coins) to the government, where they are re-spent (that is, in some sense "used" to finance government spending)'.[17] This is true for local governments and states that do not issue the currency. It is also not too far from the truth for nations that adopt a foreign currency or peg their own to gold or foreign currencies. However, as mentioned, this is not the case for governments that issue their own sovereign currency without a promise to convert at a fixed value to gold or a foreign currency (that is, governments that float their currencies).

While the exact institutional details can vary from nation to nation, governments typically spend by drawing on a bank account they have at the central bank – which, in itself, is a creature of the state and, irrespective of legal status, is effectively part of government. An instruction is sent to the central bank from the treasury to transfer some funds out of this account into an account in the private sector, which is held by the recipient of the public spending. Similarly, when the tax department receives revenue it asks the central bank to record the receipts in its central bank account. The private banking sector facilitates a transaction that reduces the funds available in the bank account of the taxpayer. No printing presses are involved in either transaction. Computer operators in the central bank and the private banks just type numbers that are recorded by the electronic accounting systems in the various banks to signify how much the government wishes to spend and/or how much it has received. It is a very orderly process and goes on hour by hour, day by day and year by year. All government spending is enacted in this way.

As we will see, accounting rules typically require governments to have sufficient funds in their account at the central bank before they can spend, and, if there are not sufficient funds available (that is, if expenses exceed revenues), to 'cover' the deficit through debt issuance. In the latter case, the government typically credits the private bank's account with treasury securities – the sale of government bonds usually involves a debt auction, which only a select number of banks or securities broker-dealers (known as primary dealers) are permitted to participate in – and the private bank in turn credits the treasury's account at the central bank with reserves of equal value. However, we should not be misled into thinking that a sovereign government can run out of funds or purchasers of public debt, or that the government will eventually have to raise taxes in order to pay back the debt. The government typically reimburses the debt by 'rolling it over' (that is, issuing new debt as the old debt matures), though it could simply extinguish the debt by issuing new fiat money.

Similarly, we should not fall prey to the neoliberal narrative that a fiscal surplus (revenues greater than spending) represents 'public saving', which can be used to fund future public expenditure. In rejecting the notion that public surpluses create a cache of money that can be spent later, Mitchell and Mosler note:

> Government spends by crediting a reserve account. That balance doesn't 'come from anywhere', as, for example, gold coins would have had to come from somewhere. It is accounted for but that is a different issue. Likewise, payments to government reduce reserve balances. Those payments do not 'go anywhere' but are merely accounted for. In the USA situation, we find that when tax payments are made to the government in actual cash, the Federal Reserve generally burns the 'money'. If it really needed the money *per se* surely it would not destroy it.[18]

Ultimately, this accounting smokescreen is unnecessary. Technically, the government doesn't 'need' pre-existing funds to spend; neither does it 'need' to offset the deficit by issuing debt to the private sector, given that it can create the currency out of thin air. Mainstream textbooks sometimes admit that the government doesn't need to raise taxes or borrow in order to spend. For example, the former chief economist at the IMF, Olivier Blanchard, wrote in his macroeconomics text that the government

> can also do something that neither you nor I can do. It can, in effect, finance the deficit by creating money. The reason for using the phrase 'in effect', is that … governments do not create money; the central bank does. But with the central bank's cooperation, the government can in effect finance itself by money creation. It can issue bonds and ask the central bank to buy them. The central bank then pays the government with money it creates, and the government in turn uses that money to finance the deficit.[19]

This option, which is also termed overt monetary financing (OMF), is erroneously referred to as 'money printing', a term that is used in a pejorative sense to put the policy option in a negative light. OMF is quickly dismissed and considered to be taboo because Blanchard, as with all mainstream economists, wrongly claims that it causes severe inflation. From a mainstream perspective, monetary financing is seen as a radical suggestion. From an MMT perspective, on the other hand, OMF is a desirable option that allows the currency issuer to maximise its impact on the economy in the most effective manner possible.

The idea is very simple and does not actually involve any printing presses at all: instead of selling debt to the private sector, the treasury simply sells it to the central bank, which then creates new funds in return. In this case, the bond purchases are explicitly aimed at an overt increase in the government's fiscal deficit through expansionary policies, thus implying a cooperation between fiscal and monetary authorities; and they are subordinated to employment- and/or growth-related targets, as well as inflation targets. OMF does not carry any intrinsic inflationary risk: it is the government *spending* itself that carries such a risk, regardless of how such spending is financed – by raising taxes, issuing debt to the private sector or issuing debt to the central bank. Indeed, all spending (private or public) is inflationary if it drives nominal aggregate spending faster than the real capacity of the economy to absorb it.

What most people do not understand, however, is that sovereign governments could run fiscal deficits *without issuing debt at all*: the central bank could simply credit the relevant bank accounts to facilitate the spending requirements of the treasury, regardless of whether the fiscal position is deficit or surplus. In other words, OMF means that the government does not depend on the private bond markets to support its net spending (deficits). For a currency-issuing government, borrowing from the private sector is an accounting convention, not a necessity, and contributes nothing positive in terms of advancing the primary goals of such a government. Moreover, the issuance of treasury bonds effectively amounts to a form of corporate welfare for the purchasers, who tend to be financial institutions, wealthy individuals and foreign governments. Why should they enjoy a risk-free government annuity? This idea should become ingrained in the progressive mindset given the way that government debt is demonised by neoliberals and used as a pretext to impose fiscal austerity. The ability to spend without issuing debt is intrinsic to a currency-issuing government and the act of issuing bonds to the non-government sector is an unnecessary act.

Adair Turner, the former chair of the British Financial Services Authority, describes this form of monetary financing – which he considers to be 'an always available and always effective option for stimulating nominal demand' – as 'running a fiscal deficit (or a higher deficit than would otherwise be the case) which is not financed by the issue of interest-bearing debt, but by an increase in the monetary base – i.e., of the irredeemable fiat non-interest-bearing monetary liabilities of the government/central bank'.[20] OMF thus has the added benefit of flushing out a lot of debt-related paranoia, however unfounded it may be, since the deficit would not add to the overall debt.

To optimise the implementation of OMF, the central bank and treasury could (and should) effectively be 'consolidated' into a single government body. Technically, there is no need for one wing of the state (the central bank) to 'lend' money to another wing of the state (the government). However, it makes little difference from an operational perspective whether OMF is implemented in a non-consolidated fashion – that is, by getting the central bank to facilitate the government's spending needs by underwriting government bonds or by directly crediting private bank accounts as instructed by the treasury, without the government offsetting this with bond-issuance – or in a consolidated fashion, by allowing the treasury to directly create new fiat money and credit the reserve accounts held by the commercial bank. In either case, this would make macroeconomic policy wholly accountable to voters instead of being managed by central bankers that are largely unaccountable and dominated by vested interests, as it is today. As we will argue in Chapter 9, democratic institutions need to assert their control over markets first and foremost through clear rules and regulations, but also to a certain extent by regaining the levers of economic, industrial and investment policy. A precondition for this is reclaiming a degree of democratic control over monetary policy itself.

Although most people would balk at the idea of OMF – because it is so removed from the current economic and monetary doctrine, especially in Europe – monetary financing is not a new idea. A number of well-known and diverse economists advocated similar policies as a response to the Great Depression in the 1930s. These include Harry Dexter White, Henry Simon, Irving Fisher, John Maynard Keynes and Milton Friedman. The idea was developed in the 1940s by the Russian-born British economist Abba Lerner, one of the forefathers of MMT. Lerner advocated that the government should 'print money' to match the government deficit spending needed to achieve and sustain full employment. In his seminal 1943 article, 'Functional Finance and Federal Debt', Lerner noted:

The central idea is that government fiscal policy, its spending and taxing, its borrowing and repayment of loans, its issue of new money and its withdrawal of money, shall all be undertaken with an eye only to the results of these actions on the economy and not to any established traditional doctrine about what is sound or unsound. This principle of judging only by effects has been applied in many other fields of human activity, where it is known as the method of science opposed to scholasticism. The principle of judging fiscal measures by the way they work or function in the economy we may call Functional Finance. ... Government should adjust its rates of expenditure and taxation such that total spending in the economy is neither more nor less than that which is sufficient to purchase the full employment level of output at current prices. If this means there is a deficit, greater borrowing, 'printing money', etc., then these things in themselves are neither good nor bad, they are simply the means to the desired ends of full employment and price stability.[21]

In 1948, none other than Milton Friedman argued not only that government deficits should sometimes be financed with fiat money, but that they should always be financed in that fashion, on the basis that such a system would provide a surer foundation for a low-inflation regime.[22] Friedman used the term 'helicopter drop' to describe a situation where the government would print dollar bills and then use them to make a lump-sum payment to citizens – as if they had been dropped on the population from a helicopter flying above.[23]

The former US Federal Reserve chairman, Ben Bernanke, revived the idea of a 'helicopter drop' in 2002. In a speech to the National Economists Club in Washington about methods to avoid deflation, Bernanke advocated a 'money-financed tax cut', which he said was equivalent to Friedman's anti-deflation proposal to drop money from helicopters in order to stimulate spending.[24] Bernanke said that when total spending collapses, a nation endures rising unemployment and, ultimately, deflation, as 'producers cut prices on an ongoing basis in order to find buyers'. As the recession deepens, interest rates drop to zero, which reduces the flexibility of monetary policy. Even from the conservative perspective of Ben Bernanke, these situations call for a significant increase in fiscal deficits to stimulate spending and confidence, with the central bank issuing new money to support the deficits. Bernanke reiterated his proposal in a recent article in which he called for a 'Money-Financed

Fiscal Program, or MFFP', which he describes as a policy scenario in which the treasury simply instructs the central bank to credit bank accounts on its behalf (that is, without matching the fiscal deficit with debt issued to the non-government sector or central bank).[25] He notes that this is an appealing idea because it would simulate the economy 'even if existing government debt is already high and/or interest rates are zero or negative'. Since 2008, in reaction to the post-crisis global recession, the idea has been endorsed by a number of notable economists, including: Citigroup's chief economist, William Buiter; Richard Wood; Martin Wolf; Paul McCulley and Zoltan Pozsar; Steve Keen; Ricardo Caballero; John Muellbauer; Paul Krugman, and others. Though most authors view monetary financing as a way to finance the government deficit directly, others have suggested using OMF to inject new money directly into citizens' bank accounts, bypassing the government altogether.

Even though historical data on monetary financing is somewhat limited, there are a number of case studies that illustrate the positive effects of OMF. Various analyses show that in the 1930s Japanese finance minister Korekiyo Takahashi was able to jump-start the Japanese economy by allowing the central bank to create money to fund public works. Korekiyo is famous for abandoning the gold standard in 1931 and introducing a major fiscal stimulus with central bank credit that 'was found to have been crucial in ending the depression quickly'.[26] Ellen Brown has demonstrated how the German government used its currency-issuing powers to finance public investment from 1933 to 1937, transforming a bankrupt country into the strongest European economy in just four years.[27] While Ryan-Collins and others have shown that OMF was critical to the economic development of Canada (1935–71) and New Zealand (1935–9).[28]

The main argument against OMF, and expansionary monetary and fiscal policies in general, is that they inevitably lead to inflation – or hyperinflation, in the case of OMF. However, there is no reason to believe that a monetary financing programme would inevitably result in excessive inflation, let alone hyperinflation. The oft-quoted hyperinflation examples – such as 1920s Germany and modern-day Zimbabwe – do not support the claim that monetary financing and/or large government deficits cause inflation. In both cases, there were major reductions in the supply capacity of the economy prior to the inflation episode. As already mentioned, there is no inherent technical reason to believe that OMF would be more inflationary than any other policy stimulus, or that it would produce hyperinflation, since the impact on nominal spending and thus potentially on inflation depends entirely on the scale of the operation: there is no risk of hyperinflation as long as the total spending growth in the economy does not exceed the productive capacity of the economy. In the context of the legitimate goals of a currency-issuing government, OMF would facilitate sufficient net spending to allow the economy to sustain full employment, which means that it would be irrational for such a government to push spending beyond that productive limit deliberately.

Moreover, it is often overlooked that the current system allows private banks to create most of the digital money in circulation through loans, which create deposits and liquidity that can be spent. This freedom gives banks the power to engineer credit-driven booms at will, which in turn leads to soaring prices (especially in the housing market). When these booms inevitably go bust, triggering a crisis, the banks attempt to repair their overleveraged balance sheets by engaging in excessive deleveraging, cutting off credit when households and businesses need it the most. This exacerbates the crisis and drives the economy into what economist Richard Koo described as a 'balance sheet recession'.[29] When this happens, fiscal deficits are required for extended periods of time at elevated levels to provide the spending support to allow the non-government sector to reduce the precariousness of their balance sheet position – that is, to reduce their indebtedness. That debt-reduction process is lengthy and results in lower than normal non-government spending and the risk of extended recession unless spending is supported by higher-than-normal government deficits.

If currency-issuing governments are so free of financial constraints, then why do they continue to tax and to issue debt? While there are legitimate reasons for governments to raise taxes and issue debt – which are, however, different from the ones claimed by mainstream economists and policymakers, as we shall see – a simple answer is that most currency-issuing governments continue to impose *voluntary* constraints on themselves that resemble the spending constraints that existed under the gold standard. These ideologically motivated fiscal rules – which resemble other forms of voluntary constraints that we have analysed in previous chapters – are designed to limit the capacity of government to run deficits and/or borrow from the central bank and non-government sector. As we have seen, the two main voluntary, operational rules which are typical of many countries are: (i) the treasury must have sufficient deposits in its account at the central bank before it can spend; and (ii) if the treasury does not have sufficient deposits to cover mandated spending, it must issue bonds to 'finance' the deficit. Moreover, it cannot sell the newly issued bonds to the central bank on the primary market; it must sell them to private banks or other investors. However, the central bank can buy these bonds on the secondary market. In various countries, this goes hand in hand with 'debt ceilings' of various kinds – legislative limits on the amount of national debt that can be issued.

From a financing perspective, none of these complex accounting structures are necessary. However, governments continue to employ them to obfuscate the way government spending actually works and thus to rationalise the imposition of neoliberal fiscal policies. Politicians know that rising public debt can be politically manipulated and demonised in order to get citizens and workers to accept – *demand* even – policies that are not in their class interest. Similarly, taxation – needed, it is claimed, to 'finance' government spending – can also be (and often is) used for political ends, such as transferring wealth from the lower-middle classes to the upper classes. Nonetheless, these rules could be legislated out of existence if the public truly understood how the monetary system operates. Similarly, the EMU is itself a system of voluntary constraints that are reflected in legal statements, all of which could be changed via appropriate legislation. In this regard, MMT exposes the notion of voluntary *versus* intrinsic constraints in a fiat currency system, thus lifting the veil of ideology in the same way that Marx exposed the superficial exchange relations that overlay the production of surplus value and the essence of private profit.

That said, there are good reasons why a currency-issuing government may choose to issue debt or raise taxes. In regard to the former, debt issuance can serve an interest-maintenance function by providing investors with an interest-bearing asset that drains the excess reserves in the banking system that result from deficit spending. If these reserves were not drained (that is, if the government did not borrow) then the spending would still occur but the overnight interest rate would plunge (due to competition by banks to rid themselves of the non-profitable reserves), and this may not be consistent with the stated intention of the central bank to maintain a particular target interest rate. In this context, if the central bank desires to maintain the current target cash rate, then it must provide an alternative to this surplus liquidity by selling government debt. In other words, from an MMT perspective, bond sales by sovereign governments should be seen as an aspect of monetary policy, not as a source of funds to finance government spending. However, as has become evident in the period since the financial crisis, central banks can achieve the same outcome by paying a return on excess reserves. It does not have to offer debt to the banks – in so-called open market operations – to maintain a positive target interest rate. When we understand these points, it becomes clear that the issuing of debt and the payment of interest income is identical in impact as the central bank paying interest on excess bank reserves.

We have also seen that a sovereign government doesn't really need revenue in its own currency to spend. Some who hear this for the first time jump to the question: 'Well, why not just eliminate taxes altogether?' There are several reasons. First, it is the tax that drives the currency. If we eliminated the tax, people probably would not immediately abandon use of the currency, but the main driver for its use would be gone. The imposition of a tax obligation denominated in the currency of the government creates an immediate demand for that currency and a desire to transfers goods and services (including labour) from the non-government sector to the government sector, in order to get hold of the currency. The second reason to have taxes is that it provides the government with a capacity to manage non-government spending to ensure price stability. Taxes create real resource space – that is, free up real resources in the economy (labour and capital), which otherwise would have been used by the non-government sector for private ends – because the non-government sector is deprived of purchasing power. This 'space' is what MMT calls 'fiscal space', and it allows the government the non-inflationary access to real resources necessary for it to fulfil its socio-economic mandate. It stands in contradistinction with the neoliberal view of fiscal space, which erroneously assumes that the government can run out of money. Other reasons for raising taxes, of course, include redistributing wealth – for example, to avoid excessive concentration of wealth in the hands of the upper classes – and encouraging (or discouraging) certain industries and/or products (for example, taxes on alcohol or carbon taxes). None of these, however, have anything to do with the funding of government spending, at least as far as currency-issuing governments are concerned.

Tax revenue also tends to moves counter-cyclically – increasing in an expansion and falling in a recession. This creates an in-built or automatic stabiliser capacity within fiscal policy that attenuates the impact of sudden shifts in non-government spending. To understand this, let us imagine that non-government spending contracts sharply due to a wave of pessimism about the future. Production is cut back and employment falters. The lost tax revenue (and the increased demand for income support) pushes the government's fiscal position towards a deficit (if starting from a surplus) or a higher deficit (if already in deficit), which underpins (provides a floor) in total spending in the economy, without the government changing any discretionary policy settings. So this counter-cyclical nature of tax receipts helps to make the government's net contribution to the economy counter-cyclical, which, in turn, helps to stabilise aggregate demand. Ultimately, tax rates should be set so that the government's fiscal outcome (whether in deficit, balanced or in surplus) is consistent with full employment.

As mentioned, this does not imply that a currency-issuing government should spend or incur deficits without limits, or that fiscal deficits are desirable per se. Fiscal deficits 'in themselves are neither good nor bad', as Abba Lerner wrote.[30] Any assessment of the fiscal position of a nation must be taken in the light of the usefulness of the government's spending programme in achieving its national socio-economic goals. This is what Lerner called the 'functional finance' approach. Rather than adopting some desired fiscal outcome (such as achieving fiscal surpluses at all costs), governments ought to spend and tax with a view to achieving 'functionally' defined outcomes, such as full employment. Fiscal policy positions thus can only be reasonably assessed in the context of these macroeconomic policy goals. Attempting to assess the fiscal outcome strictly in terms of some prior fiscal rule (such as a deficit of 3 per cent of GDP) independent of the actual economic context is likely to lead to flawed policy choices. Thus, from a progressive standpoint – that is, one that assumes the government's objective to be the pursuit of full employment and increased levels of well-being of its citizens – there might indeed be circumstances in which it is sound for a government to run a fiscal surplus, though more often than not ongoing fiscal deficits will be required. To appreciate this point, we need to understand the sectoral balances (or flow of funds) approach to macroeconomics as developed by the British economist Wynne Godley.

THE SECTORAL BALANCES APPROACH:
WHY FULL EMPLOYMENT REQUIRES GOVERNMENT DEFICITS

Macroeconomists simplify the myriad transactions and relationships that comprise a socio-economic system by focusing on broad sectors, which aggregate all these transactions. If, for simplicity's sake, we split the economy into two sectors – government and non-government – then the impact of fiscal deficits and surpluses can be seen more clearly. The former is comprised of the central bank and treasury, while the latter encompasses households, firms and private banks (we will leave the rest of the world, that is, the external or foreign sector, out of our analysis for the moment). A very simple example of such an economy, which captures the essence of the relationship between the government and non-government sectors, is an economy with a population of just two: one person being government and the other being the non-government sector. If the government runs a balanced fiscal position (spends 100 and taxes 100 dollars) then non-government accumulation of fiat currency (money) is zero in that period and the non-government budget is also balanced. Thus, there is no non-government saving in the currency. Let's say the government spends 120 and taxes remain at 100, then the non-government surplus is 20, which can accumulate as financial (monetary) assets. This represents an increase in the non-government sector's net worth or wealth. The non-government saving of 20 initially takes the form of non-interest-bearing money holdings. The government may decide to issue an interest-bearing bond to encourage saving but operationally it does not have to do this to finance its deficit, as we have seen. An interest-bearing bond is just a piece of paper that says the government will repay a certain amount (the face value) at some specified time (maturity date) and will pay an interest premium in addition (the yield or coupon rate). The non-government sector exchanges cash for the bond if it wants to earn interest and has no use for the liquid funds, which may be held as deposits in private banks. The government deficit of 20 is exactly the non-government savings of 20. Now, if the government continued in this vein, accumulated non-government savings would equal the cumulative fiscal deficits. However, should the government decide to run a surplus (say, spend 80 and tax 100) then the non-government sector would owe the government a net tax payment of 20 and would need to run down its prior savings, sell interest-bearing bonds back to the government or run into debt to get the needed funds.

Either way, the accumulated non-government saving (financial wealth) is reduced when there is a government surplus – that is, when the government spends less than it withdraws via taxation. Thus, contrary to neoliberal rhetoric, the systematic pursuit of government fiscal surpluses is necessarily manifested as a systematic decline in non-government sector savings. The government surplus thus has two negative effects on the non-government sector: (i) the stock of financial assets (money or bonds) held by the non-government sector, which represents its wealth, falls; and (ii) non-government disposable income also falls in line with the net taxation impost. Some may retort that government bond purchases provide the non-government wealth-holder with cash. That is true, but the fiscal surplus forces the non-government sector to liquidate its wealth to resolve its shortage of cash that arises from the tax demands exceeding current income. The cash from the bond sales pays the government's net tax bill. The result is exactly the same when expanding this example by allowing for non-government income generation, private firms and production, and a banking sector. In other words, the national government deficit (surplus) equals the non-government surplus (deficit). It should furthermore be noted that, precisely because of the intrinsic relationship between the government and non-government sector, the fiscal outcome is largely beyond the control of government. For example, if private domestic spending is weak then the fiscal deficit will typically rise as tax revenue declines, irrespective of what government does, and vice versa. The failure to recognise this relationship is a major oversight of mainstream economic analysis.

There is another important aspect of the relationship between the government and non-government sectors that is often misunderstood but crucial to understanding the suite of options available to a currency-issuing government. In any monetary system there are financial assets and liabilities. These are specified in monetary terms and can take a multitude of forms. A financial asset could be a bank deposit, some money in your pocket, a government bond or a corporate bond. A financial asset is different from a real asset, such as property holdings or a work of art, because it has no tangible expression. For example, a bank deposit is a virtual statement of wealth. A financial liability is usually a bank loan or some other debt that is owed. The difference between total financial assets and total financial liabilities is called net financial assets. It is different to total net wealth or net worth in that it excludes real assets.

Financial transactions within the non-government sector cannot create new net financial assets or destroy previous net financial positions. For example, when a bank agrees to a loan it creates a deposit that the borrower can draw upon to fund spending. The loan is an asset to the bank but *also* an equal and offsetting liability for the borrower. There is no net gain in financial assets for the non-government sector *as a whole* from this transaction. Transactions within the non-government sector may alter who owns the financial assets and the form those assets are held in, but they do not alter the net position of that sector overall. For example, a household might use some cash it holds in a bank deposit to purchase a corporate bond. The person's financial asset is now a bond rather than cash and the liability shifts from the bank to the corporation that has borrowed the funds. But there is still the same quantity of assets and liabilities in the non-government sector overall.

For the non-government sector to accumulate net financial assets (financial wealth) or lose net financial assets, there has to be a source of financial assets that is 'outside' the non-government sector. This can only be the government sector. In this context, MMT considers the government sector to be the consolidation of the treasury function (fiscal policy) and the central bank (monetary policy). Even though this does not reflect the reality of most countries, as we have seen, consolidating the currency-issuing arm of government (central bank) and the spending and taxing arm (treasury) allows for a better understanding of how net financial assets can enter and exit the non-government sector. It is the transactions that are conducted between the consolidated government sector and the non-government sector which determine the level of net financial assets (denominated in the national currency) that are held by the non-government sector.

Only these transactions can create or destroy net financial assets in the non-government sector. In our simple two-person economy, the fundamental principle is that the non-government sector can only accumulate net financial assets if the government runs a fiscal deficit. We can now more fully appreciate that result. For example, when the treasury department purchases some equipment for a school, it will instruct the central bank to put funds into the bank account of the private supplier of the equipment. The bank entry is created because the government required it to be created. In effect, the entry was created out of thin air, notwithstanding the 'accounting' arrangements discussed earlier that make it look as if the funds were generated by, say, tax revenue. The private supplier now has a higher bank account balance (an increased asset) but there is *no offsetting liability* within the non-government sector. Net financial assets have increased in that sector as a result of the government spending.

Conversely, when the government extracts tax revenue from the non-government sector, the taxpayer will, depending on the arrangements within the tax system, see more income extracted from its pay cheque or an existing bank deposit reduced by the amount of the tax liability. Either way, financial assets decline in the non-government sector without any corresponding decline in liabilities. As a result, net financial assets decrease. These transactions occur every day, and if the government spends more than it receives by way of tax revenue (a deficit) then net financial assets in the non-government sector will rise. The main thing to keep in mind about taxes is that they reduce liquidity in the private sector. Fiscal deficits increase the financial wealth of the non-government sector. Fiscal surpluses, clearly, have the opposite effect: they destroy net financial assets and financial wealth in the non-government sector. So, when conservatives and misguided progressives call for deficit reduction and a shift to fiscal surplus, what they are really calling for, probably unwittingly, is the reduction in non-government financial assets – our wealth.

We are now able to understand how mass unemployment arises and why government is central to its solution. There is no unemployment in traditional non-monetary economies or in non-monetary segments of a modern economy. For example, an unpaid childcarer can never be unemployed. In monetary economies, however, the output of goods and services responds to spending. Firms and other organisations do not produce if they are not confident of selling their output. The production process generates a flow of income (paid to the various production inputs). One person's spending is another person's income. A basic macroeconomic rule is that total spending must equal total income for all the goods and services produced in any period to be sold. If total spending in a period is less than the total income generated, then firms will have unsold output in the form of unwanted inventory accumulation and will reduce future production and employment.

Why would total spending fall below total income in any period? A simple reason might be that households desire to save some of their income for future use or to purchase imports, which means income generated in the domestic economy is spent abroad. The result of this spending deficiency is a rise in involuntary unemployment, which is idle labour offered for sale with no buyers at current wages. In this situation, making labour cheaper (cutting wages) will not reduce unemployment, unless those cuts somehow increase total spending. Clearly, wages are an important component of total income and spending is dependent on income. Cutting wages is thus likely to worsen a spending shortfall.

In our simplified two-sector economy, if the non-government sector desires to save overall, it will spend less than its income. That shortfall in each period has to be eliminated by the government spending more than it receives in revenue (that is, running a fiscal deficit) to prevent a rise in mass unemployment. There is another complication. The non-government sector may desire to save overall but it also has to pay taxes from its income, which further reduces the amount that can be recycled back into the non-government spending stream in each period. The imposition of taxation thus reduces the spending power of the non-government sector. That gap also has to be filled by government spending, which means 'taxes in aggregate will have to be less than total government spending'.[31]

Therefore, if the objective is to maintain full employment, while there may indeed be circumstances that require a fiscal surplus (for example, if private sector spending is strong or if the country is running a large current account surplus), for most countries this will typically require *continuous fiscal deficits* of varying proportions of GDP as the overall saving desires of the private domestic sector vary over time. By the same token, *unemployment occurs when net government spending is too low* relative to the current tax receipts, or taxes are too high relative to the level of government spending, after taking into account the overall saving desires by the non-government sector that have to be matched by government deficits.

There is a parable that allows us to understand better the relationship between the government and non-government sector. Imagine a small community comprising 100 dogs. Each morning they set off into the field to dig for bones. If there are enough bones for all the dogs buried in the field then they would each succeed in their search no matter how fast or dexterous they were. Now imagine that one day the 100 dogs set off for the field as usual, but this time they find there are only 90 bones buried. As a matter of accounting, at least ten dogs will return home bone-less. Now imagine that the government decides that this is unsustainable and decides that it is the skills and motivation of the bone-less dogs that is the problem. They are not skilled enough. They are idlers, skivers and just need to 'bone-seek' harder. So, a range of dog psychologists and dog trainers are called in to work on the attitudes and skills of the bone-less dogs. The dogs undergo assessment and are assigned case managers. They are told that unless they undergo training they will miss out on their nightly bowl of food that the government provides to them while bone-less. They feel despondent. Anyway, after running and digging skills are imparted to the bone-less dogs, things start to change. Each day, as the 100 dogs go in search of 90 bones, we start to observe different dogs coming back bone-less. The composition of the bone-less queue changes. However, on any particular day, there are still 100 dogs running into the field and only 90 bones buried there. At least ten dogs will always return bone-less. The only way for all dogs to get a bone is for the government to increase the number of bones.

The conclusion that mass unemployment is the result of the government deficit being too low also defines the limits on responsible government spending. It is clear that government spending has to be sufficient to allow taxes to be paid. In addition, net government spending is required to meet the non-government desire to save (accumulate net financial assets). The government should aim to maintain total spending such that firms are willing to produce and employ at levels sufficient to engage the available labour resources fully. Not a penny more need be spent by government. This logic also allows us to see why the pursuit of government fiscal surpluses will be contractionary. Pursuing fiscal surpluses is necessarily equivalent to the pursuit of non-government sector deficits. They are two sides of the same coin. For a time, inadequate government deficits can continue without rising unemployment. In these situations, as is evidenced in many countries in the pre-crisis period, GDP growth can be driven by an expansion in private debt. The problem with this strategy is that when the private debt-service levels reach some threshold percentage of income, the private sector will 'run out of borrowing capacity' as incomes limit debt service and banks become risk-averse. Typically, this will then provoke efforts to reduce the debt exposure (a so-called 'balance sheet restructuring') and render the household and/or firm finances less precarious. As a consequence, total spending from private debt expansion slows and unemployment rises unless the government increases its deficit. If the government refuses to show fiscal leadership then recession follows. In other words, in some circumstances credit finance can indeed expand to accommodate growth in the private sector in the presence of insufficient fiscal deficits, but this growth will be inherently unstable. Only fiscal deficits can provide the foundation for stable growth and employment.

Things get a little more complicated when we consider that the non-government sector in an open economy is not just composed of the private domestic sector. We must add the impact of the external sector (sometimes referred to as the rest of the world). We should thus understand modern economies as being composed of three sectors: the government (or public) sector, the private domestic sector and the foreign (or external) sector. This last sector represents the portion of a country's economy that interacts with the economies of other countries, and is thus the one that influences the country's current account balance (a broad measure of the balance of trade). In this model, the government sector's deficit (surplus) is still equal to the non-government sector's surplus (deficit). Except that we now say that the government sector's deficit (surplus) is equal to the private domestic sector's surplus (deficit) *plus* the current account balance. That is because, in an open economy, the net income of the private domestic sector is composed by the government deficit *and* the current account surplus (if there is one).

Therefore, in the presence of an external deficit – that is, if the country imports more than it exports – the government balance necessarily has to be in deficit for the private domestic sector to be in surplus – that is, for the private domestic sector to be able to save overall. By the same token, in the presence of an external deficit and a simultaneous government surplus, the private domestic sector must necessarily run a deficit, that is, dis-save or spend more than it earns. Under these conditions, private spending can persist for a time only if the private domestic sector accumulates ever-increasing levels of debt. This, however, will eventually become unsustainable and lead to a financial crisis. Moreover, as surpluses destroy net financial assets, this increase in private sector debt will be matched by a continuous decline in its net financial assets or wealth. On the other hand, in the presence of a current account surplus – that is, if the country exports more than it imports – the private domestic sector may able to net save even in the presence of a government surplus. Thus, in an open economy, the correct discretionary fiscal stance can only be determined by taking into account the current account balance (the rest of the world's desire to save/dis-save) as well as the private domestic sector's desire to save/dis-save. However, just like in our simplified two-sector model, we should understand that the fiscal outcome for a currency-issuing government is largely residual, rising when private domestic and foreign demand shrinks and falling when demand is rising. By the same token, a nation's current account deficit is largely a function of the rest of the world's desire to spend.

For example, let us assume that the external or foreign balance equals zero. Let us further assume that the private domestic sector's income is 100 while its spending is equal to 90, which delivers an overall surplus of ten over the year. The government sector's fiscal deficit for the year must be equal to ten as a consequence of the national accounting conventions that tie these three sector balances together. We know that the private domestic sector will accumulate ten currency units of net financial wealth during the year, consisting of ten units of domestic government sector liabilities (given that the external balance is zero). As another example, let us assume that the foreign sector spends less in the nation in question relative to the income it receives from that nation (via exports and/or net income transfers), which generates a current account deficit of 20 in the nation in question. At the same time, the government sector also spends less than its income, running a fiscal surplus of ten. From our sectoral balances accounting identity, we know that over the same period the private domestic sector must have run an overall deficit equal to 30 (20 plus 10). At the same time, its net financial wealth will have fallen by 30 units as it sold assets and/or issued debt. Meanwhile, the government sector will have reduced its outstanding debt or increased its claims on the other sectors by ten, and the foreign sector will have reduced its net financial position by 20 (also raising its outstanding debt or reducing its claims on the other sectors). Given a current account deficit of 20, the only way for the private domestic sector to run a surplus – that is, to net save – over the year is for the government sector to run a deficit higher than 20.

It is apparent that it is impossible for all sectors to run surpluses (that is, to 'save overall' – spend less than their income) simultaneously. That is, it is impossible, over any given period of time, for all sectors to accumulate net financial wealth by running surpluses. For one sector to run a surplus (in the example offered above, the government) at least one other sector (in this case the private sector) must run a deficit. To put it differently, if one sector spends more than its income, at least one of the others must spend less than its income because, for the economy as a whole, total spending must equal total receipts or income. While there is no reason why any one sector must run a balanced position (spending equal to income), the sectoral balances framework shows that the system as a whole must.

Often, but not always, the private domestic sector tends to run a surplus – spending less than its income. This is how it accumulates net financial wealth. Overall private domestic sector saving (or surplus) is a leakage from the overall expenditure cycle that must be matched by an injection of spending from another sector. The current account deficit (the so-called external sector account) is another leakage that drains domestic demand. That is, the domestic economy is spending more overseas than foreigners are spending in the domestic economy. Thus, in the presence of a private sector surplus, demand must either come from the external sector, in the form of a surplus, or from the government, in the form of a fiscal deficit. Similarly, in the presence of an external deficit, in order for households and firms together (that is, the private domestic sector) to run a surplus it is necessary for the government to run a deficit.

The accounting structures that underpin the sectoral balances framework thus allow us to test the logic of statements made by policy-makers. For example, if a politician says that the government and non-government sectors should simultaneously reduce their net indebt-edness (increase their net wealth), assuming neoliberal public debt issuance strategies, we know that the statement is an accounting impossibility, unless the country is running a very large current account surplus. We don't have to resort to theory to reach such a conclusion.

An analysis of the sectoral balances of the US and Japan over the past two decades can help to better understand this point. Wynne Godley and Alex Izurieta, for example, have shown the adverse consequences (for other sectoral balances) that resulted from the dramatic shift in the US federal government's fiscal balance over the 1992–2000 period, from borrowing levels of 6 per cent of GDP to a budget surplus of over 1.5 per cent of GDP in 2000.[32] As a result, given that the country registered a constant current account deficit during the same period, the private sector's saving levels inevitably plummeted, while its debt levels increased dramatically. As the government surplus began to diminish after 2000, private sector debt levels began to recover, although the situation began to deteriorate once again after 2003. In contrast, Japan's experience over the same period shows that the private sector surplus increased on a par with the long-term increase in the fiscal deficit. In other words, persistent and substantial fiscal deficits (along with a modest current account surplus) financed the saving desires of the private sector and helped to maintain positive levels of real activity in the economy. These relationships demonstrate the strength of fiscal policy to underwrite economic activity.

In the real world, of course, the correct discretionary fiscal stance also depends on the underlying economic structure of any given country – that is, on the relative weight of the export sector. Nations that will typically have a current account deficit at full employment (such as Australia, the US and the UK) will normally have a fiscal deficit at full employment (equal to the sum of the current account deficit and the domestic private sector surplus). Countries like Japan (with a modest current account surplus at full employment) will have a relatively smaller fiscal deficit at full employment (equal to the domestic private sector surplus minus the current account surplus). Countries with larger current account surpluses at full employment, such as Norway, will typically have a fiscal surplus at full employment, so as not to push the economy past the inflation barrier.

We have thus limited ourselves to identifying an accounting relationship between the various sectoral balances. However, this says little about the *causal relationships* between the flows of income and expenditure and the impact on the stocks of the various sectors. Now, it is a basic fact of economics that spending is mostly determined by income. It is thus fairly straightforward to assume that in an open economy deficit spending by the government – because it raises the income of the private sector (particularly if the spending is aimed at attaining and maintaining full employment) and because a portion of that income is likely to be spent on foreign goods and services – will lead to a smaller current account surplus (if the country has one) or, as is most often the case, a (larger) current account deficit. This basic economic reality is usually used – by mainstream as well as, alas, left commentators and politicians – to disprove the notion that governments can use fiscal stimulus to achieve and sustain full employment and the overall well-being of the citizenry. The underlying assumption is that sustained current account deficits are intrinsically bad and unsustainable, since they will inevitably push the nation in question into a balance-of-payments crisis, which, in turn, will require it to adopt painful recessionary measures to compress internal demand, reduce imports and bring the country back into current account (balance-of-payments) equilibrium. This argument – known as the balance-of-payments constraint – is used to suggest that full employment and domestic income growth (which, as we have seen, usually requires sustained fiscal deficits), and progressive policies more generally, are possible only insofar as the country maintains a balance-of-payments equilibrium, that is, if exports are more or less matched by imports. So-called progressive economists, in particular, are enamoured with the idea that MMT is flawed because it doesn't recognise the fiscal limits imposed by the need to maintain a stable external balance. In the following section, we will clarify why the notion that monetarily sovereign governments that float their currency face a balance-of-payments constraint is just as unfounded as the notion that they face a solvency constraint.

BALANCE-OF-PAYMENTS CONSTRAINTS – OR NOT: WHY CURRENT ACCOUNT DEFICITS ARE (ALMOST) NEVER A PROBLEM

Steve Suranovic, associate professor of economics and international affairs at the George Washington University, notes that one of the most popular and pervasive myths about international trade, 'simply stated, is that trade deficits are bad and trade surpluses are good':

> The presence of a trade deficit, or an increase in the trade deficit in a previous month or quarter, is commonly reported as a sign of distress. Similarly, a decrease in a trade deficit, or the presence of or increase in a trade surplus, is commonly viewed as a sign of strength in an economy.[33]

However, Suranovic writes,

> these perceptions and beliefs are somewhat misguided. In general, it is simply not true that a trade deficit is a sign of a weak economy and a trade surplus is a sign of a strong economy. Merely knowing that a country has a trade deficit, or that a trade deficit is rising, is not enough information to say anything about the current or future prospects for a country – and yet that is precisely how the statistics are often reported.[34]

There are two main reasons why trade deficits are considered deleterious: (i) because they are considered to result in the loss of domestic jobs, due to domestic income being spent on foreign firms' goods/services rather than domestic firms' goods/services, and thus to compromise the long-term growth prospects and welfare of a nation; and (ii) because, as mentioned, they are considered to lead inexorably to balance-of-payments crises, that is, given that current account deficits are necessarily associated with an increase in the country's level of foreign debt, it is assumed that large and persistent trade deficits will require a significant fall in living standards when the loans finally come due. As we will see, both arguments are largely unfounded.

Let us first look at the claim that trade deficits lead to job losses. A first point to acknowledge is that a trade deficit on the current account necessarily has to be matched by an equal and opposite *net financial inflow* on the capital (or financial) account, representing an increase in foreign claims against the country in question. That is because a current account deficit necessarily needs to be financed with capital inflows from abroad. This means that foreigners – usually those residing in countries that run a trade surplus on the current account, which necessarily has to be matched by an equal and opposite net financial outflow on the capital account – are purchasing domestic financial (or other) assets denominated in the deficit country's currency of issue, either by lending money to the country's citizens and/or government or by purchasing equities such as stocks and real estate. Thus, the capacity of a nation to run a current account deficit on an ongoing basis of any size is reliant on the desire of foreigners to accumulate financial claims in the currency issued by that nation. In this sense, from a MMT perspective, a current account deficit signifies the willingness of foreigners to 'finance' the saving desires of the deficit country's foreign sector. In other words, current account deficits and surpluses can only be understood in relational terms: since the current account of the world as a whole must necessarily be in balance in each period (until we figure out a way to export to other planets), it follows that for some countries to run current account surpluses others must be willing to run current account deficits (financed by the former), and vice versa. Surpluses and deficits are consequently two sides of the same coin: it is economically impossible for all countries to be in surplus at the same time. In fact, when countries that trade with each other attempt to run surpluses at the same time, this usually leads to trade wars (which historically have been the prelude to all-out military conflicts).

In any case, the money flowing into the deficit country is ultimately spent by someone and '[w]hen it is spent, it creates demands for goods and services that in turn create jobs in those industries'.[35] Thus, while it is legitimate to assume that a trade deficit will lead to job losses in the export sector, there is no reason to believe that it will lead to an overall loss of jobs at the aggregate level. In fact, evidence from various countries points to the contrary, with the unemployment rate falling as the trade deficit rises, and vice versa.[36] Moreover, the 'trade deficits cause job losses' narrative ignores a crucial point: not only can the government *always* support domestic demand and thus maintain positive levels of real activity in the economy even in the face of an external spending drain resulting from a current account deficit; it can also *always* compensate any job losses in the private sector by directly employing any idle labour for sale in the currency of issue, thus ensuring full employment, as we discuss in more detail in Chapter 9.

Ultimately, however, whether trade deficits depress domestic demand or not, and to what degree, is a moot point. As mentioned, the causality usually works in reverse, with increased domestic consumption leading to (larger) current account deficits. Jobs aside, is this a problem for the country's overall welfare? To answer this question, we first have to define what we mean by 'national welfare'. As Suranovic notes, in materialistic terms this is 'best measured by the amount of goods and services that are "consumed" by households': in other words, 'the standard of living obtainable by the average citizen' is 'affected not by how much the nation *produces* but by how much it *consumes*'.[37] Whether the goods consumed are domestically produced or imported makes little difference from the perspective of the domestic citizens, since they add to their well-being and standard of living in equal measure. It thus follows that a current account deficit – which corresponds to higher consumption than would be possible under conditions of trade equilibrium or surplus – *raises the material welfare of a nation* in the period in which it occurs. This holds particularly true for developing countries, which often lack the real resources (such as best-practice technology) necessary to fuel industrialisation and productive capacity. As even the IMF acknowledges, for these countries a trade deficit may be the only way to raise average living standards.[38]

Conversely, a current account surplus – which corresponds to lower goods and services (both domestic and foreign) being consumed domestically than would be possible under conditions of trade equilibrium or surplus, usually as a result of demand-compressing (that is, mercantilist) policies (low wages and/or government spending) – *reduces the material welfare of a nation* in the period in which it occurs. As Suranovic writes:

> The excess of exports over imports represents goods that could have been used for domestic consumption, investment, and government spending but are instead being consumed by foreigners. This means that a current account surplus reduces a country's potential for consumption and investment below what is achievable in balanced trade. If the trade surplus substitutes for domestic consumption and government spending, then the trade surplus will reduce the country's average standard of living. If the trade surplus substitutes for domestic investment, average living standards would not be affected, but the potential for future growth can be reduced. In this sense, trade surpluses can be viewed as a sign of weakness for an economy, especially in the short run during the periods when surpluses are run. Surpluses can reduce living standards and the potential for future growth.[39]

Germany provides a good case in point. Even though the country is often touted as a success – and as a model for other countries to follow – for its massive current account surplus, in his book *Die Deutschland Illusion*, Marcel Fratzscher, head of the German Institute for Economic Research (DIW), writes that Germany's obsession for trade surpluses has resulted in chronic private underinvestment in the country's economy, as the whole system depends on German capital fuelling demand abroad.[40] This has caused private investment to fall from 22.3 per cent of GDP in 2000 to 18 per cent in 2016, less than most comparably rich countries, which – combined with one of the lowest levels of gross government investment in Europe – is responsible for low productivity growth (because it discourages workers from upgrading skills and companies from investing in higher-value production) and for what a *Spiegel* article described as 'Germany's ailing infrastructure', with highways, bridges and even the Kiel Canal in desperate need of maintenance.[41] According to DIW calculations, the investment shortfall between 1999 and 2012 amounted to about 3 per cent of GDP, the largest 'investment gap' of any European country.[42] Furthermore, Germany's current account surplus is largely a result of the wage-compressing policies pursued by the government from the mid-2000s onwards, which led to a proliferation of precarious, low-paid, low-skilled jobs, and to the stifling of internal demand – and thus of imports. German citizens have therefore experienced – and continue to experience – considerably lower living standards than they would have enjoyed under conditions of trade equilibrium or surplus. As Philippe Legrain wrote, this demonstrates that Germany's external surpluses, far from being an example of superior competitiveness, 'are in fact symptomatic of an ailing economy'.[43]

We are thus in a position to appreciate MMT's claim that *exports represent real costs* for the surplus nation, while *imports represent real benefits* for the deficit nation. This notion is based on the distinction between real resources measured in accumulated goods and services and nominal wealth measured in accumulated financial credits. Exports represent real resources being denied to the country's citizens and sent to other nations, in return for nominal wealth received from them (financial credits), while imports represent real resources being received from other nations, in return for nominal wealth. In this sense, the oft-heard claim that deficit countries are 'living beyond their means' makes little sense; if anything, it is the surplus countries that are 'living below their means'. Ultimately, the question is whether a country prefers to ship fiat money abroad in exchange for goods and services or to ship goods and services abroad in exchange for fiat money.

The mainstream response to this is that trade deficits – regardless of whether they are beneficial or not to the deficit country in the period in which they occur – are inherently unsustainable in the long run, because an excessive accumulation of foreign debt will eventually precipitate a balance-of-payments crisis, as the country will find itself unable to service its growing level of foreign debt or will be subject to a sudden outflow of capital, as international capital markets lose confidence in the nation's ability to service the debt. This will force a contraction in demand and a severe depreciation of the currency, causing a significant fall in living standards. In turn, the government will be forced to adopt recessionary policies (including higher interest rates to attract capital inflows) that reduce the growth rate (and therefore imports) and push up the unemployment rate. It is only once the country's balance-of-payments position has come back into balance or surplus that the nation will regain access to international capital markets. It is therefore claimed that countries should eschew running current account deficits to avoid the painful rebalancing that will inevitably be required. The argument is persuasive because there is an element of truth to it. However, as we will see, it is another example of applying outdated gold standard logic to the radically different world of fiat currency systems with floating exchange rates.[44]

As we saw, under the Bretton Woods system of fixed exchange rates, where the central bank had to manage its foreign currency reserves to maintain the agreed parity with other currencies, the balance of payments was indeed a constraining influence on real GDP growth. In this situation, a nation could not run persistent external deficits because it would soon run out of the foreign currency reserves and/or gold stock that were necessary to defend the parity. That is one of the reasons why the system broke down. External deficit nations were forced to suppress domestic demand via higher interest rates, fiscal austerity and/or wage compression both to reduce imports and/or attract capital inflows to alleviate their balance-of-payments problems. The result was that these countries were prone to extended periods of mass unemployment, which were politically unsustainable. The same applies today to countries that peg their currency to foreign currencies (usually the US dollar).

In a flexible exchange rate system, however, no such constraints exist. Under such a system, the mainstream claim that 'a country cannot go on borrowing indefinitely' makes little sense – and is in fact constantly defied by reality. As noted above, a current account deficit reflects the fact that a country is building up liabilities to the rest of the world that are reflected in net financial inflows on the capital account. While it is commonly believed that these must eventually be paid back, this is obviously false. As the global economy grows, there is no reason to believe that the rest of the world's desire to diversify its portfolios will not mean continued accumulation of claims on any particular country. As long as a nation continues to develop and offers a sufficiently stable economic and political environment so that the rest of the world expects it to continue to service its debts, its assets are likely to remain in demand.

Therefore, the key is whether the private sector and external account deficits are associated with productive investments that increase the country's ability to service the associated debt. As acknowledged even by the IMF, a country's ability to run persistent current account deficits ultimately depends on 'whether the borrowing will be financing investment that has a higher marginal product than the interest rate (or rate of return) the country has to pay on its foreign liabilities'.[45] If this condition is met, a country can continue to run a current account deficit even in the face of a rising foreign debt-to-GDP ratio. It is thus possible for a country's standard of living to be increased in the short term *and*

208 · RECLAIMING THE STATE

in the long term as a result of a current account deficit. This explains why so many countries – the vast majority of the world's countries, in fact – have been able to run persistent current account deficits for years without incurring balance-of-payments crises. Australia provides a good case in point. The country has run a current account deficit of varying sizes relative to the economy for most of the period for which data are available. As a result, its foreign debt has grown exponentially over the years (in absolute terms and as a percentage of GDP). However, as noted in a report by the Parliament of Australia, this is not a cause of concern for the country:

> The size of Australia's foreign debt would be a cause for concern if it was mainly caused by increased consumption rather than increased investment, raising concerns that Australia was living beyond its means. However, Australia's national saving and national investment levels are both above their long-term average, suggesting Australia is well able to cover the servicing of its debt.[46]

This is illustrated by the fact that the country's debt-service ratio has been steadily declining for years despite the growing level of foreign debt.[47] Of course, if a country's spending pattern yields no long-term productive gains – if, that is, the borrowed funds are used simply to fuel consumption rather than investment – then its ability to service the debt might indeed come into question. However, we need to distinguish between foreigner-held private sector debt and foreigner-held government debt. As we have seen, the national government can always service its debts so long as these are denominated in the domestic currency. In the case of national government debt, it makes no significant difference for solvency whether the debt is held domestically or by foreign holders because it is serviced in the same manner in either case – by crediting bank accounts. In the case of private sector debt, on the other hand, this must be serviced out of income, asset sales or further borrowing. This is why long-term servicing is enhanced by productive investments and by keeping the interest rate below the overall growth rate. It should be noted, however, that private sector debts are always subject to default risk – and should they be used to fund unwise investments, or if the interest rate is too high, private bankruptcies are the 'market solution' (though the government can always soften the impact of these on the wider economy).

It is also important to distinguish between foreign debt held in the domestic currency and debt held in a foreign currency. If the foreign debt is denominated in a foreign currency, then a depreciation of the domestic currency, falling income (for example due to falling export prices) or higher world interest rates can render the country – including the government – unable to make interest and principal repayments. However, if the external debt is denominated in the domestic currency, then the depreciation would have no effect on the value of the debt. This implies that countries with large external debts are in greater danger of default if the external debt is largely denominated in a foreign currency, and therefore that the use of foreign-denominated debt should be kept to a minimum. Not surprisingly, most balance-of-payments and currency crises in developing countries – such as Mexico in the 1980s and the East Asian countries in the 1990s – were associated with high levels of dollar-denominated debt, along with various forms of currency pegs.

It should further be noted that the world's desire to accumulate claims against the deficit country can decline independently of the country's underlying trade and/or economic fundamentals. That is because in today's world the impact of the former on the exchange rate is generally overwhelmed by the impact of cross-border gross financial flows, which can behave rather irrationally. In this sense, all open economies are susceptible to balance-of-payments fluctuations. That is, while there is no such thing as a balance-of-payments growth constraint in a flexible exchange economy in the same way as it exists in a fixed exchange rate environment, the external balance still has implications for foreign reserve holdings via the level of external debt held by the public and private sectors. For this reason, nations facing continual current account deficits should also foster conditions that will reduce their dependence on imports, through well-targeted import substitution policies. However, while these fluctuations were terminal during the gold standard era for deficit countries because they meant that governments had to keep the domestic economy is a permanently depressed state to keep imports down, in a flexible exchange rate environment movements in the exchange rate respond to balance-of-payments states and are therefore able to make the adjustment much less painful. This does not mean that a flexible exchange rate delivers an automatic rebalancing of the current account, as Milton Friedman and others claimed. In fact, evidence shows that current account deficits can persist even in the face of a depreciating currency. That is because the trade balance is largely demand-driven

– that is, it is based on the level of domestic and foreign demand (the residents' and foreigners' desire to save/dis-save) – not price-driven, and therefore the ability of a depreciation to improve a country's balance of trade by making exports more competitive is often overstated, although it may indeed play a role in some circumstances. It does mean, however, that if, for whatever reason, the world's desire to accumulate claims against the deficit country were to decline – which means that the nation in question would have to reduce its excess of imports over exports, which may indeed prove painful in the short term – currency depreciation (even though this usually implies a fall in real wages due to rising import costs) is a *less painful* option than internal devaluation (lower nominal wages and/or government spending), which is the only option available to countries operating in a fixed exchange rate regime.[48]

Another oft-heard claim is that currency depreciation is intrinsically inflationary: that in a system of flexible exchange rates, as the currency begins to lose value relative to all other currencies, the rising import prices (in terms of the local currency) are passed through to the domestic price level – with accelerating inflation being the result. It is thus claimed that if the government persists in pursuing domestic full employment policies in the face of a depreciating currency, domestic inflation will worsen and the country will end up with a chronically depreciated currency, resulting in a collapse of material living standards. This argument is particularly potent in the context of the eurozone, where it is often claimed that if a country were to abandon the euro it would inevitably face severe inflationary pressures due to the depreciation of the new currency against other major currencies. In fact, empirical evidence shows that 'the correlation between changes in consumer prices and changes in the nominal exchange rate has been quite low and declining over the past two decades for a broad group of countries'.[49] A recent Bank of England paper on the topic provides three broad conclusions:

> First, contrary to common belief, exchange rate movements don't seem to consistently have larger effects on prices in sectors with a higher share of imported content. Second, exchange rates don't seem to consistently have larger effects on prices in the most tradable and internationally-competitive sectors. Third, the effects of exchange rates on inflation – and even just on import prices – do not seem to be consistent across time.[50]

The euro is a good case in point. Over the 2008–16 period, the euro has lost around 30 per cent of its value against the dollar. This, however, has not been accompanied by runaway inflation in Europe; on the contrary, the continent continues to be mired in 'lowflation' if not outright stagnation. Ultimately, it seems pretty clear that even though currency depreciation does create some exchange rate pass-through to the domestic economy, this is certainly not enough to trigger hyperinflation and certainly not enough to derail a full employment programme based on stimulating domestic demand. Moreover, as mentioned, if the debt is denominated in the local currency the depreciation would have no effect on the value of the repayments. This is consistent with our argument that a monetarily sovereign nation that floats its currency has much more domestic policy space than is considered possible by the mainstream, and can make use of this space to pursue rising living standards even if this means an expansion of the current account deficit and a deprecia-tion of the currency. Ultimately, the best way to stabilise the exchange rate is to build sustainable growth through high employment with stable prices and appropriate productivity improvements, even if the higher growth is consistent with a lower exchange rate. A low-wage, export-led growth strategy, on the other hand, sacrifices domestic policy indepen-dence to the exchange rate – a policy stance that at best favours a small segment of the population.

Of course, in extreme cases, the world's desire to accumulate claims against a deficit country could disappear entirely, in which case the country's current account deficit would get forcibly squeezed down to zero. It might also happen relatively quickly. This is known as a 'sudden stop' and is usually associated with a sudden slowdown or reversal of short-term speculative capital flows, also known as 'hot money'. This harks back to the distinction drawn above between capital inflows that manifest themselves as FDI in productive infrastructure – which are relatively unproblematic, since they create employment and physical aug-mentation of productive capacity that becomes geographically immobile – and capital inflows that are not connected to the real economy and are purely speculative in nature, which tend to fuel unsustainable consump-tion booms (that inevitably go bust). Most boom–bust financial crises in developing countries in recent decades were associated with capital inflows of this nature, with foreign investors rushing into a country in search of short-term profits and then rushing out when things turned sour. A flexible exchange rate *per se* provides no defence against these destructive flows. However, evidence shows that 'sudden stop' episodes are much more common in fixed exchange rate regimes.[51] In fact, it is often forgotten that the Bretton Woods system was ultimately derailed precisely by speculative capital flows that threatened the exhaustion of the foreign exchange and/or gold reserves of nations running external deficits. That said, countries can – and should – defend themselves from the destructive macroeconomic impact of rapid inflows and/or withdrawals of financial capital, regardless of the currency regime. There are a number of tools that nations can employ to that end, first and foremost capital controls.

Up until the 1970s, capital controls – that is, mechanisms or instruments to limit the amount of capital that is flowing into and/or out of a country – were an integral part of the post-war Bretton Woods system, and at the time were endorsed by most mainstream economists and international institutions (including the IMF), since unfettered cross-border capital flows were considered inherently volatile and destabilising. As Carmen Reinhart and Kenneth Rogoff explain, the relative calm that characterised the period between the late 1940s and early 1970s 'may be partly explained by booming world growth, but perhaps more so by the repression of the domestic financial markets (in varying degrees) and the heavy-handed use of capital controls that followed for many years after World War II'.[52] Throughout the 1970s, though, as neoliberalism gained strength worldwide, the United States, other Western governments and the international financial institutions (such as the IMF and the World Bank) began to take an increasingly critical view of capital controls. The idea was that capital account liberalisation would allow for more efficient global allocation of capital, from capital-rich industrial countries to capital-poor developing economies. Thus, throughout the 1980s and 1990s, most of the restrictions limiting movement of capital were lifted, with Europe leading the way. As a result, financial crises started reoccurring with increased frequency, especially in the developing world. This has led the IMF to reverse its long-standing position on capital controls – somewhat. In a 2010 Staff Paper, the IMF argued that capital inflow surges compromise sound macroeconomic management, by pushing the exchange rate up and undermining trade competitiveness.[53] It also acknowledged that 'large capital inflows may lead to excessive foreign borrowing and foreign currency exposure, possibly fueling domestic credit booms (especially foreign exchange denominated lending) and asset bubbles (with significant adverse effects in the case of a sudden reversal)'.[54] It concluded that 'if the flows are likely to be transitory, then use of capital controls ... is justified as part of the policy toolkit to manage inflows'.[55]

More recently the IMF further developed its position, claiming that FDI that 'may include a transfer of technology or human capital' can 'boost long-term growth'.[56] Speculative debt inflows, on the other hand, not only increase the likelihood of 'a crash' but also increase inequality and reduce growth, and warrant the use of direct controls on capital movements. The IMF acknowledges that capital controls are particularly useful for countries that have little room for economic manoeuvre, such as those that are part of a fixed exchange rate system, because they are less equipped to deal with economic shocks.[57] However, even in a flexible exchange rate regime, capital controls can be used to isolate capital inflows that support productive investment from speculative inflows, and to avoid destabilising exchange rate swings. It is our position that financial flows that are not connected to the real economy and are unproductive in nature, along with a whole other range of financial transactions that drive cross-border capital flows, should not simply be 'controlled' – they should be declared illegal (the issue of financial repression is discussed in further detail in Chapter 10). This may be considered an extreme form of direct control. Ideally, this should be introduced on a multilateral basis spanning all nations rather than being imposed on a country-by-country basis. However, in the absence of such international commitments, nations should consider unilaterally imposing capital controls as beneficial bulwarks against the destructive forces of speculative financial capital. While it is usually claimed that imposing such controls would automatically cut a country off from access to international capital markets, plunging the nation into autarchy, the experience of various countries (including a number of European countries) that have reimposed capital controls in recent years disproves this claim. Indeed, the evidence shows that countries that employed constraints on surging capital inflows fared better than countries with open capital accounts in the recent global financial crisis.[58]

Finally, it should be noted that there are countries – such as extremely underdeveloped countries that can only access limited quantities of real resources relative to their population and are highly dependent on imports of food and other life-sustaining goods – where the well-being of their citizens cannot be solved within those nations' own borders, especially if their export potential is limited, regardless of the measures that the country may employ to protect itself from speculative capital flows and reduce its dependence on imports. These countries may find no market for their currencies and may be forced to trade in foreign currencies. In this sense, it should be noted that not all currencies are equal. In this context, a new multilateral institution should be created to replace both the World Bank and the IMF, which is charged with the responsibility of ensuring that these highly disadvantaged nations can access essential real resources such as food and not be priced out of international markets due to exchange rate fluctuations that arise from trade deficits. This is discussed in more detail in the next section of this chapter.

A NEW INTERNATIONAL FRAMEWORK

MMT shows that the ultimate constraint on prosperity is the real resources that a nation can command, which includes the skills of its people and its natural resource inventory. If a country's resource base is very limited, there is relatively little that a country can do to pull itself out of poverty, even if the government productively deploys all the resources available to the nation. However, this is not a balance-of-payments constraint in the classical sense. It is a *real resource constraint* arising from the unequal distribution of resources across geographic space and the somewhat arbitrary lines that have been drawn across that space to delineate sovereign states. The world must take responsibility to ensure that it alleviates any real resource constraints that operate through the balance of payments.

Imposing austerity on these countries is no solution. The evidence shows that the structural adjustment programmes (SAPs) that the IMF and World Bank typically impose on poor nations struggling with balance-of-payments problems – based upon fiscal austerity, elimination of food subsidies, increase in the price of public services, wage reductions, trade and market liberalisation, deregulation, privatisation of state-owned assets, etc. – have had a disastrous social, economic and environmental impact wherever they have been applied. Not only have they 'reduced health, nutritional, and educational levels for tens of millions of children in Asia, Latin America, and Africa', as a UNICEF study concludes;[59] they also foisted upon these nations unsustainable levels of external debt, which were then used to justify the imposition of destructive export-led production strategies that in many cases devastated the existing subsistence systems and led to large-scale environmental ruin (for example, massive deforestation in Mali). Masqueraded as development programmes, SAPs have actually acted as giant siphons, sucking out wealth and resources from these countries and pumping it into the pockets of the rich elites and corporations in the US, Europe and elsewhere. To add insult to injury, in many instances these policies also wrecked the borrowing countries' local productive sectors, thus creating increased import and debt dependencies.

Clearly, the IMF and the World Bank have outgrown their original purpose and have ceased to play any positive role in the management of world affairs. Rather, their interventions have undermined prosperity and impoverished millions of people across the world, and continue to do so – mostly, but not exclusively (as the IMF's participation in Greece's bailout programme testifies), in the developing world. In this context, we contend that a new multilateral institution (or series of institutions) should be created to replace both the World Bank and the IMF, charged with the responsibility of ensuring that these highly disadvantaged nations can access essential real resources such as food. There are two essential functions that need to be served at the multilateral level:

- Development aid – providing funds to develop public infrastructure, education, health services and governance support.
- Macroeconomic stabilisation – the provision of liquidity to prevent exchange rate crises in the face of problematic balance of payments.

While these functions seem to align with those currently provided by the World Bank and IMF, a progressive approach to these problems would not resemble the operational procedures currently in place. With regard to the provision of development aid, the starting point for a revised sustainable development strategy should be the complete cancellation of the debt hitherto incurred by (imposed upon) developing nations. In the future, as recommended by a 2000 report by the US Congress' International Financial Institution Advisory Commission, performance-based grants – whereby funds are granted after certain outcomes are achieved, not in order to implement an agreed set of actions – should replace traditional conditionality-based loans. In a follow-up article, two of the Commission's leading economists argued that:

Performance-based grants would cost the same as traditional loans but they would deliver more benefits to the global poor. Grants would make programs effective, monitor output, pay only for results, prevent accumulation of unpayable debt, forestall diversion of funds for unproductive ends and protect donor nation contributions from risk of loss.[60]

They would also prevent the build-up of unsustainable debt because 'there can be no outlay without benefits and no continuing financial liability if projects fail'. A progressive developmental model should also reject the current export-led corporate farming models, which are implicated in environmental degradation within less developed countries. There are many dimensions to this phenomenon, including deforestation, genetic engineering, increased use of dangerous pesticides and irrigation schemes that deplete aquifers. A progressive multilateral institution would aim to reduce (and ultimately eliminate) poverty through economic development, but within an environmentally sustainable frame. It would also allow countries to restrict imports from nations that engage in poor environmental practices – an approach that the WTO has repeatedly deemed illegal. Further, developing nations should have the right to defend and sustain their local industries. The more recent trade theories show that the presence of increasing returns to scale – where output rises proportionately more than any increase in inputs, coupled with network effects, where the creation of critical mass provides significant benefits to consumers – justifies the protection of local (and particularly nascent) industries, through the imposition of selective tariffs.[61] Indeed, contrary to the claim that trade liberalisation promotes growth, the evidence indicates a positive relationship between tariffs and economic growth in developing economies.[62] As seen in Chapter 5, no advanced nation achieved that status by following the IMF/World Bank free-market approach; rather, it did so through widespread industrial protection and government controls and supports.

Even though the post-war period saw the introduction of a series of agreements relating to the liberalisation of international trade (such as the General Agreement on Trade and Tariffs (GATT), which paved the way to the creation of the WTO in 1995), the trade landscape continued to remain laced with state intervention and protectionist policies. In fact, there has been an almost dichotomised development process among rich and poor nations, which dates back to the colonial era. The poorer nations (typically under (neo-)colonial rule) had 'free trade' forced upon them with concomitantly poor outcomes, while the (neo-)colonial powers adopted heavily protectionist positions. Further, while tariffs have come down under successive GATT and WTO rounds, the global trading terrain has been anything but level. Rich nations such as the US still maintain a complex array of tariffs on goods attempting to enter their borders. Japan, for example, maintains a highly protectionist stance with respect to its primary products (particularly rice). These cases are generalised across most nations. The reality is there for all to see: economic growth has fallen on average as the neoliberal regime has been extended; where so-called 'liberalisation' has been most acute, this fall has been larger. A progressive developmental policy should reject this approach flat-out and recognise the right of developing countries to choose their developmental path autonomously, with due regard for each countries' customs, traditions, standards and priorities. This, as history shows, will likely entail the use of 'illiberal' trade practices such as export subsidies, import controls, restrictions on capital flows, directed credit, etc.[63]

In this regard, a progressive trade policy would also ban the ISDS clauses embedded in the more recent wave of trade agreements. As previously noted, these create mechanisms through which international corporations can take out legal action against governments if they believe that a particular piece of legislation or regulation threatens their opportunities for profit. This undermines the capacity of states to regulate in the public interest in a number of areas, including labour market regulation (job protection, minimum wages, etc.), the cost of medical supplies, financial market oversight, environmental protection and standards relating to food quality. The underlying assumption is that the interests of international capital should take precedence over any other consideration. Furthermore, there is very little evidence that these agreements generate benefits in terms of growth, jobs and/or exports.[64] A progressive agenda would ban these agreements and force corporations to act within the legal constraints of the nations they seek to operate within or sell into. More generally, the current free trade framework – which pays little or no attention to labour or environmental standards and fuels a 'race to the bottom' model, where workers in poor nations are paid poverty-level wages and work in appalling and dangerous conditions, while regions in developed nations are hollowed out with entrenched unemployment and increasing poverty and social alienation – needs to be rejected in favour of a fair trade framework. The WTO has consistently avoided the inclusion of strict labour standards in its agreements, as it maintains the view that low-wage countries attract capital as a result of their comparative advantage, which leads to their development. The evidence is not supportive of this belief.[65] Corporations staunchly resist the introduction of global labour standards because they know that this would undermine the global labour arbitrage that is at the basis of their strategy of profit capture. Under a fair trade framework, all countries should respect the following principles:

- Good working conditions – wages, safety, hours.
- Right to association and to strike – formation of trade unions, etc.
- Consumer protection – safety, ethical standards, quality of product or service, etc.
- Environmental standards.

Under these conditions, what we would actually have is 'fair trade' rather than the type of trading arrangements embodied in the raft of so-called free trade agreements. To this end, the WTO should be replaced by an all-encompassing multilateral body that is charged with establishing relevant labour and environmental standards to regulate trade. While it is recognised that nations at different stages of development will have different productive methods, working standards that are acceptable across cultures can be devised. For example, in advanced countries road building is highly mechanised with high capital-to-labour ratios relative to Africa, where labour-intensive methods are better because they can produce the same standard of output with more labour. However, within these differences, some standards remain common – the right to association, the right to adequate rest and breaks, the right to holidays, the right to fair pay, the right to strike. It is beyond the scope of this book to define all the operational details, but the general principle is clear – trade should not be allowed if it violates the principles listed above. Under fair trade principles, a nation allowing capitalist firms to deny basic workers' rights becomes a sufficient condition to block trade with that nation. In this sense, the MMT view of trade – according to which imports represent a benefit (goods and services otherwise unattainable), in a materialistic sense, while exports represent a cost (real resources used by foreigners rather than domestic citizens) – does not militate against our critique of 'free trade'. Indeed, it strengthens it.

Even though, generally speaking, exports are a cost and imports are a benefit, the framework within which we make those assessments is multi-dimensional and extends the concept of material progress in ways that mainstream economics typically ignores. For example, a commercial transaction that is only considered in terms of the use value that consumers receive may involve massive damage to the producing community. So while an imported good or service might be seen in narrow terms to be a 'benefit' for the consumer, once we broaden our assessment of the costs and benefits of the overall chain of production and consumption a more nuanced view will emerge. By adopting principles that take into account the actual costs of production – including damage to the environment, destruction of local sustainable industry, damage to human dignity, etc. – the benefits of the import for a consumer will pale into insignificance relative to the costs for a producer. In these cases, import controls may be justified to limit the damage to the less developed nation, despite the material benefits to the more developed nation. A more progressive stance, however, would be to recognise that there are circumstances in which it is in the global interest to restrict the capacity of a nation to export, for example by paying a country to avoid engaging in destructive practices such as coal mining and deforestation, thus reducing the impact on that country's exporting capacities, particularly on the communities involved. A progressive policy framework has to allow all workers access to work, and the poorest members in each nation opportunities for upward mobility, if jobs are destroyed as part of an overall strategy to redress matters of global concern (whether to advance labour, environmental or broader issues). Part of these transition arrangements might also include more generous foreign aid to ensure that trade constraints do not interrupt international efforts to relieve world poverty. In general, a single nation should not be punished for the uneven pattern of geographic resource distribution.

With regard to the question of macroeconomic stabilisation – that is, the provision of liquidity to countries struggling with balance-of-payments problems – a progressive multilateral institution would recognise that all nations should maintain sovereign currencies and float them on international markets, but at the same time acknowledge that capital flows may be problematic at certain times and that some nations require more or less permanent assistance due to their limited export capacities and domestic resource bases. The starting point would be to recognise that as long as there are real resources available for use in a nation, its government can purchase them using its currency power. That includes all idle labour. So, there is no reason to have involuntary unemployment in any nation, no matter how poor its non-labour resources are. The government in each country could easily purchase these services with the local currency without placing pressure on labour costs in the country. A new multilateral institutional structure should work within that reality rather than use unemployment as a weapon to discipline local cost structures. In the case of a nation that is highly dependent on imported food and/or energy, the role of the international agency would be to buy the local currency to ensure that the exchange rate does not price the poor out of food. The international community would agree that this support would be ongoing and unconditional so long as the link between the imported food and/or energy and the foreign exchange intervention is clear. Moreover, the current conditionality requirements – spanning fiscal outcomes, interest rates, monetary growth, etc. – need to be abandoned.

This is a simple solution that is preferable to forcing these nations to run austerity campaigns just to keep their exchange rate higher. Furthermore, new international agreements are needed to outlaw speculation by investment banks on food and other essential commodities. More generally, a new framework is needed at the international level to ban illegal speculative financial flows that have no necessary relationship with improving the operation of the real economy. However, as mentioned, in the absence of such international commitments, nations should consider unilaterally imposing capital controls. Finally, this new multilateral institution would not force nations to cut taxes for high-income earners in return for aid, which is another bias in current IMF and World Bank interventions. It would recognise that the role of taxation is to create non-inflationary space for the sovereign government to command real resources in order to fulfil its socio-economic programme. The reality is that there are many idle resources in the poorer nations – land, people and materials – that can be bought by government and mobilised to reduce poverty without causing inflation. Finally, it should be acknowledged that these nations will likely have to run continuous fiscal and current account deficits for many years to allow the non-government sector to accumulate financial assets and provide a better risk management framework. A progressive international agency would help them to do just that.

I Have a Job For You:
Why a Job Guarantee is
Better than a Basic Income

There is a quasi-consensus among progressives that the solution to most of the social ills of modern capitalism – poverty, income insecurity, unemployment – lies in the provision of a universal basic income (UBI): that is, an income unconditionally granted by the state to all citizens on an individual basis, irrespective of income. This idea has gathered strength in recent years due to the widespread belief that we are on the verge of a 'second machine age' that, unlike the first machine age – the industrial revolution – will render obsolete most of human involvement in the production process, not simply in the manufacturing sector – where the process has been ongoing for a long time – but also, crucially, in the service sector, potentially taking over millions of jobs for which human 'cognitive functions' were hitherto deemed indispensable, thanks to the development of highly intelligent software-driven machines and robots. It is claimed that the capacity of these new machines to replace human tasks is unlike anything that we have previously witnessed and exceeds the ability of humans to envisage and create new jobs that will replace those displaced by robots.

The IMF recently published an article arguing that the second machine age or 'robot revolution could have profound negative implications for equality'.[1] The conventional economic argument deployed by the IMF is based on a competitive labour market framework where the introduction of robots, which are perfect or near-perfect substitutes for human labour, effectively increases the supply of 'labour' and thus inevitably leads to higher unemployment and lower wages – hence the term technological unemployment. According to this line of reasoning, the second machine age raises the question – even from a mainstream perspective – of how to maintain sufficient levels of income and aggregate demand in the face of massive unemployment and declining wages. According to the IMF – and, interestingly, to most progressives – the solution lies in taxing the rising income on capital and then redistributing that income via the introduction of a UBI guarantee. As we will see, however, there are serious problems both with the 'machines will cause mass unemployment' narrative as well as with the notion that the solution to this (alleged) problem lies in a UBI.

With regard to the former, the American economist David Autor, who is a leading authority on the issue of automation and employment, recently concluded that the substitution process is likely to be finite 'because there are many tasks that people understand tacitly and accomplish effortlessly but for which neither computer programmers nor anyone else can enunciate the explicit "rules" or procedures'.[2] He refers to this as 'Polanyi's paradox'. In his 1966 book, *The Tacit Dimension*, the economist-turned-philosopher Michael Polanyi wrote that we should 'reconsider human knowledge by starting from the fact that *we can know more than we can tell*'.[3] Accordingly, he conjectured that much of human knowledge is 'tacit' in nature and that the rules that allow us to 'know' things 'cannot be put into words'.[4] In a sense, we don't know why we know things. Much of our knowledge is the product of culture and tradition that is infused into our subconscious and filters reality in particular ways that we are not immediately aware of. This is the tacit dimension. Polanyi's thesis, if correct, has significant ramifications for the claim that robots will take over the labour market. Autor says that '[f]ollowing Polanyi's observation, the tasks that have proved most vexing to automate are those demanding flexibility, judgment, and common sense – skills that we understand only tacitly'.[5]

Accordingly, he notes that the implications about the use of robots go beyond a discussion of the extent of substitution of machine for labour. He argues that 'jobs are made up of many tasks and while automation and computerisation can substitute for some of them, understanding the interaction between technology and employment requires thinking about more than just substitution'.[6] In other words, there are tasks that rely on our tacit knowledge, which constrains the capacity of robots to replace humans in the workplace. Those who argue that the second machine age is somehow different must also demonstrate that the new wave of technologies has been able to overcome the Polanyi constraint.

Autor expects that 'a significant stratum of middle-skill jobs combining specific vocational skills with foundational middle-skill levels of literacy, numeracy, adaptability, problem solving, and common sense will persist in coming decades'.[7] As we will see, the state has a central responsibility in this regard.

More generally, the 'robots will rule the world' argument sidesteps entirely the question of human and political agency. Of course, robots are becoming increasingly advanced and will probably be able to replace humans – particularly unskilled and low-skilled workers – in a number of areas. However, this is not a new phenomenon – it has been ongoing since the capitalists worked out better ways of securing the surplus production. But just as children were banned from the workplace in advanced nations as an act of social policy, the state has the capacity to determine how new technologies are deployed. We produce highly technological vehicles that can reach dizzying speeds but we force them to obey limits that are well below their overall capacity. Why? Because we empower the state to protect our common interests. If robots and computers threaten our very survival then it is rather far-fetched to expect that we will allow states to be totally compliant and allow robots to take over and completely drive out humans from the workplace. There will always be options and alternatives; it is the role of the state to create a legal framework that advances the overall interests of citizens.

While innovations in technology will free humans from repetitive and mind-numbing work and improve productivity in those tasks, there is no reason to believe that robots are destined to develop outside the legislative framework overseen by the state. Such arguments are in denial of the basic capacities of the state to legislate in the common interest. In this sense, the claim that robots will inevitably cause mass unemployment and wage stagnation is just as deceptive as the mainstream claim that the divergence between productivity growth and employment and wage growth witnessed from the 1970s onwards – the so-called 'great decoupling' – is an inevitable and unavoidable consequence of the 'changing nature of technological progress'.[8] In fact, as seen in Chapter 5, this divergence has much more to do with the war on labour waged by capital in the neoliberal era – which has succeeded in generating high levels of labour underutilisation as a way of disciplining workers – than with technological change per se. In other words, it was a political choice. The same is true today.

A more appropriate question when confronting the issue of disruptive innovation is how to help those displaced, unskilled workers transition into alternative skills and jobs. A progressive state needs a framework to support those transitions – what we call a 'just transition framework'. Where possible, workers should be assisted through education and training structures to find work in new high- and middle-end jobs. This would ensure that the costs of economic restructuring due to the second machine age – and to other challenges, such as the shift to more sustainable production processes to deal with the issues of climate change and environmental degradation – are shared across society rather than shouldered solely by specific categories of workers and their communities. Moreover, should it not prove possible to transition all workers into private sector high- and middle-skill jobs, then *alternative jobs will need to be created directly by the state*, and alternative visions of productive work developed. This is where the job guarantee comes into play, which we will talk about further on.

As we will see, basic income proposals do not provide a coherent or progressive response to the challenges posed by technological unemployment. There is some truth to the claim that automation is likely to render the *private sector* structurally unable to provide full employment, particularly in the transition phase, regardless of governments' efforts to retrain workers and maintain sufficient levels of demand in the economy through deficit spending. However, we will argue that it would be a mistake for progressives to passively accept the end of wage labour as an inevitable – even desirable, some would say – aspect of technological progress, as most proponents of basic income do; instead, the task of progressives should be to develop new types of employment, in accord with the human need to work and with inclusive societal goals, and more generally to develop a framework for radically re-envisaging the concept of productive work. We will now elucidate why we don't consider basic income to be a progressive solution to the problem of income insecurity and why we consider it to be an acceptance of the inevitability of mass unemployment – and thus a surrendering to the mainstream narrative. We will illustrate why it is deeply flawed from both a theoretical as well as technical standpoint, and usually reflects a failure to understand the capacity of currency-issuing states to expand employment. Finally, we will demonstrate that a job guarantee, from a progressive standpoint, is a superior approach to basic income in virtually all respects.

UNIVERSAL BASIC INCOME: FALSE PREMISES,
ERROR-PRONE MACROECONOMICS

The UBI – or basic income guarantee – proposal has been advocated by a diversity of interests on both sides of the political spectrum. Tracing the origins of the UBI proposal reveals that the motivations of its proponents at different periods of history have varied wildly, from those who desire(d) to cut government spending and push the responsibility of maintaining 'welfare' on to individuals, to those who believe(d) that unemployment is a violation of justice but there is little governments can do about it, to, more recently, those who invoke trepidation about the so-called second machine age. Voices from the left and the right weave various aspects of these motivations, often in overlapping ways, to justify their demands for a basic income to be paid by the state to all individuals. One of the pioneers of basic income was the British socialite and conservative activist Juliet Rhys-Williams. Rhys-Williams was a member of the Beveridge Committee, which sought to reform the British system of income support in the early 1940s and would later develop the framework that would become the post-war welfare state in Britain. The idea advanced by the committee was that a system of flat-rate social insurance contributions would underpin a flat-rate benefit scheme. Critics opposed to a large government arm claimed that these systems were complex, costly and promoted category bias (where a person would nurture characteristics that allowed them to 'fit' into one benefit category or another to ensure they gained the income support).

Rhys-Williams was a dissenting voice on the Beveridge Committee and resisted the proposed solution to income support. Instead, she put forward a negative income tax scheme, which in her view would eliminate the need for a welfare state by providing a guaranteed minimum income with tax incentives to earn further income.[9] Her motivation was to reduce the size and footprint of government while at the same time providing a means for reducing poverty, a major concern for conservatives of her era (which has been lost in the neoliberal era). The former motivation also underpinned Milton Friedman's later proposal for a negative income tax, where an individual would receive a refund of any unused tax deductions/ allowances up to some small maximum amount (the guaranteed income component) and then face a declining subsidy up to the threshold where he/she would pay full taxes on earned income.[10] For Friedman, the guaranteed component needed to be small because he argued that if the subsidy component was too generous the incentives would not motivate people to look for employment. Importantly, Friedman considered the cause of poverty to be excessive state intervention in the economy. Thus, he saw 'basic income' as a means to reduce the role of government to a minimum, by eliminating social programmes and replacing them with private welfare provisions. Friedman specifically argued that 'if enacted as a substitute for the present rag bag of measures directed at the same end, the total administrative burden would surely be reduced.'[11] Friedman went on to list some of the measures he would hope to eliminate: direct welfare payments and programmes of all kinds, old age assistance, social security, aid to dependent children, public housing, veterans' benefits, minimum-wage laws and public health programmes, hospitals and mental institutions.

Not all basic income proponents see it as a way of shrinking the state, of course. On the left side of the political spectrum, progressive supporters of basic income are mostly motivated by a desire to solve the problem of poverty and income insecurity. They highlight the fact that if there is a lack of employment alternatives available to citizens, then the provision of an unconditional basic income would be the easiest and most direct means of eliminating poverty and income insecurity. However, an effective solution to the problem requires that we understand 'the underlying rather than proximate causes of income insecurity.'[12] How we construct the problem conditions the way that we attempt to solve it. In this sense, Mitchell and Watts note that '[i]t is easy to pose a "false problem" and then develop rhetoric to "solve it"'.[13] Moreover, to assemble an array of possible solutions, we must understand the power that a currency-issuing state has in terms of solving the underlying causes. If we have an ill-informed understanding of those capacities we are prone to define the possible policy set too narrowly and thus exclude preferred solutions. As we will see, practically all basic income proposals fall short when it comes to identifying the structural causes of unemployment and the instruments available to governments to solve them, which in turn reflects a failure to understand the operational reality of modern fiat economies.

The basic income approach to income insecurity is based on what Mitchell and Watts call a 'false premise and a curious inconsistency'.[14] While basic income proponents concentrate on income security as an end in itself, those who promote the job guarantee consider income insecurity to be a manifestation of a broader problem in capitalism – a deliberately engineered lack of employment growth. The existence and persistence of mass unemployment and the link to income insecurity is generally recognised by basic income advocates, but the former is rarely explained. An exception is leading basic income advocate Philippe Van Parijs. Drawing on mainstream neoclassical economic theory, Van Parijs argues that unemployment arises because wage rigidities don't allow wages to be reduced when there is an excess supply of labour (that is, unemployment).[15] In his conception, unemployment exists because the going wage is too high relative to the productivity level, and therefore firms are unwilling to offer jobs to all those seeking to work at the current wage level; because wages cannot easily be cut, unemployment persists and becomes endemic. In short, Van Parijs considers unemployment to be caused by a departure from an alleged competitive equilibrium rather than any macroeconomic failure – that is, an aggregate spending deficiency. In other words, there is no recognition that mass unemployment is the result of a deficiency of total spending in the economy, resulting from the fiscal deficit being too low (or surplus being too high, depending on the circumstances in the non-government sector). This is reflective of a wider trend among progressive thinkers: by failing to understand that unemployment is largely the result of defective macroeconomic policy, they end up accepting job scarcity as an inevitability (without understanding what is driving the jobs shortage in the first place) and thus turn to basic income schemes to assuage their well-meaning equity concerns. Basic income proponents move in lockstep with the mainstream narratives in this regard.

This leads them to commit another mistake. Because they fail to understand the reality of modern money – that is, they operate under the assumption that currency-issuing governments are financially constrained – their proposals for remedying income insecurity are also deeply flawed. One of the sensitive issues for UBI proponents, for example, is its perceived 'cost'. Accordingly, the mainstream UBI literature advocates the introduction of a basic income within a so-called 'fiscally neutral' environment – that is, by financing it through taxation rather than deficit spending (with differing opinions as to who should 'fund' the programme). Given that mass unemployment is the result of inadequate aggregate spending, a basic income proposal of this nature would solidify or lock the nation into entrenched states of capacity wastage and merely replace the income support for the unemployed with the basic income. Furthermore, focusing on the 'cost' of the programme is likely to lead the basic income to be set at a level too low to lift people out of poverty.[16] It is also highly unlikely that labour participation rates would fall significantly with the introduction of a modest UBI, given the rising participation of women in part-time work (desiring higher family incomes) and the strong commitment to find work among the unemployed. So the suppression of net government spending that would accompany the introduction of a 'fiscally neutral' basic income would likely increase, not reduce, unemployment.[17] However, there could be an increase in the supply of part-time labour via full-timers reducing work hours and combining the UBI with earned income.

In that context, employers in the secondary (casualised, part-time) labour market will probably utilise this increase in the part-time labour supply to exploit the implicit UBI subsidy to further reduce wages, thus implying a redistribution of income from labour to capital. Even basic income advocates have acknowledged this probability.[18] Thus, the introduction of a basic income guarantee is likely to exacerbate the trend away from full-time work towards low-wage, low-productivity part-time jobs, deskilling and, ultimately, falling average material living standards. Thus, even a substantial basic income guarantee, if introduced in a 'fiscally neutral' environment, would have a relatively small impact on aggregate spending and employment; high levels of labour underutilisation would be likely to persist. This kind of basic income proposal thus has little to offer those that, if given a chance, would choose to work rather than take the basic income. Mitchell and Watts conclude that '[o]verall this strategy does not enhance the rights of the most disadvantaged, nor does it provide work for those who desire it'.[19]

It was recently reported that the CEOs of various big IT companies are beginning to fear 'a backlash when it comes to jobs' as they introduce new job-destroying technologies.[20] We are back to the 'robots are coming to take all your jobs' story, which has become one of the distractions that conservatives and progressives alike have fallen prey to, further distancing the issue of unemployment from government responsibility. As a result, many CEOs are now calling for a UBI because 'tech firms could be in the "firing line"'. It is argued that this 'will provide a bare minimum of living. Instead, workers will still want to get a higher standard of living by working.'[21] The logic is hard to follow, however: if the UBI is justified because robots are taking all the jobs, where will the supplemental labour income come from to ensure that the UBI is not a poverty confinement? The motivation of CEOs is clearly to maintain social control – to offer people enough food and other things to keep them alive so they won't rebel and challenge the biases in income distribution that have led to dramatically increased shares taken by capital and high-income cohorts.

Many of these problems, of course, could be overcome if the basic income were introduced within a functional finance paradigm – that is, if it were accompanied by a net government stimulus (deficit), in the knowledge that a currency-issuing government faces no revenue or solvency constraints when making its spending decisions. In this scenario, persistent unemployment could be avoided if the income guarantee was sufficient to motivate the unemployed to drop out of the labour force and take the income guarantee. But this implies a bizarre concept of full employment: mass unemployment would be solved by engineering an artificial withdrawal of the available labour supply, so that some of the unemployed are reclassified as not in the labour force and in receipt of a basic income allocation instead. Moreover, a basic income of this kind – sufficiently generous and funded by an increasing fiscal deficit – would raise serious issues from an inflationary standpoint. In a modern monetary economy, the inflation risk is related to the relationship between nominal spending growth (demand) and the capacity of the economy to respond to that demand with an increased supply of real goods and services. Within a functional finance paradigm, the government uses its fiscal capacity to increase overall spending in the economy to avoid mass unemployment. The target is output and employment growth rather than any particular fiscal outcome (in monetary terms). We have seen that mass unemployment arises when the fiscal deficit is inadequate to offset the desire of the non-government sector to save overall. Following that logic, if there is mass unemployment, then the solution is for the government to expand its net fiscal impact (spending over taxation) and allow the deficit to rise.

To reduce unemployment, the introduction of a basic income would therefore require a net government stimulus (that is, an increasing fiscal deficit). A deficit-funded UBI of this kind, however, would lack any in-built price stabilisation mechanisms (inflation anchor) and would thus lead to inflationary pressures. Let us see why. Workers who draw income from the production cycle have also added output (via their labour) to that cycle. For a given level of productivity (output per unit of input), the more people that have access to income without adding input (that is, are supported in real terms by the production of others), the greater the inflation risk. To put it differently, the greater the share of income generated in any period that is received by people who offer nothing in return, the higher the inflation risk. Under these circumstances, the more people pursue the 'freedom' of non-work under the basic income guarantee, the worse the situation becomes, because this means that the supply side of the economy keeps shrinking while the demand side remains stable (depending on the level of the stipend). The real resource space available for the stimulus is thus reduced. Moreover, the excess demand for goods would be increasingly met via imports, with consequential effects for the exchange rate and the domestic price level, which would accentuate the inflationary pressure. To minimise the inflation risk, the basic income stipend would have to be relatively small, which, in turn, would mean that the scheme would be unable to offer a dignified and/or independent life to the recipients. They would be freed from work but not poverty. These economic outcomes are consistent with indiscriminate (generalised) Keynesian policy expansions of the past. The conclusion is that the introduction of a basic income policy is likely to be highly problematic with respect to its capacity to deliver both sustained full employment and price stability.

The job guarantee, by way of contrast, is designed to provide an explicit inflation anchor and allows the government to continuously maintain full employment and provide a decent wage to those whom, from time to time, will be in the job guarantee pool. It does not rely on poverty wages or unemployment to maintain price stability. That alone is a fundamental advantage of the job guarantee over the basic income guarantee – it is sustainable.

THE JOB GUARANTEE:
A SIMPLE CONCEPT WITH FAR-REACHING CONSEQUENCES

The initial observation is that the job guarantee (JG) is designed on the basis of an explicit recognition that a monetarily sovereign government is never revenue- or solvency-constrained because it is the monopoly issuer of the currency. Starting from this point conditions the narrative that can be developed to support the introduction of a JG. It frees its proponents from arcane debates about whether the government can 'afford' the scheme or not – a problem most basic income proposals suffer from. The JG is a simple concept with far-reaching consequences. It involves the government making an *unconditional job offer to anyone who is willing to work* at a socially acceptable minimum wage and who cannot find work elsewhere. It is based on the assumption that if the private sector is unable to create sufficient job opportunities then the public sector has to stand ready to provide the necessary employment. This creates a buffer stock of paid jobs that expands (declines) when private sector activity declines (expands).

To avoid disturbing the private sector wage structure, and to ensure that the job guarantee is consistent with stable inflation, the JG wage rate is set at the minimum-wage level, defined to ensure the worker is not socially excluded. The government thus purchases labour 'off the bottom' of the non-government wage distribution. Since the JG wage is open to everyone, it effectively becomes the national minimum wage. The minimum-wage level should be an expression of what any given society deems to be the lowest acceptable material standard of living. Similar considerations should determine the appropriate basic income stipend, although the capacity of the government to maintain such a stipend without inflation is limited at best, as we have seen. JG workers would thus enjoy stable incomes, and their increased spending would boost confidence throughout the economy and underpin a private-spending recovery. By maintaining a buffer stock of employment, the JG operates according to what economists term 'a fixed price/floating quantity rule'. This means that the government's unconditional job offer is at a fixed wage (the fixed-price rule) and the buffer stock of jobs fluctuates in accordance with the strength of non-government sector spending (a floating quantity). Given that the JG hires at a fixed price in exchange for hours of work and does not compete with private sector wages, employment redistributions between the private sector and the buffer stock can always be achieved to stabilise any wage inflation in the non-JG sector. So the fundamental difference in relation to inflation between the basic income proposals and the JG is that the former spends on a quantity rule (the stimulus competes with other market prices), while the latter spends on a price rule (spending is in the form of a fixed-price offer to idle resources with no market bid).

Once the scheme is in operation, the anti-inflation mechanisms are easy to understand. If there are inflationary pressures developing in the non-government sector as it reaches full capacity, the government would manipulate its fiscal and monetary policy settings to constrain non-government sector spending to prevent the economy from over-heating. This would see labour being transferred from the inflating non-government sector to the 'fixed wage' JG sector and eventually this would resolve the inflationary pressures. Clearly, when unemployment is high this situation will not arise, since by definition this means that there is no non-government sector demand for idle resources. In general, there cannot be inflationary pressures arising from a policy that sees the government offering a fixed wage to any labour that is unwanted by other employers. By not competing with the non-government market for resources, the JG thus avoids the inflationary tendencies of traditional Keynesian pump-priming, which attempts to maintain full capacity utilisation by 'hiring off the top' – that is, by competing for resources at market prices and relying on so-called spending multipliers to generate the extra jobs necessary to achieve full employment. Of course, it is likely that without the threat of unemployment, private sector workers may have fewer incentives to moderate their wage demands, which may lead to wage–price pressures. But JG workers would retain higher skill levels than those who are forced to succumb to lengthy spells of unemployment. The JG workers would thus constitute a more credible threat to the current non-government sector employees than those who languish in the unemployment pool. When wage pressures mount, an employer would be more likely to exercise resistance if he/she could hire from the fixed-price JG pool. The only question facing the JG is whether there is enough real capacity in the economy – available resources and output space – for the extra government spending. The existence of idle workers in most countries is strong evidence that there is ample non-inflationary scope to spend. Further, the government knows when it has spent enough. Under the JG, the last person who seeks a job on any particular day defines how much government spending is required to ensure that there are enough jobs available.

While it is easy to characterise the JG as purely a public sector job-creation strategy designed to reduce income insecurity, it is important to appreciate that it is actually a macroeconomic policy framework designed to deliver full employment *and* price stability based on the principle of buffer stocks, where job creation and destruction is but one component. It is thus a macroeconomic stability framework rather than an ad hoc crisis response. The JG also provides the economy with a powerful 'automatic stabiliser' – a characteristic missing from the basic income guarantee concept. Government employment and spending automatically increases (decreases) as jobs are lost (gained) in the non-government sector. The JG thus fulfils an absorption function to minimise the employment and income losses currently associated with the flux in non-government sector spending. When non-government sector employment declines, public sector employment will automatically react and increase its payrolls. The nation always remains fully employed, with only the mix between non-government and public sector employment fluctuating as it responds to the spending decisions of the non-government sector. In short, the JG provides the government with a powerful inflation control mechanism, while avoiding the massive costs of unemployment. In this sense, it represents a minimum spending approach to full employment. Importantly, the JG does not replace conventional use of fiscal policy to achieve social and economic outcomes. The government should indeed supplement the JG wage with a wide range of social expenditures, including adequate levels of public education, health and childcare, etc. Further, as we will see, the provision of large-scale public infrastructure remains crucial; the introduction of a JG does not undermine the capacity of the government to pursue these projects.

What kind of jobs would/could the JG offer? First and foremost, it could provide jobs that are inclusive to the most disadvantaged. Gregg and Layard recognise that there is a 'mass of low-tech maintenance which needs to be done on public housing, schools, hospitals and roads'.[22] Extensive research has been done in a number of countries to identify suitable JG jobs.[23] The jobs must be accessible to the least skilled workers, who typically bear the greatest burden of unemployment. The jobs should ideally not substitute existing government or private employment. Within those constraints, JG workers could still contribute in many socially useful activities, including urban renewal projects and other environmental and construction schemes (reforestation, sand dune stabilisation, river valley erosion control, etc.), personal assistance to pensioners and other community schemes. For example, creative artists could contribute to public education as peripatetic performers. As we will see further on, a crucial aspect of the JG lies precisely in the fact that it offers an opportunity for radically rethinking the very concept of work. Moreover, future labour market policy must consider the environmental risk factors associated with economic growth. Possible threshold effects and imprecise data covering the life-cycle characteristics of natural capital suggest that a risk-averse attitude is wise. Indiscriminate (Keynesian) expansion falls short in this regard because it does not address the requirements for risk aversion. It is not increased demand per se that is necessary, but *increased demand in certain areas of activity*. The JG would thus be 'green' because it would provide jobs in environmentally sustainable activities that are unlikely to be produced by traditional private sector firms.

A common critique of large-scale public sector job-creation programmes (such as the JG) is that they are inefficient – wasteful schemes that lead to the economy's resources being utilised in suboptimal ways. This critique is based on a very narrow conception of efficiency – the type that dominates mainstream economics. However, there are a number of ways in which the concept of 'efficiency' can be understood, which in turn informs the way in which one evaluates the propositions that we are advancing. Thus, in the following section we will show why the mainstream private cost-and-benefit construction of what is and is not efficient is bereft of credibility in a progressive vision that evaluates things in terms of society rather than economy, and human well-being rather than private profit. In the following sections we will therefore present what we consider to be a progressive vision of efficiency.

TOWARDS A PROGRESSIVE CONCEPT OF EFFICIENCY

According to the dominant neoliberal view, 'people and nature exist primarily to serve the economy'.[24] In the 1980s, as the neoliberal narrative gained supremacy, we began to live in economies rather than societies or communities. It was also a period during which unemployment persisted at high levels in most OECD countries. The two things are not unrelated. We have been indoctrinated to believe that government is a burden rather than being the essential facilitator for economic well-being. We support governments that deliberately constrain aggregate spending below the level necessary to maintain jobs for all, which in turn creates a class of unemployed who become dependent on increasingly pernicious welfare regimes. Income support for the unemployed used to be considered a right of citizenship and, typically, one of brief duration, as new jobs emerged with government fiscal support. In the neoliberal era, income support is vilified as skiving off the hard work of others. This narrative is reinforced on a daily basis by a virulent media, which heaps scorn on the victims of the jobs shortfall, as if the unemployed individuals were to blame for their own plight. This ridicule of the unemployed is not confined to the popular press. For example, at a November 2011 meeting of the US Federal Reserve Bank's Open Market Committee, the discussion turned to whether the unemployment problem was one of excessive drug use and poor work habits. At one point, one committee member reported that '60 percent of [job] applicants failed to answer "0" to the question of how many days a week it's acceptable to miss work'. At which point, the committee members burst into laughter.[25]

We have been dumbed down to eschew previous understandings – that systemic constraints in the form of the failure of the system to create enough jobs renders these individuals powerless to change their circumstances. We now deny a basic reality of macroeconomics: that if there are insufficient jobs being generated, someone will miss out. Instead today we lay the blame on the attitudinal deficiencies of those standing desperately in the jobless queues. We have been schooled to think in individual terms and ignore the collective. The demise of collective will in the public setting has been a principal casualty of the rise of neoliberalism. As Margaret Thatcher famously remarked: 'There is no such thing as society.'[26] Unfortunately, this mentality has also infested progressive movements and their political organisations.

In the mainstream vision, the economy is elevated to the level of a deity, whose purpose is somehow removed from the people, even though this deity recognises our endeavours and rewards us accordingly. *We serve the economy*: that is our purpose. This narrative engenders a particular concept of efficiency. Students learn by rote that a 'freely competitive market' will maximise efficiency because individuals determine how much they value particular goods and services through their desire to buy, and the prices firms offer for these goods and services are an indication of the cost of resources used in their production. The desire of consumers is to maximise their satisfaction from the goods and services they buy, while the desire of producers is to maximise their profits by minimising their costs while supplying what the consumers demand. By coming together, the two sides of the market (demand and supply) ensure that the available productive resources are allocated to production in such a way that the economy maximises the production of goods and services at the lowest cost. This is what mainstream economists consider to be a state of efficiency. It is based on the 'costs' that the private producers incur rather than the total costs of production (and so-called negative externalities, such as environmental pollution and resource depletion) and is focused on private profits and the satisfaction of those who have the resources available to facilitate purchases.

Within this framework, the plight of mass unemployment is ignored or redefined as a maximising outcome of free choices taken by rational individuals seeking to achieve the best outcomes for themselves and their families. Accordingly, mainstream economists claim that unemployment is largely a voluntary state reflecting the free choice of workers to trade off income for leisure (non-work). Rational individuals consider the benefits they gain from not working, which they construct as enjoying leisure against the costs arising from the loss of income. They are conceived as continually monitoring the wages on offer and adjusting their labour supply to maximise satisfaction. There is no hint that the economy may not offer sufficient jobs, which would render these choices, if they do indeed occur, redundant. Mainstream economists further claim that this individual choice is often distorted by the provision of income support payments by governments to the unemployed. They claim that if the government withdrew these benefits then it would alter the calculation individuals make when choosing to remain unemployed – that is, leisure would become more 'expensive' relative to work once the subsidies against job search (the income support) are withdrawn. Moreover, complex models are elaborated to demonstrate that double-digit unemployment levels, such as those registered in many eurozone countries, reflect the economy's 'natural rate of unemployment' – that is, the level of unemployment above which inflation would inevitably start to rise.

Further, economists measure success in terms of GDP, which measures the total flow of spending on goods and services over any given period valued at market prices. We continually use GDP as if it measures something that really matters. It is a vastly imperfect measure of societal well-being. According to this measure, an economy can achieve high rates of GDP growth by producing large quantities of military equipment, while polluting its natural environment, subjecting its workers to gross violations of human rights and enduring mass unemployment, high levels of income and wealth inequality, and elevated levels of poverty. Another economy can achieve low rates of GDP growth, but provide high levels of first-class health care, education and quality of life, with reduced negative impacts on the natural environment, an advanced appreciation of human rights, reductions in income and wealth inequality, and full employment. The mainstream vision tells us that the former economy is the most successful. This narrative is so powerful that progressive politicians and commentators have become seduced into offering 'fairer' alternatives to the mainstream solutions rather than challenging mainstream assumptions root-and-branch. For example, progressives timidly advocate more gradual fiscal austerity – the so-called 'austerity lite' approach – when they should be comprehensively rejecting it and advocating larger deficits to solve the massive rates of labour underutilisation that burden most economies.

So what would a *progressive concept of efficiency* look like? Just like mainstream theories, it would aim to get as much output as possible from the inputs mustered in the economy. No one wants to see human and natural resources go to waste – not even mainstream economists, in theory at least. The question is: what do we mean by 'as much output as possible'? And what are the inputs that we are acknowledging? This is what sets a progressive vision of efficiency a world apart from the narrow mainstream concept of efficiency. By placing society rather than private firms at the centre of our framework, we gain a broader understanding of the costs and benefits, which then conditions how we assess the efficiency of an activity. A progressive vision of the relationship between the people, the natural environment and the economy leads to a solidaristic and collective approach to problems, which has a deep tradition in Western societies. It recognises that an economic system can impose constraints on individuals that render them powerless. If there are not enough jobs to go around then focusing on the ascriptive characteristics of the unemployed individuals totally misses the point. Above all, it shifts our attention back on to society rather than narrowing the focus to 'the economy' and the corporations operating within it. Corporations are just one part of the economy, which is one part of the human settlement. Once we work within this vision, our notion of efficiency becomes markedly different from that espoused by the neoliberal vision. Within this construction of reality, the economy is just one part of society and it is seen as being *our* construction, with people organically embedded and nurtured by the natural environment. As Anat Shenker-Osorio notes, a progressive vision of efficiency acknowledges that:

> we, in close connection with and reliance upon our natural environment, are what really matters. ... The economy should be working on our behalf. Judgments about whether a suggested policy is positive or not should be considered in light of how that policy will promote our well-being, not how much it will increase the size of the economy.[27]

In this view, the economy is seen as a 'constructed object' – that is, a product of our own endeavours and policy interventions, which should be appraised in terms of how functional they are in relation to our broad goals. Those broad goals are expressed in societal terms rather than in narrow 'economic' terms. In the neoliberal vision, we are schooled to believe that what is good for the corporate, profit-seeking sector is good for us. Within the progressive vision, society's goals are articulated in terms of advancing public well-being and maximising the potential for all citizens within the limits of environmental sustainability. The focus shifts to one of placing our human goals at the centre of our thinking about the economy, while at the same time recognising that we are embedded and dependent on the natural environment. In this narrative, *people create the economy*. There is nothing natural about it.

Concepts such as the 'natural rate of unemployment', which suggest that governments should not interfere with the market when there is mass unemployment and leave it to its own self-equilibrating forces to reach its natural state, are erroneous. Governments can always choose and sustain a particular unemployment rate. Within this framework, the role of the government is that of doing things that we cannot easily do ourselves; furthermore, we understand that the economy will only serve our common purposes if it is subject to active oversight and control. In the progressive vision, collective will is important because it provides the political justification for more equally sharing the costs and benefits of economic activity. Progressives have historically argued that the government has an obligation to create work if the private market fails to create enough employment. Accordingly, collective will means that our government is empowered to use net spending (deficits) to ensure that there are enough jobs available for all those who want to work. The government is therefore not a moral arbiter but a *functional entity serving our needs*.

How does the progressive vision expand our understanding of efficiency? Once society becomes the objective and we recognise that people and the natural environment are the major components of attention, with the economy being a vehicle to advance societal objectives rather than maximising the profits of the private sector, then our conceptualisation of what is efficient and what is not changes dramatically. This is especially the case once we understand that our national government is the agent of the people and has the fiscal and legislative capacity (as the currency issuer) to ensure resources are allocated and used to advance general well-being irrespective of what the corporate or foreign sector might do. It is clearly ludicrous to conclude that a society is operating efficiently when there are elevated levels of unemployment – people wanting to work who cannot find work – and large swathes of a nation's youth are denied access to employment, training or adequate educational opportunities. It is inconceivable that we would consider a nation successful if income and wealth inequality is increasing, poverty rates are rising and basic public services are degraded. In each of these cases, the neoliberal definition of efficiency could be satisfied, despite the overall well-being of citizens being compromised by the behaviour of the capitalist sector and the policy responses of government.

The tolerance of high levels of unemployment, a relatively recent phenomenon, exemplifies the policy dominance of neoliberal ideology. The empirical evidence clearly shows that most advanced economies have not provided enough jobs since the mid-1970s, as deflationary policies have been foisted upon the working classes. While these have been effective in bringing inflation down, they have also imposed – even from a mainstream standpoint – huge unemployment costs on the economy, and particularly on certain classes and demographic groups that are rarely computed or discussed in official circles. It is well documented that sustained unemployment imposes significant economic, personal and social costs that include: loss of current output; social exclusion and the loss of freedom; skill loss; psychological harm, including increased suicide rates; ill health and reduced life expectancy; loss of motivation; the undermining of human relations and family life; racial and gender inequality; and loss of social values and responsibility.

Many of these 'costs' are difficult to quantify but clearly are substantial given qualitative evidence. Further, there is evidence that the 'quality' of the unemployed buffer stock (defined in terms of its capacity to discipline price pressures) deteriorates over time. Just as soggy, rotting wool is useless in a wool price stabilisation scheme, the quality of labour resources can deteriorate if unemployed for lengthy periods. The more employable are the unemployed, the greater is the price level discipline of the unemployment buffer stock. There is overwhelming evidence that the skill losses and related circumstances associated with long-term unemployment undermine the quality of the jobless buffer stock and require higher and higher levels of unemployment to be created to maintain the same downward pressure of prices. A JG, on the other hand, if well managed, would allow workers to maintain a continuous involvement in paid work, which would lead to improved physical and mental health, more stable labour market behaviour, reduced burdens on the criminal justice system, more coherent family histories and useful output. A progressive concept of efficiency thus leads to the conclusion that unemployment is incomparably more inefficient than any public sector job-section programme could ever be. In the simplest possible terms, *an efficient economy is one where there is full employment* – where everyone that wants a job can find one.

THE JOB GUARANTEE: A MEANS OF ENSLAVEMENT OR A SOURCE OF FREEDOM?

Another criticism that is often levelled at the JG – particularly by progressive supporters of basic income – is that it aims to 'enslave' workers in pointless jobs, in contrast to basic income, which aims to 'liberate' human beings from the 'tyranny' of wage labour. Needless to say, we strongly disagree. Notwithstanding the theoretical and technical flaws of basic income proposals, these essentially view individuals as mere consumption units. However, human beings are much more than that. There is an extensive research literature that stresses the role of work in advancing the well-being of individuals and their families. David L. Blustein, one of the world's foremost experts on the importance of work for psychological health, concluded that the empirical evidence shows that 'working is important, and indeed can be essential, for psychological health' and 'can promote connection to the broader social and economic world, enhance well-being, and provide a means for individual satisfaction and accomplishment'.[28] The literature is replete with analyses where 'individuals who lose their jobs often struggle with mental health problems (such as depression, substance abuse, and anxiety)'.[29] Blustein documents the findings of a plethora of research studies that have focused on the importance of work for psychological health. From an anthropological perspective, Blustein noted that 'working is a central ingredient in the development and sustenance of psychological health. The nature of working is inextricably linked to our evolutionary past, as our survival was (and still is) dependent on our ability to locate food, find shelter, and develop a community for mutual support and nurturing'.[30]

In short, working is, in many ways, intrinsic to human existence. Proponents of employment guarantees share the conclusion of Blustein and other researchers that for many people 'working is the "playing field" of their lives, where their interactions with others and with existing social mores are most pronounced, with opportunities for satisfaction and even joy, as well as major challenges and, at times, considerable psychological and physical pain'.[31]

In other words, work plays a much more significant role in society and in the lives of individuals than merely providing an income. That said, a progressive vision clearly cannot ignore the historical context in which a discussion of the benefits of work is being conducted. Obviously, in a broad sense, the current mode of production, where workers are divorced from ownership of the means of production and have to subject themselves to the whims of capital in order to gain a living, is oppressive and coercive. In identifying the importance of work for psychological well-being, we are not oblivious to this oppressive aspect. However, it is also clear that people operate at multiple levels simultaneously. In this regard, Blustein argues that 'working is the social role in which people generally interact with the broader political, economic, and social contexts that frame their lives, working often becomes the nexus point for social oppression as well as a source of rewards, resilience, and relationships'.[32]

In this sense, we recognise that work as an organised activity is an essential aspect of human well-being, notwithstanding the dominant socio-economic context. We therefore need to distinguish the specific form that work has taken under capitalism – where it is certainly oppressive and the anathema of liberation – from the intrinsic meaning of work for people. People will still seek ways to 'work' and will have to continue working even if we liberate ourselves from the yoke of capitalism. In this context, the case for the JG leaves two outstanding and important issues to be discussed: is a compulsory JG overly coercive, and does the UBI model introduce dynamics that can take us beyond the oppressive reliance on wage labour for income security? With regard to the first question, we should start by noting that a society can choose to have whatever transfer system it sees fit (including the provision of unemployment benefits) running parallel with the introduction of a JG. The latter does not demand a total abandonment of the existing income support schemes. But a strong case can be made that individuals in any coherent society have an obligation to give back to the community that is guaranteeing them a job and the broad benefits that accompany that guarantee. Most societies are not yet ready to create a class of individuals of working age and amenable health to draw a living income without directly contributing something back to society, irrespective of the macroeconomic problems that this would raise, which we discussed above. This premise conditions the way we might think about coercion within the context of a JG.

So is a compulsory JG overly coercive? One of the essential criteria for a sustainable full employment policy is that it not violate the current social attitudes towards work and non-work. Robert Van der Veen and Philippe Van Parijs argued that the introduction of a universal income guarantee can provide a 'capitalist road to communism', which relates to the need to move beyond the oppression of the capitalist workplace and 'to move toward distribution according to needs'.[33] However, they qualify that notion by noting that there is a 'constraint on the maximization of the relative share of society's total product distributed according to needs' and that 'some economies are unable to meet this constraint',[34] which means that the basic income guarantee is not a general path to a better future for all. Moreover, their interpretation of the communist conception of freedom is questionable. In 1851, the French socialist politician and historian Louis Blanc laid out a scheme whereby cooperative workshops under workers' control would be supported by the state to provide guaranteed employment for the impoverished citizens in French cities.[35] He wrote that, when assessing the practicality of such a scheme, we need to consider what the fundamental principles of a future society might be. As part of his view of the role of the state and the responsibilities of individuals, he noted that a fundamental principle should be the following: 'From each according to his/her abilities, to each according to their needs.'[36]

Marx also incorporated that fundamental principle in Part I of his *Critique of the Gotha Program*.[37] Basic income proposals completely ignore the 'each according to one's ability' part. We don't consider this to be a sound basis for a healthy society based on reciprocity. Thus, the basic income 'capitalist road to communism', by abandoning the principle that individuals who are able to work should do so for the benefit of all, would appear to be a very partial interpretation of the communist conception of freedom.

Furthermore, there has been considerable research done by social scientists that suggests that people still consider work to be a central aspect of life and hold deep-seated views about deservingness and responsibility. These views translate into very firm attitudes about mutual obligation (reciprocity) and how much support should be provided to the unemployed. While these attitudes are at times expressed in unpleasant ways, and are exploited by the right to divide and conquer the working class, the fact remains that they are deeply ingrained in our societies and will take time to change. More importantly, however, most unemployed workers indicate in surveys that they would prefer to work rather than be provided with income support. In other words, the poor and the unemployed *want to work*. In this regard, Amartya Sen has shown that what matters is not just freedom but *substantive* freedom.[38] Thus, policy choices should first and foremost take into account what individuals themselves want and value, and should then provide them with the means to realise their aspirations. In this regard, the JG is a source of freedom, capitalist property relations notwithstanding.

Young people must be encouraged to develop skills and engage in paid work rather than be the passive recipients of social security benefits. The failure to ensure that there is enough paid work excludes the unemployed from fully participating in society's economic, social and cultural life, which has highly detrimental consequences. There are substantial social benefits that arise from the provision of stable work with decent wages and health and retirement benefits. Moreover, by creating circumstances in which an individual's opportunity to engage in paid employment and earn a living wage is guaranteed, the JG dampens any resentment that may be felt towards that proportion of unemployed people who are currently perceived as undeserving of state support and assistance. The JG approach thus overrides the free-rider option that is available under an unconditional basic income. In a society which accords value to the notion of reciprocity, the guaranteed work model ensures that no social group or individual is solely viewed as a consumption unit – to be fed and clothed by the state but ignored in terms of his/her social needs for work and human interaction within the workplace.

Of course, there will always be people who do not value work in any intrinsic sense, and if confronted with the choice between the JG and a basic income guarantee would always choose the latter option. A blanket JG is thus coercive in its impact on this particular group. Basic income advocates would likely suggest 'merely' making the JG voluntary within the context of a UBI guarantee. To understand this criticism of the JG we should note that the underlying unit of analysis in the basic income literature is an individual who appears to resemble McGregor's theory X person. Theory X people are found in mainstream microeconomics textbooks and are constructed as self-centred, rational maximisers.

Lester Thurow noted that this neoliberal conception of the X person views man as 'basically a grasshopper with a limited, short-time horizon who, liking leisure must be forced to work and save enticed by rewards much greater than those he gets from leisure'.[39] This is a staunchly libertarian conception of human freedom, which requires an individual to have free choice; in this regard, basic income proponents see the decoupling of income from work as an essential step towards increasing the choice and freedom of individuals. However, for the state to permit individualism at this level – to support individuals in their consumption but not require any reciprocation – severely limits the possibilities for social change and community engagement. Progressives should be at the forefront of collective engagement rather than advocating policies that smack of individualism.

Of course, the provision of a basic income guarantee does not preclude community action. Individuals may adopt a whole range of campaigns and activist agendas while being supported on the barest income guarantee. However, we cannot help but note that a characteristic of the neoliberal era has been the elevation of 'volunteerism' to some virtuous heights. Morality runs deep through neoliberal narratives when it works to reinforce the redistribution of income towards the top. The reality is that many functions that are now considered to be the ambit of volunteers, despite their value to society, were previously, in many cases, paid jobs. So if the basic income recipients are engaged in these activities why wouldn't they want to be paid for their work? Basic income advocates see their approach as a way of rejecting the capitalist 'gainful worker' approach, by breaking the nexus between surplus value creation and income at the individual level. Now, we fully agree that the traditional moral views about the virtues of work – which are exploited by the capitalist class – need to be recast. However, we believe that a non-capitalist system of work and income generation is needed before the yoke of the work ethic and the stigmatisation of non-work can be fully expunged.

In this sense, the JG offers a great opportunity for radically, albeit gradually, recasting what is considered to be meaningful work. With private sector job opportunities destined to decline due to technological change, a central question becomes how can societies broaden the definition of productive work and reduce the stigma of not being engaged in traditional work? Clearly, there is a need to embrace a broader concept of work in the first phase of the decoupling of work from income. Basic income proposals fall short in this respect, since the stigma of being unemployed does not disappear when one is not working and is receiving an income guarantee. Current social norms are unlikely to digest this new culture of non-work very easily. The resentment currently directed towards the unemployed will only be transferred towards Van Parijs' 'surfers of Malibu'. By way of contrast, the JG would provide a means to establish a new employment paradigm where community development and other non-traditional jobs would become valued. Over time, and within this new employment paradigm, public debate and education can help broaden the concept of valuable work until activities which we might construe today as being 'leisure' would become considered to be 'gainful employment'. Struggling musicians, artists, surfers, thespians and the like could all be employed within the JG framework. In return for income security, the surfer might be required to conduct water safety awareness lessons for school children; and musicians might be required to rehearse some days a week in school halls and thus impart knowledge about band dynamics and appreciation of music to young schoolchildren. Thinking even more laterally, community activism itself could become a JG job. For example, organising and managing a community garden to provide food for the poor could be considered a paid job. We would see more of this sort of beneficial activity if it were rewarded in this way.

In other words, through the JG, society can begin to redefine the concept of productive work well beyond the realms of 'gainful work', which in the current parlance specifically relates to activities that generate private profits for firms. Over time, productivity would become more of a social, shared, public concept, limited only by our imagination. In this way, the JG becomes an evolutionary force that provides income security to those who want it, but also allows us to broaden the very concept of work. Social attitudes take time to evolve; the social fabric must be rebuilt over time. The change in the mode of production through evolutionary means will not happen overnight; concepts of community wealth and civic responsibility that have been eroded over time need to be restored. In the UBI approach, the intrinsic social and capacity-building role of participating in paid work is ignored and hence undervalued. It is sometimes said that beyond all the benefits in terms of self-esteem, social inclusion, confidence building, skill augmentation and the like, a priceless benefit of creating full employment through job creation is that children see at least one parent going to work each morning. In other words, it creates an intergenerational stimulus that the basic income approach can never attain. Ultimately, the JG provides a strong evolutionary dynamic in terms of establishing a broader historical transition away from the unemployment (and income insecurity) that is intrinsic to the capitalist mode of production. It provides a short-run palliative and a longer-term force for historical change. The basic income guarantee is found lacking in this regard on all counts.

There is a final issue that remains to be addressed. As we have seen, government can, through the use of fiscal policy and particularly through the use of the JG, achieve and maintain full employment without major problems to the economy. However, as Kalecki insightfully noted in the 1940s and as the crisis of Keynesianism in the 1970s – examined in Chapter 2 – demonstrated, 'although the achievement of full employment is essentially an economic matter, its maintenance becomes a political one'.[40] That is because full employment tilts the balance of power in favour of the working classes and the masses more generally. It emboldens them to challenge the institutions of capitalist power, not only within the workplace but also, and more importantly, at the institutional level. This is what happened in the 1970s, as an increasingly militant working class linked up with other social movements to challenge the institutional structure of capitalist power and demand a radical democratisation of society. In other words, full employment represents a threat to the interests of the capitalist class, which are likely to respond to it by using their power – within the workplace and at the political level – to bring the working class under control once again.

One of the most powerful weapons at the disposal of the capitalist class, in this regard, is their control over investment. Given that, in a capitalist economy, investment is a fundamental prerequisite for growth and employment, by choosing *not* to invest – in what is known as a capital strike – capitalists can bring great pressure to bear on governments. From the 1970s onwards, capitalists made widespread use of this weapon to get governments to abandon their commitment to full employment. For Kalecki – but a similar opinion was expressed by a number of other thinkers, from Keynes to Minsky – the key to solving the underlying social and political tensions resulting from the maintenance of full employment in a capitalist economy lies in a degree of *state control over investment* (what Keynes called 'a somewhat comprehensive socialisation of investment'), which would severely reduce the political and economic power wielded by the capitalist class and consequently its ability to derail a progressive political platform. In the 1970s and 1980s, as we saw with regard to the experience of the socialist governments of Britain and France, the left proved unwilling to go this way. This left it no other choice but to 'manage the capitalist crisis on behalf of capital'.[41] Any progressive government that wants to avoid taking the same ignominious path must thus be ready to target investment, not simply employment. This is what we will address in Chapter 10.

10

We Have a (Central) Plan:
The Case of Renationalisation

As we saw in Chapter 1, the post-war development of core capitalist countries – particularly in Europe – was based on extensive industrial policy. Not only did the state heavily support private firms through financial and investment aid, R&D funds, public procurement, market protection, consortiums, public education strategies, telecommunications, transport and energy networks, etc. National policy tools also included the creation or expansion of a vast array of state-owned firms in strategic industries, key infrastructures and natural monopolies. France was probably the most significant example of this strategy. The centrepiece of France's post-war reconstruction effort was a massive nationalisation programme, put in place by Charles De Gaulle's government, which saw the state take 'control of businesses in energy, transportation, and finance'.[1] Paul Cohen, who teaches history at the University of Toronto, notes that in 1946 the French state directly controlled 98 per cent of coal production, 95 per cent of electricity, 58 per cent of the banking sector, 38 per cent of automobile production and 15 per cent of total GDP.[2] State-owned firms at the time included EDF (electricity), France Télécom (telecommunications), Renault (auto) and Aérospatiale (aerospace). Moreover, under the direction of Jean Monnet, the first director of the General Commissariat for Planning, the government started 'draft[ing] five-year plans in order to shape long-term economic development'.[3] Cohen concludes that the French experience was, by all measures, 'a great success':

> Nationalised industries and five-year plans may transgress the treasured tenets of neoliberal orthodoxy, but they didn't stop France from enjoying three decades of sustained economic growth and prosperity. In the period between 1950 and the first oil shock in 1973, recalled in France today as *les trente glorieuses* (the 'thirty glorious years'), its economy grew at the impressive clip of 5 percent a year

(while United States growth averaged 3.6 percent), unemployment was virtually unknown (2 percent in France, compared to 4.6 percent in the United States), and French women and men experienced dramatic increases in their standard of living.[4]

Moreover, the French state 'used planning as a flexible tool to restructure companies and save jobs, to create new industries from scratch and promote job growth, to soften deindustrialisation's blow to workers and their communities, and to orient transportation and energy policy onto more sustainable pathways'.[5] Then, in the 1980s and 1990s, the economic policy debate in France and elsewhere started being dominated by neoliberal views that argued that industrial policies – and particularly state-owned firms – are inefficient and inappropriate. The argument was (and still is) that markets are able to operate more efficiently both in the short term and in the long term.

As a result, in recent decades state-owned firms have been privatised in most countries, 'leading to extensive closing down of capacity, foreign takeovers and greater market concentration' – a process that continues to this day.[6] Public assets put up for privatisation around the world included: state banks, publicly owned airlines and airport infrastructure; state prison systems; energy generation, distribution and retailing; public transport systems; public hospitals and healthcare facilities; public employment services; public telecommunications; public water and sewerage utilities; and public postal services, among others. As we saw in Chapter 4, the long-term process of privatisation of the French state's once-large collection of public assets commenced under Mitterrand – following his government's 'turn to austerity' in 1983 – but reached its pinnacle in the late 1990s under the Socialist-Communist-Green coalition led by Lionel Jospin, which 'undertook the privatisation of Crédit Lyonnais and other corporations, as well as selling minority stakes in Aérospatiale, Air France, and France Télécom'.[7] Cohen notes that 'these wide-ranging privatisations represent[ed] nothing less than a rejection of the postwar edifice of French capitalism that De Gaulle helped erect'.[8] He further notes that '[t]he move away from state ownership was not in fact born of a rational economic calculus but rather of specific political choices.'[9]

Privatisation promised to deliver lower costs and prices, improved services and better working conditions. Moreover, it was argued that privatisation would simply shift workers from the public to the private sector and thus would not lead to an overall loss of jobs. The reality is that some 40 years or so into the privatisation experiment, none of these claims have been realised: on the contrary, there is a litany of evidence to show that the experience of privatisation 'has been one of poor performance, under-investment, disputes over operational costs and price increases ... monitoring difficulties, lack of financial transparency, workforce cuts and poor service quality causing public health risks and creating environmental problems'.[10] Especially when it comes to utility companies, the effect of privatisations on the product price has proven to be extremely negative. In the 34 OECD countries, for example, the average price for energy charged by private companies is 23.1 per cent higher than the price charged by public companies.[11]

Moreover, in many cases the wage losses, redundancies and erosion of labour rights that have resulted from privatisation have further exacerbated the recent economic crisis and led to increased levels of inequality. All in all, the evidence suggests that *none* of these transfers to private ownership have resulted in improvements to societies' well-being. Meanwhile, research by the IMF and by European universities shows that there is no evidence that privatised firms are more efficient.[12] In fact, in many cases privatised firms rely on higher public subsidies than they needed when they were in public hands. To add insult to injury, despite the rhetoric in favour of private management, many of the firms involved in the acquisition of privatised assets are, in fact, other countries' state-owned companies: Chinese, German and French state-owned companies, for example, own large stakes in Europe's formerly public utilities.

Arguments that the public sector could fund enterprises more cheaply (both because it could borrow more cheaply and because it didn't need to generate profit) were dismissed by proponents of privatisation. The privatisation lobby claimed that the difference in funding costs lay in the fact that the private sector would now explicitly assume the risk of the enterprise – a factor they said was buried in public accounts but was ultimately a liability to the 'taxpayer'. It was a lie. In many cases, the privatisation failed outright and the asset was returned to public ownership (Swissair, for example) because the state maintained the risk of the activity, despite the claims by proponents of privatisation to the contrary. The indelible fact is that in the case of large-scale national infrastructures and systemically important industries – such as the financial sector – the risk can never be shifted from the public to the private domain. For these, private ownership amounts to little more than a case of privatisation of the profits and socialisation of the losses.

Even more crucially, privatisation and the abandonment of national industrial policies have meant that governments have voluntarily constrained their ability to determine the level and composition of investment, demand and production. This can be considered one of the root causes of the massive (and interrelated) social, economic, political and ecological crises that the world is facing, since it means that crucial decisions about the future of biological life on earth – such as what is produced and consumed and how – are essentially left to the private sector and to the financial markets, which have repeatedly proven themselves unable to determine prices efficiently and allocate resources between the various sectors of the economy, fuelling the cancerous growth of socially and environmentally destructive (but very profitable) industries and practices. Private markets inherently prioritise private profit over societal and environmental well-being. All studies show that solving the ecological crisis requires a radical and profound socio-ecological transformation process. A recent report by the New Economics Foundation notes that:

> despite the slowdown of economic activity ... the environmental crisis is becoming more severe. The recent human made greenhouse gas emissions are the highest in history, the earth's temperature is increasing and natural resources are continuously deteriorating. These crises have called into question the sustainability of our societies. They cannot be tackled in isolation, as has mostly been the case so far. Any attempt to deal with the economic crisis by using the traditional growth policies will lead to more pollution and a higher use of natural resources, risking further economic and financial crises. Any attempt to deal with the environmental crisis by ignoring the potential adverse effects on unemployment and inequality will damage our societies and lead to more severe economic and financial crises. And any attempt to regulate the financial sector without transforming the way that it interacts with the ecosystem and the macroeconomy will fail to ensure financial stability in the long run. There is, therefore, a clear need for a new approach that will promote policies capable of dealing with all these crises simultaneously.[13]

Clearly, we cannot expect markets, with their focus on short-term profits, to lead this transition. This requires a drastic expansion of the state's role – and an equally drastic downsizing of the private sector's role – in the investment, production and distribution system. A progressive agenda for the twenty-first century must thus necessarily include a broad renationalisation of key sectors of the economy and a new and updated notion of planning. The case for state ownership is particularly strong in those sectors that are characterised by a so-called natural monopoly. A natural monopoly arises when a certain industry's infrastructure costs of setup are very high and the resulting market can only support one supplier, which thus gains an overwhelming advantage over potential competitors. Examples of natural monopolies include telecommunications, mass transport, postal services, highways and public utilities such as electricity and water services. These industries often produce essential goods and services that should be available to everyone, irrespective of income, and thus cannot be run according to a strict profit-based logic. Therefore, when transferred to private ownership, they need to be heavily regulated and subsidised to ensure that they deliver socially beneficial outcomes. Moreover, many of these industries create what economists call 'negative externalities' – such as pollution – that are much easier to control when they are under public control. In common parlance, negative externalities mean that 'the market' has failed; even mainstream economists accept that in these instances government intervention is justified (in the form of regulation, etc.).

The experience of France's state-owned industries illustrates many of the benefits of renationalisation. Paul Cohen writes that 'successive governments used their stakes in France's traditional smokestack industries to guide industrial reorganisations', shifting from coal-powered electricity generation to nuclear power without loss of employment or regional dislocation.[14] Public ownership thus allows the government to shift technologies within the energy sector more easily than if the sector is privately owned and operated. This is particularly relevant for progressive aspirations for a green, sustainable energy sector based on renewables. Public ownership also allows governments to manage the transition from labour-intensive coal- and nuclear-powered electricity generation plants to less labour-intensive renewable energy plants with less cost to workers and their families, given that the public sector can absorb the displaced workers more readily. Cohen compares the gradual and relatively painless shift away from coal in France with 'Thatcherite Britain's brutal mine closures and bloody union-police confrontations'.[15]

Publicly owned firms can also ride out economic cycles more easily than profit-based firms. The subsidies to keep a public operation functioning in bad times are typically lower than those needed to socialise private losses. During the financial crisis, many governments effectively had to nationalise several large banks in order to protect depositors. The fear of collapse would disappear if these were held in public hands – a point we will return to. This raises the question of the rate of return. As a general rule, state-owned firms and particularly those that deliver essential public goods should not be expected to earn commercial returns: a currency-issuing government should not concern itself with the *monetary return* on its investments – given that it faces no financial constraints – but should rather focus first and foremost on the *social return*. However, Cohen provides evidence that, even in commercial terms, publicly owned enterprises that produce for a consumer market can be very successful. He cites the example of Renault, fully state-owned up until the 1990s, noting that '[s]tate management is no small part of the reason why France today is home to profitable automobile manufacturers whose product lines are focused on small, innovative, fuel-efficient cars'.[16] This shows 'public investment to be an invaluable tool for creating new industries and stimulating growth'.[17]

In today's context, renationalisation thus means using the state to promote new environmentally sustainable, knowledge-intensive, high-skill and high-wage economic activities – and more generally to promote the wider socio-ecological transformation of the current system of production and consumption. Specific activities that could be targeted include: (i) the protection of the environment, sustainable transportation, energy efficiency and renewable energy sources; (ii) the production and dissemination of knowledge, applications of ICTs and web-based activities; (iii) health, welfare and caring activities, and much more.

To be clear, we are not trying to paint an idyllic picture of state-owned firms – in France or elsewhere. In Chapter 1, we analysed in detail the many problems that plagued the state-heavy economies of the Fordist-Keynesian era. The growth of heavy industry was encouraged without any real understanding of the long-term consequences for the natural environment. Work was, in many instances, repetitive and mind-numbing, and often conducted in unsafe and harsh conditions. In many cases, state-owned firms were riddled with cronyism and nepotism.

Some were utter disasters. But these problems were (are) not exclusive to the public sector. The financial crisis is a testament to the colossal inefficiency of the private sector – and the cost that its failures impose on society and the economy, which surpass by far any cost that may derive from the well-publicised failures of the public sector (corruption, excessive bureaucracy, etc.). The point is that the ownership status of an activity is not the reason for its success or lack thereof. A public enterprise can be as well or as badly managed as a private enterprise, with the crucial difference that the former allows for a degree of democratic control and oversight over key sectors of the economy. This, in itself, justifies reversing the privatisation process of recent decades, particularly where key public utilities are concerned – the appalling track record of privatisation notwithstanding.

Renationalisation and planning could also be used to promote a greater degree of national self-sufficiency and reduce a country's dependence on imports. Keynes himself famously wrote that the he sympathised 'with those who would minimise, rather than with those who would maximise, economic entanglement among nations. ... Ideas, knowledge, science, hospitality, travel – these are the things which should of their nature be international. But let goods be homespun whenever it is reasonably and conveniently possible, and, above all, let finance be primarily national.'[18]

However, such a programme must take into account 'the (merciless) fact that the average product today is much more complicated and diverse in components and origin(s), and is much more knowledge-based', as Trond Andersen of the Norwegian University of Science and Technology writes.[19] In other words, the global economy today is much more 'entangled' than it was at Keynes' time. To overcome this problem, Andersen outlines a series of tasks that a government could undertake:

- Charting the domestic and import share of production of different categories of goods, to establish whether the import content could be reduced.
- Charting where the imports come from, and researching the possibilities for cooperative agreements with well-reputed and global suppliers, so that they could help set up manufacturing plants for domestic manufacture of their products, in exchange for which they could, for instance, receive a licence fee for every unit sold. The agreement could also contain clauses prohibiting export of the same product. Andersen notes that 'the main point of the

idea is import substitution, but not by inventing the wheel anew and forcing an inferior "people's tractor no. 1" on an unwilling population. Instead this would mean that a modern, high-quality product that the domestic market already desired, would mainly be made domestically.'[20] Intermediate goods and components for the plant could be supplied by the foreign partner.

- Charting where the need for new employment is largest, and locating plants there.
- Planning for and building energy, transport and communications infrastructure to service these new manufacturing plants.

We have thus examined very broadly the question of renationalisation in the context of the production and supply of natural monopolies and vital public services. However, we have left out the industry where renationalisation is most urgent and necessary, since all the other sectors of the economy arguably depend on it: the banking sector. Today, over 90 per cent of the money in circulation is created out of thin air by private banks. When a bank makes a new loan, it simply makes an entry into a ledger – Keynes called this 'fountain pen money'; nowadays it usually involves tapping some numbers into a computer – and creates brand new money, which it then deposits into the borrower's account. In other words, contrary to popular opinion, loans lead to newly created deposits and not the other way around. The money supply is therefore largely controlled by private banks, not central banks. The ability to create credit (and money) – in effectively unlimited amounts – gives banks an incomparable power over the rest of the economy. That is because banks don't simply control how much money is created; they also control *where this money goes* – that is, who can access credit and who cannot. This gives banks the power to determine, to a large degree, the level and composition of investment, demand and production within the economy and thus its overall direction; it also gives them the power to engineer credit-driven booms at will, which in turn leads to soaring prices (especially in the housing market). When these booms inevitably go bust, triggering a crisis, the banks attempt to repair their overleveraged balance sheets by engaging in excessive deleveraging, cutting off credit when households and businesses need it the most, and further exacerbating the post-crisis recession.

A Federal Reserve Bank of New York paper notes that the impact of banking shocks on aggregate lending and investment is further exacerbated when 'a few banks account for a substantial share of an economy's loans'[21] – a reality that today characterises all advanced countries. By their very nature, financial markets pursue short-term profit, which is why, in the years leading up to the financial crisis, banks pumped huge amounts of money into the most profitable sector of all, the housing market. This pushed prices up year after year, at the expense of all the other sectors of the economy, laying the ground for the financial crisis of 2007–9, which had such a devastating impact on the living conditions of millions of people around the world. As Adair Turner writes, '[b]anks which can create credit and money to finance asset price booms are thus inherently dangerous institutions'[22] Moreover, by having commercial banking and investment under the same roof, the money-creation process inherent in commercial banking enables the development of investment banking, as the newly created money can then be used to feed speculative banking activities. It should also be noted that none of the underlying problems that caused the 2007–9 financial crisis have been resolved. In fact, the situation has got worse in many respects, with the post-crisis restructuring of the financial sector having led to an even more concentrated financial landscape marked by even larger banks that continue to expose the economy – and, more importantly, millions of citizen and workers – to huge systemic risks.

Given the crucial and systemically relevant role that banks play in the economy, for all intents and purpose they can – and should – be considered public institutions. In many ways, both *de jure* and *de facto*, they already are: not only are bank deposits formally guaranteed by governments, but financial institutions also have access to almost unlimited public funds when faced with bankruptcy, as the recent financial crisis vividly demonstrated. Even worse, today the financial sector is essentially dependent on continuous state support simply to stay afloat, as we saw in Chapter 5. This creates an unresolvable tension, where banks are not allowed to fail by dint of government support (implicit or otherwise) yet at the same time behave just like any other risk-taking, profit-seeking firm, paying exorbitant salaries and bonuses to management and skewing their operations to the interests of their shareholders. Most progressives would agree that radical financial reform – breaking up the big banks, separating commercial and investment banking, etc. – is necessary. However, this is not enough. As Eric Toussaint and others argue, even if these measures were applied, 'capital will do everything possible to recover part of the ground it will have lost, finding multiple ways of getting around the regulations, using its powerful financial resources to buy the support of lawmakers and government leaders in order to deregulate, once again, and increase profits to the maximum without regard for the interests of the majority of the population.'[23]

This means that the fundamental incompatibility between the essentially public nature of finance and the profit motive intrinsic to the private ownership of the banks – which has led to the global financial crisis and its very destructive aftermath, and results in a continuous privatisation of profits and socialisation of losses – needs to be addressed head-on. The only structural solution to this incompatibility – which represents a huge impediment to the construction of a society 'guided by the pursuit of the common good, social justice and the reconstitution of balanced relations between human beings and the other components of nature'[24] – is the nationalisation (socialisation) of the banking sector. As Frédéric Lordon proposes, nothing less than a 'total deprivatisation of the banking sector' needs to be carried out.'[25]

Simply put, banks should be publicly owned and democratically controlled. Toussaint and others note that socialising the banking sector means: (i) expropriating the large shareholders without compensation; (ii) granting a monopoly of banking activities to the public sector, with one single exception – the existence of a small cooperative banking sector (subject to the same fundamental rules as the public sector); and (iii) creating a public service for savings, credit and investment. Public ownership in itself is no panacea, of course. There are countless examples around the world of public banks that behave no differently than their private counterparts. Therefore, measures should be introduced to ensure that the public system does not replicate the profit-seeking model of the private banks. In terms of operational guidelines, the only useful function that a bank should perform is to participate in the payments system and provide loans to creditworthy customers. In other words, banks should return to their original purpose: allocating money to businesses and families and aiding the growth of the economy.

So how might we ensure that the operations of the public banking system satisfy our conception of social/public purpose? First, the newly nationalised banks should only be permitted to lend directly to borrowers. Attention should always be focused on what is a reasonable credit risk, with the aim of avoiding some of the Minskian fluctuations in credit availability over the business cycle. Moreover, all loans should be kept on the banks' balance sheets. This would stop all third-party commission deals that might involve banks acting as 'brokers' and on-selling loans or other financial assets for profit. Banks should not be permitted to speculate as counter-parties with other banks. Moreover, new social, labour and environmental criteria, such as the working conditions that business borrowers provide to their workforce, should be introduced to determine how the banking system allocates credit. Second, banks should not be allowed to accept any financial asset as collateral to support loans. The collateral should be the estimated value of the income stream on the asset for which the loan is being advanced. This will force banks to appraise the credit risk more fully. One of the factors that led to the financial crisis was the increasing inability of the banks to appraise this risk properly. Further, the foreclosure scandal that followed the financial crisis would not have occurred if these stipulations had been in place. Third, banks should be prevented from having off-balance sheet assets. Fourth, banks should never be allowed to trade in credit default insurance. Fifth, banks should not engage in any other commercial activity. Sixth, banks should not be allowed to underwrite contracts in foreign interest rates nor issue foreign currency-denominated loans. There is no public benefit achieved in allowing them to do this. The result of these suggestions would be to render illegal a huge raft of transactions that are currently considered part of normal banking. On the question of bank governance, bank management should also be restructured to include representatives of unions, community and social movements, and elected officials. More generally, a new bank charter should be democratically drafted, with citizen participation, laying out the wider societal goals that the public banking system should serve. Steering the activities of banks towards the advancement of the common good would go a long way towards eliminating the dysfunctional, antisocial nature of private banking and ensuring that these 'public' institutions serve the public purpose. The socialisation of banks should thus 'be part of an expansive vision that reshapes the practices and uses of credit along egalitarian lines'.[26] In this regard, Toussaint and others write:

> Because banks are today an essential tool of the capitalist system and of a mode of production that is devastating our planet and grabbing its resources, creating wars and impoverishment, eroding, little by little, social rights and attacking democratic institutions and practices, it is essential to take control of them so that they become tools placed at the service of the greater number of people.[27]

The case for bank nationalisation is also based on an acknowledgement of the fact that the fundamental responsibility of government macro-economic policy is to maximise real national output in a way that is sustainable (socially, economically and environmentally). This in turn requires financial stability. An economy's financial system is stable if its key financial institutions and markets function 'normally'. To achieve financial stability two broad requirements must be met: (i) the country's key financial institutions must be stable and engender confidence so that they can meet their contractual obligations without interruption or external assistance; and (ii) the key markets must be stable and support transactions at prices that reflect economic fundamentals. There should be no major short-term fluctuations where there have been no changes in economic fundamentals. In other words, the stability of financial institutions requires them to absorb shocks and avoid potential widespread economic losses, while the stability of the financial system as a whole requires levels of price volatility that do not cause widespread economic damage. Prices should move to reflect changes in economic fundamentals. The essential requirements of a stable financial system are: clearly defined property rights; central bank oversight of the payments system; capital adequacy standards for financial institutions; bank depositor protection; an institutional lender of last resort that can intervene when private institutions refuse to lend to solvent borrowers in times of liquidity crisis; an institution to ameliorate coordination failure among private investors/creditors; and the provision of exit strategies to insolvent institutions. While some of these requirements can be provided by private institutions, they all fall within the domain of government. As a consequence, there is nothing intrinsically 'private' that has to be present in the banking system for these requirements to be met. The stability of the financial system is fundamentally a public good and should thus be the legitimate responsibility of government.

BEYOND BANK NATIONALISATION

The reforms to the ownership and operations of the commercial banking system that we have outlined only go so far. By forcing the banks to return to a retail focus and preventing them from operating as casino players represents a considerable improvement over the current situation. However, there is a vast array of financial institutions that would fall outside the prudential regulation dragnet and which account for the bulk of global financial transactions. These include large investment banks such as Goldman Sachs and other Wall Street institutions. Throughout the neoliberal era, as a result of financial market deregulation and lack of supervision of financial flows from authorities, the volume of global financial transactions increased from 15.3 times nominal world GDP in 1990 to 73.5 times by 2008.[28] Stephen Schulmeister notes that 'the overall increase in financial trading is exclusively due to the spectacular boom of the derivatives markets'.[29] In other words, most of the financial flows comprise wealth-shuffling speculative transactions which have nothing to do with the facilitation of trade in real goods and services across national boundaries. One might characterise these transactions as being simply unproductive. Yet, as the global financial crisis demonstrated, they have the capacity to derail the entire real economy when their engineered speculative bubbles burst.

It would be wrong to consider all hedging and speculation to be damaging. When it accompanies trade flows and provides security to a trading concern that has cross-border exposure (either in revenue or costs) to exchange rate fluctuations, it can be beneficial. When we talk about hedging in this context we are referring to a strategy that aims to avoid foreign exchange risk. By entering forward contracts, the producer of real goods and services (for export) or an importer can transfer the risk of unforeseen exchange rate changes to a speculator, and it is likely that such arrangements increase the volume of international trade. But these types of transactions are a tiny fraction of the total volume of financial transactions, which are dominated by a few large multinational firms that have no other motivation than to expand their reach and profits. As Matt Taibbi argued, financial firms like Goldman Sachs are 'huge, highly sophisticated engine[s] for converting the useful, deployed wealth of society into the least useful, most wasteful and insoluble substance on Earth – pure profit for rich individuals'.[30]

The robber barons of the industrial era have been replaced, in the era of financial capital, by the banksters. The question that arises is how a progressive state should deal with this destructive influence. In the same way as the basic income guarantee has become popular among progressives as a solution to income insecurity arising from mass unemployment (see Chapter 9), the idea of a Robin Hood or Tobin Tax is today championed by progressives as a means of addressing the unfettered greed of these large investment banks and the destruction they wreak, especially among poorer nations. Neither solution is desirable; they both reflect a failure to understand the intrinsic capacity of the sovereign state.

The idea of a Tobin Tax (named after the Nobel Prize-winning economist James Tobin) is simple. It involves imposing a small tax on foreign financial transactions. Part of the motivation relates to the increasing awareness that short-termism or high-frequency trading is now becoming dominant in global financial markets. High-frequency trading is driven by computer algorithms, automatically programmed to follow rules that can generate a multitude of (usually small) trades per second. The resulting asset prices that emerge have little correspondence to any economic fundamentals. Rather, they reflect speculation, herding and 'technical trading', which can erode the long-term fortunes of companies and economies in general.

It is argued that a Tobin Tax would discourage these short-term hot capital flows but not interfere with long-term investments, because a small tax would be relatively minor compared to the total scale of these projects. Short-term speculators who move in and out of a currency, sometimes within hours of taking their positions, would be more exposed to the tax. By discouraging these short-term capital flows, it is argued that exchange rate volatility would decline and significant revenue would be raised, which could be used to alleviate poverty and improve public services and make national economic policies less vulnerable to external shocks.

Why is this approach an inferior option for progressives to adopt? First, it would be futile to deter speculative behaviour that assists international trade in goods and services. Second, an important question that is begged by the discussions about the Tobin Tax is why should we allow these destabilising financial flows to occur in the first place? If they are not facilitating the production and movement of real goods and services what public purpose do they serve? It is clear that they have made a small number of people fabulously wealthy. It is also clear that they have damaged the prospects of disadvantaged workers in many less developed countries. More obvious to all of us now is that, when the system comes unstuck through the complexity of these transactions and the impossibility of correctly pricing risk, real economies across the globe suffer. The consequences have been devastating in terms of lost employment, income and wealth. So there is no public purpose being served by allowing these trades to occur even if the imposition of the Tobin Tax (or something like it) might deter some of the volatility in exchange rates. Third, the progressives who focus on the funds such a tax would provide for governments fail to understand the spurious nature of these arguments when applied to a currency-issuing government.

A superior progressive option would be to outlaw all non-productive financial flows. As part of a more general reform of the international institutional architecture, governments should agree to make all financial transactions that cannot be shown to facilitate trade in real goods and services illegal. Speculative attacks on a nation's currency would be judged in the same way as an armed invasion of the country – illegal. This would smooth out the volatility in currencies and allow fiscal policy to pursue full employment and price stability without destabilising external sector transactions. This would also have the benefit of ensuring greater food security for the poorer nations. One of the most hideous aspects of the speculative mania is the way in which large investment banks reap huge profits by betting on food prices on financial markets. This drives up food prices and creates shortages, leaving millions going hungry and facing deeper poverty. There is no justification for allowing these transactions to take place.

Conclusion: Back to the State

As the reader will have surmised by now, what we have outlined in the second part of the book is not a *political programme*. With the exception of the job guarantee, we have not put forward specific policies. It is not our job to do so; besides, every country has different needs and requirements in that respect. A one-size-fits-all left-wing programme would therefore make little sense. Rather, what we have done is to provide what we consider to be the necessary requirements – in theoretical, political and institutional terms – for conceiving a political-institutional framework within which the achievement of a socially and economically progressive agenda – whatever that may be – is technically possible. As we have seen, this requires:

(i) A correct understanding of the capacities of monetarily sovereign (or currency-issuing) governments, and more specifically an understanding that such governments are never revenue- or solvency-constrained because they issue their own currency by legislative fiat and therefore can never 'run out of money' or become insolvent. These governments always have an unlimited capacity to spend in their own currencies: that is, they can purchase whatever they like, as long as there are goods and services for sale in the currency they issue. At the very least, they can purchase all idle labour and put it back to productive use (for example, through a job guarantee). This also means understanding that there is no such thing as a balance-of-payments growth constraint in a flexible exchange economy in the same way as it exists in a fixed exchange rate environment: a monetarily sovereign nation that floats its currency has much more domestic policy space than the mainstream considers, and can make use of this space to pursue rising living standards, even if this means an expansion of the current account deficit and a depreciation of the currency. As we have seen, through capital controls and other instruments, the aspirations of global finance can be brought into line with the demands of a government intent on advancing the well-being of its citizens. Understanding the operational reality of modern fiat economies is therefore a *conditio sine qua non* for envisioning a progressive, emancipatory vision of national sovereignty – one based on popular sovereignty, democratic control over the economy, full employment, social justice, redistribution from the rich to the poor, inclusivity and more.

(ii) A drastic expansion of the state's role – and an equally drastic downsizing of the private sector's role – in the investment, production and distribution system. A progressive agenda for the twenty-first century must thus necessarily include a broad renationalisation of key sectors of the economy – including, and most importantly, the financial sector – and a new and updated notion of planning, aimed at placing the commanding heights of economic policy under democratic control. We consider this to be an equally necessary condition for the pursuit of a progressive agenda, and in particular for the socio-ecological transformation of production and society that is desperately needed to deal with the ongoing – and worsening – environmental crisis.

These two elements, in our opinion, provide the foundations on which to build a radical and progressive alternative to neoliberalism, the specific details of which should be the outcome of a broad debate among progressive thinkers, social movements and political parties in each country and at the international level. This goes to the heart of the malaise of the contemporary left: its inability to conceive radical solutions to the problems we face, for the reasons that we have outlined throughout the book. Instead of telling the people that governments cannot run out of money, left politicians and activists demand that we 'tax the rich' to pay for essential services, thus fuelling the myth that taxes fund government expenses. Yes, we should tax the rich, but to ensure that wealth is distributed more equitably, *not* because the revenue is needed to fund healthcare, education or public services. Similarly, they opt for an 'austerity lite' solution, where they tell people that while deficit and debt reduction is necessary to ensure 'fiscal sustainability', they will make the fiscal cuts fairer and the adjustment path less painful, when they should be telling people to stop worrying about fiscal deficits altogether and educating them about the need for *higher* deficits in order to achieve societal progress. They talk of taxing speculative financial flows when they should be declaring these transactions illegal. They promise to 'bring the unemployment rate down', when they should be saying that there is never a reasonable excuse for a monetarily sovereign country to have anything less than full employment at all times.

By buying into neoliberal macroeconomic myths, the left has become unable to articulate radical alternatives. However, that is exactly what we need, and what – we hope – this book will contribute to. As Perry Anderson recently noted: 'For anti-systemic movements of the left in Europe' – though the same applies elsewhere as well – 'the lesson of recent years is clear. If they are not to go on being outpaced by movements of the right, they cannot afford to be less radical in attacking the system, and must be more coherent in their opposition to it'.[1] In other words, *the left needs to get radical again.* Recent events demonstrate this. In the US, Bernie Sanders has shown the potential of breaking out of the 'responsible' political discourse. Becky Bond and Zack Exley, the leading organisers behind Sanders' 2016 presidential nomination campaign, write in their book *Rules for Revolutionaries: How Big Organizing Can Change Everything*:

> What set Bernie apart from the start of his campaign was his message and his authenticity as a messenger. Then he unleashed the makings of a real political revolution – he asked for one. He outlined radical solutions our moment calls for, not the tepid incrementalist compromises that most politicians think is all that is feasible. Bernie didn't talk about education tax credits or even debt-free college. He demanded free college tuition. He didn't advocate for complicated health insurance schemes, he said 'healthcare is a human right'. Bernie called for an end to mass incarceration, not incremental changes in sentencing laws. He had no 10-point plan to regulate fracking to the point that it wouldn't be feasible in most places in the United States. He simply said we should ban fracking.[2]

Similarly, the recent French presidential elections saw the surge of a new radical, oppositional and 'populist' left under the leadership of Jean-Luc Mélenchon. Mélenchon articulated what the Socialist Party – which was virtually wiped off the political map – failed to articulate: a progressive vision of the future, which included radical alternatives to the straightjacket of the monetary union. Instead of siding with capital to undermine the rights and welfare of French workers, Mélenchon articulated a vision for restoring workers' rights, a radical redistribution of wealth, a free national healthcare system, full employment and other policies that in the context of the current orthodoxy appear 'radical' but were considered garden-variety left policies a few decades ago. The same can be said of Jeremy Corbyn, who in the June 2017 UK general elections delivered Labour its best result in 20 years on the basis of a programme which includes the renationalisation of mail, rail and energy firms. All these leaders are cognisant of the need to address the growing tensions between global capitalism and the state system by articulating a positive, progressive vision of national sovereignty. As we have argued throughout this book, a renewed focus on national sovereignty is crucial to the resurgence of the left. As Wolfgang Streeck notes, in the coming years the growing masses of citizens dispossessed by the forces of neo-liberalism will increasingly 'choose the reality of national democracy, imperfect as it may be, over the fantasy of a democratic global society'.[3] Whether that reality will be one based on hatred, intolerance and authoritarianism or social, economic and environmental justice depends on us.

Finally, even though in this book we have focused mainly on the economic and technical aspects of a progressive national strategy, it is clear that having a compelling socio-economic programme is not enough to win over the hearts and minds of the people. Beyond the centrality of the state from a political-economic point of view, the left has to come to terms with the fact that for the vast majority of people that don't belong – and never will belong – to the globetrotting international elite, their sense of citizenship, collective identity and common good is intrinsically and intimately tied to nationhood. Ultimately, being a citizen means to deliberate with other citizens in a shared political community and hold decision makers accountable. As Michael Ignatieff writes:

> Most citizens don't love the state or identify with it, and thank goodness they look to their families, their neighbourhoods, and traditions for the belonging and loyalties that give life meaning. But they also know that they need a sovereign with the power to compel competing sources of power in society to serve the public good. People don't want big government but they do want protection. They're perfectly willing to take responsibility for the risks they take themselves, but they want some public authority to protect them from the systemic risks imposed on them by the powerful. They refuse to see why large corporations should privatise their gains, but socialise their losses. They want to have a competent sovereign, and what goes with this, they want to feel that they are sovereign.[4]

The right today is also winning because it is capable of weaving powerful narratives of *collective identity* in which national sovereignty is defined in nativist, nationalist or even racist terms. Progressives must thus be able to provide equally powerful narratives and frames, which recognise the human need for belonging and connectedness. In this sense, a progressive vision of national sovereignty should aim to reconstruct and redefine the national state as a place where citizens can seek refuge 'in democratic protection, popular rule, local autonomy, collective goods and egalitarian traditions', as Wolfgang Streeck argues, rather than a culturally and ethnically homogenised society.[5] This is also the necessary prerequisite for the construction of a new international(ist) world order, based on interdependent but independent sovereign states.

Notes

INTRODUCTION

1. See Perry Anderson, 'Why the System Will Win', *Le Monde diplomatique*, March 2017.
2. Ray Dalio et al., *Populism: The Phenomenon*, Bridgewater, 22 March 2017.
3. 'Rose Thou Art Sick', *The Economist*, 2 April 2016.
4. Paolo Gerbaudo, 'Post-Neoliberalism and the Politics of Sovereignty', *openDemocracy*, 4 November 2016.
5. Marc Saxer, 'In Search of a Progressive Patriotism', *Medium*, 15 April 2017.
6. Adaner Usmani, 'The Left in Europe: From Social Democracy to the Crisis in the Euro Zone: An Interview with Leo Panitch', *New Politics*, Vol. 14, No. 54 (Winter 2013).
7. Stuart Hall, 'The Great Moving Right Show', *Marxism Today*, January 1979, p. 18.
8. Colin Hay, 'Globalisation, Welfare Retrenchment and the "Logic of No Alternative": Why Second-Best Won't Do', *Journal of Social Policy*, Vol. 7, No. 4 (1998), p. 529.
9. John Ardagh, *France in the New Century*, London: Penguin, 2000, pp. 687-8.
10. Stephen Gill, 'The Geopolitics of Global Organic Crisis', *Analyze Greece!*, 5 June 2016.
11. Nancy Fraser, 'The End of Progressive Neoliberalism', *Dissent*, 2 January 2017.
12. Jonathan Haidt, 'When and Why Nationalism Beats Globalism', *The American Interest*, Vol. 12, No. 1 (July 2016).
13. Wolfgang Streeck, 'The Return of the Repressed', *New Left Review*, Vol. 104 (March–April 2017).
14. Yanis Varoufakis and Lorenzo Marsili, 'Varoufakis: "A un anno dall'Oxi, non rifugiamoci nei nazionalismi. Un'Europa democratica è possibile"', *la Repubblica*, 8 July 2016.
15. J. W. Mason, 'A Cautious Case for Economic Nationalism', *Dissent*, Spring 2017.
16. Fraser, 'The End of Progressive Neoliberalism'.
17. Wolfgang Streeck et al., 'Where Are We Now? Responses to the Referendum', *London Review of Books*, Vol. 38, No. 14 (July 2016).

CHAPTER 1

1. Adam Przeworski and Michael Wallerstein, 'Democratic Capitalism at the Crossroads', in Thomas Ferguson and Joel Rogers (eds), *Political Economy:*

    Readings in the Politics and Economics of American Public Policy, New York: M. E. Sharpe, 1984, p. 339.

2. Nouriel Roubini and Stephen Mihm, *Crisis Economics: A Crash Course in the Future of Finance*, London: Penguin, 2011, p. 24.

3. John Maynard Keynes, *The General Theory of Employment, Interest, and Money*, New York: Classic House, 2008, chapter 24.

4. Quoted in Roubini and Mihm, *Crisis Economics*, p. 158.

5. Ibid.

6. Roubini and Mihm, *Crisis Economics*, p. 159.

7. Niall Ferguson and Nouriel Roubini, 'The Perils of Ignoring History: This Time, Europe Really Is On the Brink', *Spiegel Online*, 12 June 2012.

8. Quoted in Harriet Torry and Margit Feher, 'Nowotny Links Austerity With Rise of Nazism', *Wall Street Journal*, 19 June 2012.

9. Steven Bryan, 'The Historical Appeal of Austerity', Columbia University Press blog, 1 October 2010.

10. Chris Harman, 'The State and Capitalism Today', *International Socialism*, Vol. 2, No. 51 (Summer 1991), pp. 3–57.

11. Ibid.

12. Pierre Larrouturou, *Svegliatevi!*, Milan: Piemme, 2012, p. 15 (authors' translation, emphasis added).

13. Roubini and Mihm, *Crisis Economics*, p. 161.

14. Joan Robinson, 'The Second Crisis of Economic Theory', *American Economic Review*, Vol. 62, No. 2 (1972), pp. 1–10.

15. The term is attributed to Joan Robinson.

16. Simon Clarke, *Keynesianism, Monetarism and the Crisis of the State*, Aldershot: Edward Elgar, 1988, p. 275.

17. David Harvey, *A Brief History of Neoliberalism*, Oxford: Oxford University Press, 2005, p. 10.

18. Michel Aglietta, *A Theory of Capitalist Regulation: The US Experience*, London and New York: Verso, 1979, p. 20.

19. Clarke, *Keynesianism, Monetarism and the Crisis of the State*, pp. 9–10.

20. Bob Jessop, 'Fordism and Post-Fordism: A critical Reformulation', in A. J. Scott and M. J. Storper (eds), *Pathways to Regionalism and Industrial Development*, London: Routledge, 1992, pp. 43–65.

21. Mariana Mazzucato, *The Entrepreneurial State*, London: Anthem, 2013.

22. Stuart Hall et al., *Policing the Crisis: Mugging, the State, and Law and Order*, London and Basingstoke: Macmillan, 1978, p. 214.

23. Ibid.

24. Ibid., p. 236.

25. Richard Westra, 'From Imperialism to Varieties of Capitalism', in Richard Westra et al. (eds), *The Future of Capitalism After the Financial Crisis*, Milton Park: Routledge, 2015.

26. Przeworski and Wallerstein, 'Democratic Capitalism at the Crossroads', p. 336.

27. Ibid., p. 338.

28. Quoted in Przeworski and Wallerstein, 'Democratic Capitalism at the Crossroads', p. 338.
29. Al Campbell, 'The Birth of Neoliberalism in the United States', in Alfredo Saad Filho and Deborah Johnston (eds), *Neoliberalism: A Critical Reader*, London: Pluto, 2005, p. 189 (emphasis added). Quoted in Chris Harman, 'Theorising Neoliberalism', *International Socialism*, No. 117 (Winter 2008).
30. Clarke, *Keynesianism, Monetarism and the Crisis of the State*, p. 276.
31. Campbell, 'The Birth of Neoliberalism in the United States', p. 188. Quoted in Harman, 'Theorising Neoliberalism'.
32. Harman, 'Theorising Neoliberalism'.
33. Ibid.
34. Robinson, 'The Second Crisis of Economic Theory'.
35. Ibid.
36. Keynes, *The General Theory*, chapter 24.
37. John Maynard Keynes, broadcast lecture, 14 March 1932.
38. Ibid. (emphasis added).
39. John Maynard Keynes, 'Economic Possibilities For Our Grandchildren', in John Maynard Keynes, *Essays in Persuasion*, New York: W. W. Norton, 1963, pp. 358–3.
40. Robinson, 'The Second Crisis of Economic Theory'.
41. Lars P. Syll, 'Why IS-LM Doesn't Capture Keynes' Approach to the Economy', author's blog, 25 November 2016.
42. Ibid.
43. David C. Colander et al. (eds), *The Coming of Keynesianism to America*, Aldershot: Edward Elgar, 1996.
44. Paul Davidson, 'Post World War II Politics and Keynes's Aborted Revolutionary Economic Theory', *Economia e Sociedade*, Vol. 35 (2008).
45. Robinson, 'The Second Crisis of Economic Theory'.
46. Paul A. Baran and Paul M. Sweezy, *Monopoly Capital*, New York and London: Monthly Review, 1966.
47. See Riccardo Bellofiore, 'The Socialization of Investment: From Keynes to Minsky and Beyond', Working Paper No. 822, Levy Economics Institute, 2014.
48. *Business Week*, 12 February 1949.
49. Keynes himself, in a 1945 article published in the *New Republic*, had conceded that it might be 'politically impossible for a capitalistic democracy to organise expenditure on the scale necessary to make the grand experiments which would prove my case – except in war conditions'.
50. Robinson, 'The Second Crisis of Economic Theory'.
51. The term is used by Peter Gowan in 'The American Campaign for Global Sovereignty', *Socialist Register*, Vol. 39 (2003).
52. Bellofiore, 'The Socialization of Investment'.
53. Karl Marx, *A Contribution to the Critique of Hegel's Philosophy of Right*, first published in *Deutsch-Französische Jahrbücher*, 7 and 10 February 1844.
54. David Riesman, *The Lonely Crowd: A Study of the Changing American Character*, New Haven, CT: Yale University Press, 1950.

55. Clarke, *Keynesianism, Monetarism and the Crisis of the State*, pp. 271–2.
56. Adaner Usmani, 'The Left in Europe: From Social Democracy to the Crisis in the Euro Zone: An Interview with Leo Panitch', *New Politics*, Vol. 14, No. 54 (Winter 2013).
57. Anthony Crosland, *The Future of Socialism*, London: Jonathan Cape, 1956.

CHAPTER 2

1. Milton Friedman, 'The Role of Monetary Policy', *The American Economic Review*, Vol. 58, No. 1 (March 1968).
2. Quoted in Paul Krugman, 'Who Was Milton Friedman?', *The New York Review of Books*, 15 February 2007.
3. Michael Kumhof and Zoltán Jakab, 'Banks Are Not Intermediaries of Loanable Funds – and Why This Matters', Working Paper No. 529, Bank of England, 2015, p. iii.
4. Ibid., p. 5.
5. John Maynard Keynes, *Treatise on Money*, New York: Harcourt, Brace & Company, 1976.
6. Milton Friedman and Anna Jacobson Schwartz, *A Monetary History of the United States, 1867–1960*, Princeton, NJ: Princeton University Press, 1963.
7. Friedman, 'The Role of Monetary Policy'.
8. Krugman, 'Who Was Milton Friedman?'
9. Friedman, 'The Role of Monetary Policy'.
10. *The Banker*, Vol. 118, No. 514 (December 1968).
11. *The Report of the Committee on the Working of the Monetary System*, 1959, p. 132.
12. Aled Davies, 'The Evolution of British Monetarism, 1968–1979', Discussion Papers in Economic and Social History No. 104, University of Oxford, 2012.
13. Harold James, *International Monetary Cooperation Since Bretton Woods*, Washington, DC: International Monetary Fund, 1996, p. 191.
14. Simon Clarke, *Keynesianism, Monetarism and the Crisis of the State*, Aldershot: Edward Elgar, 1988, p. 329.
15. Leo Panitch and Sam Gindin, 'Global Capitalism and American Empire', *Socialist Register*, Vol. 40 (2009).
16. See Guido Giacomo Preparata and Domenico D'Amico with Evelyn Ysais, 'The Political Economy of Hyper-Modernity', in Giacomo Preparata and Domenico D'Amico (eds), *New Directions in Catholic Social and Political Research*, New York: Palgrave Macmillan, 2016.
17. Quoted in 'Galbraith Urges Wage-Price Curb', *The New York Times*, 20 July 1970.
18. John Cornwall, *The Conditions for Economic Recovery*, Armonk, NY: M. E. Sharpe, 1983, pp. 200–1.
19. Franco Modigliani and Tommaso Padoa-Schioppa, 'La politica economica in una economia con salari indicizzati al 100 o più', *Moneta e Credito*, Vol. 30, No. 117 (1977); 'The Management of an Open Economy with "100%

Plus" Wage Indexation', *Essays in International Finance*, No. 130 (December 1978).
20. Luigi L. Pasinetti, 'How Much of John Maynard Keynes Can We Find in Franco Modigliani?', *BNL Quarterly Review*, Vol. 58, Nos. 233–4 (June–September 2005), pp. 21–39.
21. James O'Connor, *The Fiscal Crisis of the State*, Piscataway, NJ: Transaction, 1973.
22. Ibid., p. 1.
23. Eric Hobsbawm, *Age of Extremes*, London: Abacus, 1995, p. 411.
24. Raymond Vernon, *Sovereignty at Bay: The Multinational Spread of US Enterprises*, New York: Basic, 1971.
25. Raymond Vernon, 'Economic Sovereignty at Bay', *Foreign Affairs*, October 1968.
26. Ibid.
27. Ibid.
28. Ibid.
29. Alan Blinder, 'The Fall and Rise of Keynesian Economics', *The Economic Record*, Vol. 64, No. 187 (1988), pp. 278–94.
30. Philip Mirowski and Dieter Plehwe (eds), *The Road from Mont Pèlerin*, Cambridge, MA and London: Harvard University Press, 2009, p. 8.
31. Clarke, *Keynesianism, Monetarism and the Crisis of the State*, pp. 1 and 329.
32. Gérard Duménil and Dominique Lévy, 'The Neoliberal (Counter-) Revolution', in Alfredo Saad Filho and Deborah Johnston (eds), *Neoliberalism: A Critical Reader*, London: Pluto, 2005, p. 12.
33. Blinder, 'The Fall and Rise of Keynesian Economics', p. 278.
34. Interview by Adam Curtis for the 1992 documentary *Pandora's Box* (emphasis added).
35. David Harvey, *A Brief History of Neoliberalism*, Oxford: Oxford University Press, 2005, p. 15.
36. Andrew Glyn, *Capitalism Unleashed*, Oxford: Oxford University Press, 2006, p. 18.
37. Michał Kalecki, 'Political Aspects of Full Employment', *Political Quarterly*, 1943.
38. Ibid.
39. Michel J. Crozier et al., *The Crisis of Democracy*, New York: NYU Press, 1975.
40. Ibid., p. 8.
41. Ibid., pp. 113–14 and 40.
42. Naomi Klein, *The Shock Doctrine*, New York: Metropolitan, 2007, p. 141.
43. Glyn, *Capitalism Unleashed*, p. 7.
44. Ibid., p. 5.
45. Richard B. Freeman (ed.), *Working Under Different Rules*, New York: Russell Sage, p. 15.
46. Karl Marx, *Value, Price and Profit*, New York: International Co. Inc., 1865.
47. Ibid.

48. Robert Rowthorn, *Capitalism, Conflict and Inflation*, London: Lawrence and Wishart, 1980, p. 133.

49. Ibid., p. 134.

50. David Harvey, *The Condition of Postmodernity*, Oxford: Basil Blackwell, 1989, p. 142.

51. Clarke, *Keynesianism, Monetarism and the Crisis of the State*, pp. 304–5.

CHAPTER 3

1. Robert Rowthorn, *Capitalism, Conflict and Inflation*, London: Lawrence and Wishart, 1980, p. 68.

2. Asad Haider, 'Law and Order: Make Marxism Great Again', *Viewpoint Magazine*, 28 July 2016.

3. Simon Clarke, *Keynesianism, Monetarism and the Crisis of the State*, Aldershot: Edward Elgar, 1988, p. 305.

4. Ibid., p. 311.

5. Stuart Hall et al., *Policing the Crisis: Mugging, the State, and Law and Order*, London and Basingstoke: Macmillan, 1978, p. 260.

6. Hugo Radice (ed.), *Global Capitalism: Selected Essays*, Milton Park and New York: Routledge, 2015.

7. David Harvey, *A Brief History of Neoliberalism*, Oxford: Oxford University Press, 2005, pp. 14–15.

8. Clarke, *Keynesianism, Monetarism and the Crisis of the State*, p. 304.

9. Davies, *The Evolution of British Monetarism*, p. 12.

10. 'On Labour's Programme 1973', *Guardian*, 3 October 1973.

11. John Medhurst, *That Option No Longer Exists: Britain 1974–76*, London: John Hunt, 2014.

12. Ibid., p. 103.

13. Martin Holmes, *The Labour Government, 1974–79*, Houndmills and London: Macmillan, 1985, p. 41.

14. Ibid., p. 40.

15. Medhurst, *That Option No Longer Exists*, p. 116.

16. Glyn, *Capitalism Unleashed*, p. 8.

17. Stuart Hall, 'The Great Moving Right Show', *Marxism Today*, January 1979, p. 17.

18. Ibid., p. 18.

19. Jim Tomlinson, 'Crowding Out', *History & Policy*, 5 December 2010.

20. British Cabinet, 'Conclusions of a Meeting of the Cabinet', 10 June 1976, p. 6.

21. International Monetary Fund, *Annual Report 114*, 1974, p. 112.

22. Peter Riddell, *The Thatcher Government*, Oxford: Martin Robertson, 1983, p. 59.

23. United States Senate, 'US Foreign Economic Policy: The United Kingdom, France, and West Germany', Washington, DC: US Government Printing Office, p. 4.

24. British Cabinet, 'Conclusions of a Meeting of Cabinet', 6 July 1976.

25. United States Senate, 'US Foreign Economic Policy', p. 1.
26. Clarke, *Keynesianism, Monetarism and the Crisis of the State*, p. 314.
27. Steve Ludlum, 'The Gnomes of Washington: Four Myths of the 1976 IMF Crisis', *Political Studies*, Vol. 40, No. 4 (1992), p. 724.
28. Ibid.
29. United States Senate, 'US Foreign Economic Policy'.
30. James Heartfield, 'European Union: A Process Without a Subject', in Christopher J. Bickerton et al. (eds), *Politics Without Sovereignty*, London: UCL Press, 2007, pp. 140–1.
31. Colin Hay, 'Globalisation, Welfare Retrenchment and the "Logic of No Alternative": Why Second-Best Won't Do', *Journal of Social Policy*, Vol. 7, No. 4 (1998), p. 528.
32. Ibid., p. 529.
33. Ibid.
34. Ibid.
35. United States Senate, 'US Foreign Economic Policy'.
36. Duménil and Lévy, 'The Neoliberal (Counter-)Revolution'.
37. Preparata and D'Amico, 'The Political Economy of Hyper-Modernity', p. 14.
38. Ibid., p. 16.
39. William Greider, *Secrets of the Temple*, New York: Simon & Schuster, 1989, p. 506.
40. Kees van der Pijl, 'Rebellion in Athens', June 2015.
41. Panitch and Gindin, 'Global Capitalism and American Empire', p. 22.
42. James M. Boughton, *The IMF and the Force of History*, Washington, DC: International Monetary Fund, 2006, p. 30.
43. John Williamson, 'What Washington Means by Policy Reform', in John Williamson (ed.), *Latin American Readjustment: How Much has Happened*, Washington, DC: Peterson Institute for International Economics, 1990.
44. See, for example, Joseph E. Stiglitz, *Globalization and its Discontents*, New York: W. W. Norton, 2002; and Jagdish Bhagwati, 'The Capital Myth', *Foreign Affairs*, Vol. 77, No. 3 (1998), pp. 7–12.
45. Francis Fukuyama, 'The End of History?', *The National Interest*, No. 16 (1989), pp. 3–18.
46. Panitch and Gindin, 'Global Capitalism and American Empire', p. 20 (emphasis added).

CHAPTER 4

1. The prevailing wisdom of the time on the relationship between capital and the common market was spelled out by the European Court of Justice in 1981, when it ruled on the case of an Italian arrested for attempting to take 24,000 German marks in cash out of the country (Italian law prohibited the unauthorised exportation of foreign currency worth more than 500,000 lire). The European Court of Justice ruled that the Treaty of Rome contained no 'general principle' favouring capital freedom, and that

the Italian regulations were consistent with EEC laws: 'At present, it cannot be denied that complete freedom of movement of capital may undermine the economic policy of one of the member states or create an imbalance in its balance of payments, thereby impairing the proper functioning of the common market.' The Court thus found that, at least in 1981, the success of the common market depended in part on restricting capital mobility.

2. Rawi E. Abdelal, *Capital Rules: The Construction of Global Finance*, Cambridge, MA: Harvard University Press, 2007, p. 58.

3. *Business Week*, 23 March 1981.

4. Quoted in Jonah Birch, 'The Many Lives of François Mitterrand', *Jacobin*, 19 August 2015.

5. Birch, 'The Many Lives of François Mitterrand'.

6. Abdelal, *Capital Rules*, p. 61.

7. Ibid., p. 60.

8. Ibid.

9. Will Hutton, *The World We're In*, London: Little Brown, 2002, p. 296, quoted in James Heartfield, 'European Union: A Process Without a Subject', in Christopher J. Bickerton et al. (eds), *Politics Without Sovereignty*, London: UCL Press, 2007, pp. 140–1.

10. Abdelal, *Capital Rules*, p. 59.

11. John Ardagh, *France in the New Century*, London: Penguin, 2000, pp. 687–8, quoted in Heartfield, 'European Union: A Process Without a Subject'.

12. Christian De Boissieu and Jean Pisani-Ferry, *The Political Economy of French Economic Policy in the Perspective of EMU*, Document de travail n. 95-09, Centre d'Etudes Prospectives et d'Informations Internationales, October 1995, p. 23.

13. Ibid.

14. Quoted in Charles Grant, *Delors: Inside the House that Jacques Built*, London: Nicholas Brealey.

15. Abdelal, *Capital Rules*, p. 64.

16. Nicolas Jabko, 'In the Name of the Market: How the European Commission Paved the Way for Monetary Union', *Journal of European Public Policy*, Vol. 6, No. 3 (1999), p. 476, quoted in Abdelal, *Capital Rules*.

17. Horst Ungerer et al., *The European Monetary System: Developments and Perspectives*, Washington, DC: International Monetary Fund, 1990, p. 10.

18. Quoted in Abdelal, *Capital Rules*.

19. Ibid.

20. Jacques Melitz, 'Financial Deregulation in France', *European Economic Review*, Vol. 34, Nos. 2–3 (1990), pp. 394–5, quoted in Abdelal, *Capital Rules*.

21. Jabko, 'In the Name of the Market', p. 475.

22. Abdelal, *Capital Rules*, p. 77.

23. Elena Rodica Danescu, *The Werner Report and the Delors Report*, Centre Virtuel de la Connaissance sur l'Europe, 2013, p. 4.

24. David Howarth and Peter Loedel, *The European Central Bank: The New European Leviathan?* Houndmills: Palgrave Macmillan, 2003, p. 36.
25. Amy Verdun, 'The Role of the Delors Committee in the Creation of EMU: An Epistemic Community?', *Journal of European Public Policy*, Vol. 6, No. 2 (1999), p. 308.
26. Peter M. Haas, 'Introduction: Epistemic Communities and International Policy Coordination', *International Organization*, Vol. 46, No. 1 (Winter 1992), p. 3.
27. European Commission, *Pierre Werner – Testimonies at the Threshold of the 21st Century*, 1999.
28. European Commission, *Report to the Council and the Commission on the Realization by Stages of Economic and Monetary Union in the Community* (also known as the *Werner Report*), 1970, p. 10.
29. Ibid., p. 12.
30. European Commission, *Report of the Study Group on the Role of Public Finance in European Integration* (also known as the *MacDougall Report*), 1977.
31. European Commission, *Report on Economic and Monetary Union in the European Community* (also known as the *Delors Report*), 1989, p. 13.
32. Ibid., pp. 20–1.
33. Quoted in Richard McAllister, *European Union: An Historical and Political Survey*, New York: Taylor & Francis, 2009, p. 58.
34. Abdelal, *Capital Rules*, p. 85.
35. Ibid., p. 84.
36. Valerio Lintner, 'The European Community: 1958 to the 1990s', in Max Schulze (ed.), *Western Europe: Economic and Social Change Since 1945*, London: Longman, 1999, p. 153, quoted in Heartfield, 'European Union: A Process Without a Subject' (emphasis added).

CHAPTER 5

1. Ronald Reagan's first inaugural address, January 1981.
2. See Kean Birch, 'Have We Ever Been Neoliberal?', working paper, May 2011.
3. Ibid.
4. Ibid.
5. Ibid.
6. Miguel A. Centeno and Joseph N. Cohen, 'The Arc of Neoliberalism', *Annual Review of Sociology*, Vol. 38 (August 2012), pp. 317–40.
7. Susan Strange, *Casino Capitalism*, Oxford: Basil Blackwell, 1986, chapter 2.
8. James A. Baker III, remarks before a conference at the Institute for International Economics, 14 September 1987.
9. Noam Chomsky, 'How Free is the Free Market?', *Resurgence*, No. 173 (1995).
10. Friedrich Hayek, *The Road to Serfdom*, London: Routledge, 1944, p. 39.
11. Milton Friedman, *Capitalism and Freedom*, Chicago: University of Chicago, 1962, p. 27.

12. Joao Rodrigues, 'The Political and Moral Economies of Neoliberalism', *Cambridge Journal of Economics*, Vol. 37 (2013), p. 1008.

13. Mario Pianta, *Nove su dieci: Perché stiamo (quasi) tutti peggio di dieci anni fa*, Bari: Laterza, 2012, p. 60 (author's translation).

14. Giovanni Arrighi, *The Long Twentieth Century*, London and New York: Verso, 1994, p. 10.

15. Karl Marx, *Manifesto of the Communist Party*, 1848.

16. See Colin Hay, 'Marxism and the State', in Andrew Gamble et al. (eds), *Marxism and Social Science*, Urbana and Chicago: University of Illinois, 1975, pp. 152–74.

17. Leo Panitch and Sam Gindin, 'Global Capitalism and American Empire', *Socialist Register*, Vol. 40 (2009), p. 7.

18. Karl Polanyi, *The Great Transformation*, New York: Farrar & Reinhart, 1944.

19. Ibid., pp. 139–41.

20. See Chris Harman, 'The State and Capitalism Today', *International Socialism*, Vol. 2, No. 51 (Summer 1991), pp. 3–57.

21. Adam Smith, *An Inquiry into the Nature and Causes of the Wealth of Nations*, 1776, book 4, chapter 9.

22. Fernand Braudel, *Afterthoughts on Material Civilization and Capitalism*, Baltimore, MD: Johns Hopkins University Press, 1977, pp. 64–5, quoted in Arrighi, *The Long Twentieth Century*.

23. Arrighi, *The Long Twentieth Century*, p. 10.

24. Fernand Braudel, *The Perspective of the World*, New York: Harper & Row, 1984, p. 92.

25. Hay, 'Marxism and the State'.

26. Elmar Altvater, 'Notes on Some Problems of State Interventionism', *Kapitalistate*, No. 1 (1973), pp. 97–108.

27. Hay, 'Marxism and the State'; see also Bob Jessop, *The State*, Cambridge and Malden, MA: Polity, 2016, chapter 4.

28. Arrighi, *The Long Twentieth Century*, p. 20.

29. Ibid.

30. Naomi Klein, *The Shock Doctrine*, New York: Metropolitan, 2007, pp. 59, 7.

31. Quoted in George Monbiot, 'Neoliberalism: The Ideology at the Root of All Our Problems', *Guardian*, 15 April 2016.

32. Oxfam, *Be Outraged: There Are Alternatives*, May 2012, pp. 13–15.

33. Ibid.

34. IMF Independent Evaluation Office (IEO), *Fiscal Adjustment in IMF-Supported Programs*, 2003.

35. Klein, *The Shock Doctrine*, p. 15 (emphasis added).

36. Stefania Vitali et al., *The Network of Global Corporate Control*, ETH Zurich, September 2011.

37. Panitch and Gindin, 'Global Capitalism and American Empire', p. 29.

38. Thomas L. Friedman, 'A Manifesto for the Fast World', *The New York Times Magazine*, 28 March 1999.

39. Project for a New American Century, *Rebuilding America's Defenses*, Washington, DC: PNAC, 2000.
40. Michael Hardt and Antonio Negri, *Empire*, Cambridge, MA: Harvard University Press, 2000, pp. 137–8.
41. David Harvey, *A Brief History of Neoliberalism*, Oxford: Oxford University Press, 2005.
42. Stephen Gill, 'The Geopolitics of Global Organic Crisis', *Analyze Greece!*, 5 June 2016.
43. 'Five Minutes with Noam Chomsky', London School of Economics' EUROPP blog, 3 December 2012.
44. Hugo Radice, 'Reshaping Fiscal Policies in Europe: Enforcing Austerity, Attacking Democracy', *Social Europe Journal*, 11 February 2013.
45. Mario Seccareccia, 'The ECB and the Betrayal of the Bagehot Rule', *Economia e Politica*, 12 August 2015.
46. Lukas Oberndorfer, 'A New Economic Governance through Secondary Legislation? Analysis and Constitutional Assessment: From New Constitutionalism, via Authoritarian Constitutionalism to Progressive Constitutionalism', in Niklas Bruun et al. (eds), *The Economic and Financial Crisis and Collective Labour Law in Europe*, Oxford and Portland, OR: Hart, 2014, pp. 25–47.
47. John Maynard Keynes, *The General Theory of Employment, Interest, and Money*, New York: Classic House, 2008, p. 26.
48. Seán Healy, 'Is Austerity Working?' *Irish Examiner*, 7 August 2013.
49. ETUI, *Benchmarking Working Europe 2013*, Brussels: ETUI, 2013.
50. Aaron Pacitti, 'Austerity and the Consolidation of Elite Power', *Huffington Post*, 23 December 2012.
51. 'Five Minutes with Noam Chomsky'.
52. Paul Krugman, 'The 1 Percent's Solution', *New York Times*, 25 April 2013.
53. For 2010 data see Credit Suisse, *Global Wealth Report*, October 2010, p. 17; for 2012 data see Credit Suisse, *Global Wealth Report 2012*, October 2012, p. 20; for 2013 data see Credit Suisse, *Global Wealth Report 2013*, October 2013, p. 23.
54. ILO, *World of Work Report 2013: Repairing the Economic and Social Fabric*, 2013, pp. 79–84.
55. Ibid., pp. 79–80.
56. Pedersen & Partners, 'Top Executive Compensation in Top 100-Companies Averages 1.3 Million Euros', 2012.
57. Ibid.
58. See Richard Peet, 'Contradictions of Finance Capitalism', *Monthly Review*, Vol. 63, No. 7 (December 2011).
59. John Ardagh, *France in the New Century*, London: Penguin, 2000, pp. 687–8, quoted in James Heartfield, 'European Union: A Process Without a Subject', in Christopher J. Bickerton et al. (eds), *Politics Without Sovereignty*, London: UCL Press, 2007, pp. 140–1.
60. Susan Strange, *The Retreat of the State*, Cambridge: Cambridge University Press, 1996.

61. Ibid., p. 4.
62. Göran Therborn, 'Globalizations: Dimensions, Historical Waves, Regional Effects, Normative Governance', *International Sociology*, Vol. 15, No. 2 (2000), p. 153.
63. https://en.wikipedia.org/wiki/Globalization.
64. Therborn, 'Globalizations', p. 155.
65. Marx, *Manifesto of the Communist Party*, 1848 (emphasis added).
66. Chris Brown, Foreword to Bickerton et al. (eds), *Politics Without Sovereignty*. As Brown notes, the problems of national sovereignty in political science have played an essential role since the late sixteenth century and the publication of Jean Bodin's *Six Books of the Commonwealth*.
67. John Quiggin, 'Globalization and Economic Sovereignty', *Journal of Political Philosophy*, Vol. 91, No. 1 (2000), pp. 58–60.
68. Arrighi, *The Long Twentieth Century*, p. 28.
69. Sam Gindin, 'Unmaking Global Capitalism', *Jacobin*, 1 June 2014.
70. David Harvey, *The Condition of Postmodernity*, Oxford: Basil Blackwell, 1989.
71. Dani Rodrik, 'The Inescapable Trilemma of the World Economy', author's blog, 27 June 2000. A full academic argument is presented in Dani Rodrik, 'How Far Will International Economic Integration Go?', *Journal of Economic Perspectives*, Vol. 14, No. 1 (2000), pp. 177–86.
72. Ibid.
73. Ibid.
74. Ibid.
75. Arrighi, *The Long Twentieth Century*, p. 82.
76. Ibid., p. 75.
77. Peter F. Drucker, 'The Global Economy and the Nation-State', *Foreign Affairs*, Vol. 76, No. 5 (1997), pp. 167–8.
78. Ibid.
79. Strange, *The Retreat of the State*, p. 4.
80. Intan Suwandi and John Bellamy Foster, 'Multinational Corporations and the Globalization of Monopoly Capital', *Monthly Review*, Vol. 68, No. 3 (July–August 2016).
81. Charles P. Kindleberger, *American Business Abroad*, New Haven, CT: Yale University Press, 1969, p. 27.
82. Ibid., p. 207.
83. Richard Vernon, *Sovereignty at Bay*, New York: Basic Books, 1971.
84. These include Stephen Hymer, Samir Amin, Richard Barnet and Ronald Müller.
85. Paul A. Baran and Paul M. Sweezy, 'Notes on the Theory of Imperialism', *Monthly Review*, Vol. 17, No. 10 (March 1966), pp. 15–31.
86. Ibid., p. 18.
87. James O'Connor, *The Corporations and the State*, New York: Harper and Row, 1974, pp. 195–6.
88. https://en.wikipedia.org/wiki/Transnationality_Index.
89. Peter Dicken, *Global Shift*, London: Sage, 2003, pp. 221–4.

90. Harman, 'The State and Capitalism Today'.
91. Strange, *The Retreat of the State*, pp. 44–5 (emphasis added).
92. Robert B. Reich, *Saving Capitalism*, New York: Alfred A. Knopf, 2015, Introduction.
93. Gindin, 'Unmaking Global Capitalism'.
94. Harvey, *A Brief History of Neoliberalism*, pp. 3–4.
95. Herman E. Daly, 'The Perils of Free Trade', *Scientific American*, November 1993.
96. See John Bellamy Foster et al., 'The Global Reserve Army of Labor and the New Imperialism', *Monthly Review*, Vol. 63, No. 6 (November 2011).
97. Ibid.
98. Ibid.
99. Louis Uchitelle, 'Is Manufacturing Falling Off the Radar?', *New York Times*, 11 September 2011.
100. Sources: Federal Reserve Economic Data and World Wealth and Income Database.
101. Kate Bronfenbrenner, *Uneasy Terrain*, Ithaca, NY: ILR Collection, 2000.
102. Ibid.
103. OECD, *Growing Unequal? Income Distribution and Poverty in OECD Countries*, Paris: OECD, 2008, p. 128.
104. Luciano Gallino, *Finanzcapitalismo*, Turin: Einaudi, 2011, p. 163.
105. OECD, *Employment Outlook 2012*, Paris: OECD, 2012, p. 110.
106. ILO, *Global Wage Report 2016/2017*, Geneva: ILO, 2016.
107. OECD, *An Overview of Growing Income Inequalities in OECD Countries: Main Findings*, Paris: OECD, 2011, p. 38.
108. Ibid., p. 22.
109. OECD, *Growing Unequal?*, p. 32.
110. Oxfam, 'Wealth: Having It All and Wanting More', 2015.
111. Only after the 1997 East Asian crisis did the IMF require developing countries to switch to large trade surpluses. See Dean Baker, *Rigged*, Washington, DC: Center for Economic and Policy Research, 2016.
112. Ha-Joon Chang, *Bad Samaritans*, New York: Bloomsbury, 2008, p. 14.
113. See Ha-Joon Chang, *The Myth of Free Trade and the Secret History of Capitalism*, London: Bloomsbury, 2007.
114. Baker, *Rigged*, p. 7.
115. John Smith, *Imperialism in the Twenty-First Century*, New York: Monthly Review, 2016.
116. Ibid., p. 10.
117. Ibid, p. 22.
118. UNCTAD, *World Investment Report*, 2013, p. 122.
119. Chomsky, 'How Free is the Free Market?'
120. Joan Robinson, 'What Are the Questions?', *Journal of Economic Literature*, Vol. 15, No. 4 (December 1977), pp. 1318–39.
121. Baker, *Rigged*, p. 9.
122. Gallino, *L'impresa irresponsabile*, Turin: Einaudi, 2005, p. 35, quoted in Christian Marazzi, *The Violence of Financial Capitalism*, Cambridge, MA: Semiotext(e), 2011.

123. Harry Magdoff and Paul M. Sweezy, *Stagnation and the Financial Explosion*, New York: Monthly Review, 1987, p. 13.
124. Riccardo Bellofiore et al., 'A Credit-Money and Structural Perspective on the European Crisis: Why Exiting the Euro is the Answer to the Wrong Question', *Review of Keynesian Economics*, Vol. 3, No. 4 (2015), p. 6.
125. Marazzi, *The Violence of Financial Capitalism*, p. 34.
126. Nouriel Roubini, 'Economic Insecurity and Inequality Breed Political Instability', in Janet Byrne (ed.), *The Occupy Handbook*, New York: Back Bay, 2012, pp. 156–7.
127. Özlem Onaran, 'From Wage Suppression to Sovereign Debt Crisis in Western Europe: Who Pays for the Costs of the Crisis?', 3 December 2010.
128. Riccardo Bellofiore et al., 'A Credit-Money and Structural Perspective on the European Crisis', pp. 476–7.
129. Ibid., p. 475.
130. See Emmanuel N. Roussakis, *Commercial Banking in an Era of Deregulation*, Westport, CT and London: Praeger, 1997, p. 407.
131. Riccardo Bellofiore, 'The Socialization of Investment: From Keynes to Minsky and Beyond', Working Paper No. 822, Levy Economics Institute, 2014.
132. Ibid.
133. John Bellamy Foster, 'The Age of Monopoly-Finance Capital', *Monthly Review*, Vol. 61, No. 9 (February 2010).
134. J. G. Palma, 'The Revenge of the Market on the Rentiers: Why Neo-Liberal Reports on the End of History Turned Out to be Premature', *Cambridge Journal of Economics*, Vol. 33, No. 3 (2009), p. 2.
135. Gallino, *Finanzcapitalismo*, p. 167.
136. *Economist*, 'Reforming Derivatives', 2013.
137. BIS, *Triennial Central Bank Survey: Report on Global Foreign Exchange Market Activity in 2010*, December 2010, p. 7.
138. Hyman P, Minsky, *Stabilizing an Unstable Economy*, New Haven, CT: Yale University Press, 1986.
139. François Chesnais, *La finance mondialisée*, Paris: La Découverte, 2004.
140. François Chesnais, *La mondialisation du capital*, Paris: Syros, 1997, p. 74, quoted in Chris Harman, 'Theorising Neoliberalism', *International Socialism*, No. 117 (Winter 2008) (Harman's translation).
141. Ibid., p. 304, quoted in Harman, 'Theorising Neoliberalism' (Harman's translation).
142. Michael Hudson, 'The Paradox of Financialized Industrialization', author's blog, 16 October 2015.
143. Gerald Epstein, 'International Capital Mobility and the Scope for National Economic Management', in Robert Boyer and Daniel Drache (eds), *States Against Markets*, New York: Routledge, 1996, p. 157.
144. See Franco Bassanini and Edoardo Reviglio, *National States Sovereignty, Democracy and Global Financial Markets: The European Issues*, Rome: Astrid, December 2013.

145. Ibid.
146. Rudolf Hilferding, *Das Finanzkapital*, Berlin: Dietz, 1955.
147. Giovanni Arrighi, 'Globalization, State Sovereignty, and the "Endless" Accumulation of Capital', revised version of a paper presented at the Conference on 'States and Sovereignty in the World Economy', University of California, Irvine, 21–3 February 1997.
148. Epstein, 'International Capital Mobility', p. 212.
149. Braudel, *The Perspective of the World*.
150. Arrighi, 'Globalization', p. 8.
151. Marazzi, *The Violence of Financial Capitalism*, pp. 27–8.
152. Giovanni Arrighi, *Adam Smith in Beijing: Lineages of the 21st Century*, London: Verso, 2007, p. 140.
153. Arrighi, *The Long Twentieth Century*, p. 308.
154. Michael C. Webb, *The Political Economy of Policy Coordination*, Ithaca, NY and London: Cornell University Press, 1995, p. 95.
155. Ibid., p. 96.
156. Ibid., p. 97.
157. Epstein, 'International Capital Mobility', p. 157.
158. Ibid., p. 212.
159. Jessop, *The State*, p. 193.
160. Ibid., p. 198.
161. Leonard E. Grinin, 'State Sovereignty in the Age of Globalization: Will it Survive?', *Journal of Globalization Studies*, Vol. 3, No. 1 (2012), pp. 3–38.
162. Hugo Radice (ed.), *Global Capitalism: Selected Essays*, Milton Park and New York: Routledge, 2015.
163. Simon Clarke, *Keynesianism, Monetarism and the Crisis of the State*, Aldershot: Edward Elgar, 1988, p. 305.
164. Ibid., p. 311.
165. Gordon Brown, *Red Paper on Scotland*, Edinburgh: EUSPB, 1975, p. 7.
166. Michel J. Crozier et al., *The Crisis of Democracy*, New York: NYU Press, 1975, pp. 113–14 and 40.
167. Thomas L. Friedman, *The Lexus and the Olive Tree*, New York: Farrar, Straus and Giroux, 1999, pp. 103–4.
168. Colin Crouch, *Post-Democracy*, Cambridge: Polity, 2004.
169. Stephen Gill, 'Theoretical Foundations of a Neo-Gramscian Analysis of European Integration', in Hans-Jürgen Bieling and Jochen Steinhilber (eds), *Dimensions of a Critical Theory of European Integration*, Marburg: FEG am Institut für Politikwissenschaft des Fachbereichs Gesellschafts-wissenschaften und Philosophie der Phillips-Universität Marburg, 2000, pp. 15–33 and 30.
170. Stephen Gill, 'New Constitutionalism, Democratisation and Global Political Economy', *Pacifica Review: Peace, Security & Global Change*, Vol. 10, No. 1 (1998), pp. 23–38.
171. Heartfield, 'European Union: A Process Without a Subject', p. 138.
172. Ibid.

173. Andrew Moravcsik, *The Choice for Europe*, Ithaca, NY: Cornell University Press, pp. 264, 288, 338 and 386.

174. Heartfield, 'European Union: A Process Without a Subject', p. 141.

175. Quoted in Paul Ginsborg, *Italy and Its Discontents*, London: Allen Lane, 2001, p. 243.

176. Heartfield, 'European Union: A Process Without a Subject', p. 138; speech before the National Assembly, 12 October 1977.

177. Nigel Lawson, *The View from No. 11*, London: Corgi, 1993, p. 1024, quoted in Heartfield, 'European Union: A Process Without a Subject'.

178. Ibid., p. 111.

179. Bernhard Kempen, 'Art. 125, N. 1', in Rudolf Streinz, *EUV/AEUV: Vertrag über die Europäische Union und Vertrag über die Arbeitsweise der Europäischen Union*, Munich: CH Beck, 2012 (translation by Lukas Oberndorfer).

180. Heartfield, 'European Union: A Process Without a Subject', p. 144.

181. Oberndorfer, 'A New Economic Governance through Secondary Legislation?'.

182. Ulrich Häde, 'Art. 4 EGV, N. 8', in Christian Calliess and Matthias Ruffert (eds), *EUV/ EGV – Kommentar*, Munich: CH Beck, 2007 (translation by Lukas Oberndorfer).

183. Friedrich Hayek, 'The Economic Conditions of Interstate Federalism', 1948.

184. Karl Marx, 'The Constitution of the French Republic Adopted November 4, 1848', 1851.

185. Stephen Gill, 'European Governance and the New Constitutionalism', *New Political Economy*, Vol. 10, No. 1 (1998), p. 13.

186. Oberndorfer, 'A New Economic Governance through Secondary Legislation?', p. 38.

187. Wolfram Elsner, 'Financial Capitalism: At Odds with Democracy', *RealWorld Economics Review*, Vol. 62 (2012), p. 158.

188. Oberndorfer, 'A New Economic Governance through Secondary Legislation?', p. 53.

189. Edgar Grande, 'Das Paradox der Schwäche: Forschungspolitik und die Einflusslogik europäischer Politikverflechtung', in Markus Jachtenfuchs and Beate Kohler-Koch (eds), *Europäische Integration*, Wiesbaden: Springer, 1997, quoted in Alberto Bagnai, 'Europe's Paradoxes', *Phenomenology and Mind*, No. 8 (2015), p. 114.

190. Kevin Featherstone, 'The Political Dynamics of the Vincolo Esterno: The Emergence of EMU and the Challenge to the European Social Model', 2001, quoted in Bagnai, 'Europe's Paradoxes'.

191. Ellen Meiksins-Wood, *Democracy Against Capitalism: Renewing Historical Materialism*, Cambridge: Cambridge University Press, 1995, pp. 1–2.

192. Nancy Fraser, 'The End of Progressive Neoliberalism', *Dissent*, 2 January 2017.

193. Ibid.

194. Ibid.

CHAPTER 6

1. Paul Krugman, 'What Secular Stagnation Isn't', *New York Times*, 24 October 2014.
2. Philip Stephens, 'The Trumpian Threat to the Global Order', *Financial Times*, 22 September 2016.
3. Álvaro García Linera, 'La globalización ha muerto', *La Razón*, 27 December 2016 (authors' translation).
4. James Meadway, 'What If We've Reached Peak Globalisation?', *Guardian*, 28 September 2015.
5. Ibid.
6. Bjørn Lomborg, 'The Free-Trade Miracle', *Project Syndicate*, 21 October 2016.
7. Ibid.
8. Vassilis K. Fouskas and Bulent Gokay, 'Class, Trump, Brexit, and the Decline of the West', *openDemocracy*, 13 November 2016.
9. Alexander Naumov, 'Bitesize: Global growth: The *old* normal?', *Bank Underground*, 1 December 2016.
10. See, for example, Paul Arbair, '#Brexit, the Populist Surge and the Crisis of Complexity', author's blog, 5 July 2016.
11. Fouskas and Gokay, 'Class, Trump, Brexit'.
12. Mark Blyth, 'Global Trumpism', *Foreign Affairs*, 15 November 2016.
13. Antonio Gramsci, *Selections from the Prison Notebooks*, New York: International Publishers, 1971, pp. 275–6.
14. Paolo Gerbaudo, 'Post-Neoliberalism and the Politics of Sovereignty', *openDemocracy*, 4 November 2016.
15. Ibid.
16. Yanis Varoufakis and Lorenzo Marsili, 'Varoufakis: "A un anno dall'Oxi, non rifugiamoci nei nazionalismi. Un'Europa democratica è possibile"', *la Repubblica*, 8 July 2016.

CHAPTER 7

1. Jim Stanford, 'The Laws of Free Trade Are Not Immutable After All', *Real-World Economics Review Blog*, 9 January 2017.
2. Quoted in Wolfgang Münchau, 'Central Bank Independence is Losing its Lustre', *Financial Times*, 19 February 2017.
3. Quoted in George Parker and Chris Giles, 'PM Criticises "Bad Side-Effects" of Monetary Policy', *Financial Times*, 5 October 2016.
4. Wolfgang Münchau, 'Shadow Hangs Over Control of Central Banking', *Irish Times*, 20 April 2017.
5. Paul Krugman, 'The Big Fail', *New York Times*, 6 January 2013.
6. See Thomas Fazi, 'How Can Europe Change?' ISIGrowth Working Paper 33/2016, 2016.

7. Jonathan D. Ostry et al., 'Neoliberalism: Oversold?', *Finance & Development*, Vol. 53, No. 2 (2016), pp. 38–41.
8. Stanford, 'The Laws of Free Trade Are Not Immutable After All'.
9. Ibid.
10. Nancy Fraser, 'The End of Progressive Neoliberalism', *Dissent*, 2 January 2017.
11. See Fazi, 'How Can Europe Change?'
12. Richard Tuck, 'The Left Case for Brexit', *Dissent*, 6 June 2016.
13. Elias Ioakimoglou and George Souvlis, 'Greece Was the Prologue', *Jacobin*, 27 August 2016.
14. Wolfgang Münchau, 'The Wacky Economics of Germany's Parallel Universe', *Financial Times*, 16 November 2014.
15. Jürgen Habermas et al., 'Juncker is the Democratic Choice to Head the EU Commission', *Guardian*, 7 June 2016.
16. Lorenzo Del Savio and Matteo Mameli, 'Against the European Parliament', *openDemocracy*, 8 January 2015.
17. Ibid.
18. William Mitchell, *Eurozone Dystopia*, Aldershot: Edward Elgar, 2015.

CHAPTER 8

1. Robert Lucas Jr, 'Macroeconomic Priorities', *American Economic Review*, Vol. 93, No. 1 (March 2003), p. 1.
2. Ben S. Bernanke, 'The Great Moderation', speech at the meetings of the Eastern Economic Association, Washington, DC, 20 February 2004.
3. Olivier Blanchard, 'The State of Macro', *Annual Review of Economics*, Vol. 1, No. 1 (2008), p. 2.
4. Paul Romer, 'The Trouble With Macroeconomics', Commons Memorial Lecture of the Omicron Delta Epsilon Society, New York University, 5 January 2016.
5. IMF Independent Evaluation Office (IEO), *IMF Performance in the Run-Up to the Financial and Economic Crisis*, Washington, DC: IMF, 2011.
6. Ibid., p. 17.
7. Ibid., p. 18.
8. William Buiter, 'The Unfortunate Uselessness of Most "State of the Art" Academic Monetary Economics', *VoxEU.org*, 6 March 2009.
9. Paul Krugman, 'How Did Economists Get It So Wrong?', *New York Times*, 2 September 2009.
10. Joe Earle et al., *The Econocracy*, Manchester: Manchester University Press, 2016, p. 9.
11. Mark Blyth, *The History of a Dangerous Idea*, New York: Oxford University Press, 2013, p. 100.
12. Ann Pettifor, 'Brexit: Economists Dangerously Irrelevant', *Prime*, 24 June 2016.
13. John Maynard Keynes, *The General Theory of Employment, Interest, and Money*, New York: Classic House, 2008, p. 26.

14. Barack Obama, speech at the Jobs and Economic Growth Forum, 3 December 2009.
15. Deutsche Bank, *Helicopters 101: Your Guide to Monetary Financing*, 15 April 2016.
16. Quoted in the *Telegraph*, 'David Cameron: Tax Cuts Would Make Economic Situation Worse', 16 June 2011.
17. Stephanie Bell, 'Do Taxes and Bonds Finance Government Spending?', *Journal of Economic Issues*, Vol. 34, No. 3 (September 2000), p. 617.
18. William Mitchell and Warren Mosler, 'The Imperative of Fiscal Policy for Full Employment', *Australian Journal of Labour Economics*, Vol. 5, No. 2 (2002), p. 255.
19. Olivier Blanchard, *Macroeconomics*, New York: Prentice Hall, 1997, p. 429.
20. Adair Turner, *The Case for Monetary Finance: An Essentially Political Issue*, paper presented at the 16th Jacques Polak Annual Research Conference hosted by the International Monetary Fund, Washington, DC, 5–6 November 2015, 2015, p. 2.
21. Abba P. Lerner, 'Functional Finance and Federal Debt', *Social Research*, Vol. 10, No. 1 (February 1943).
22. See Adair Turner, 'Debt, Money and Mephistopheles: How Do We Get Out of This Mess?', speech given at the Cass Business School, 6 February 2013, p. 28.
23. Milton Friedman, *The Optimum Quantity of Money*, London: Macmillan, 1969, p. 4.
24. Ben S. Bernanke, 'Deflation: Making Sure "It" Doesn't Happen Here', speech to the National Economists Club, Washington, DC, 21 November 2002.
25. Ben S. Bernanke, 'What Tools Does the Fed Have Left? Part 3: Helicopter Money', Brookings, 11 April 2016.
26. Myung Soo Cha, 'Did Korekiyo Takahashi Rescue Japan from the Great Depression?', Discussion Paper Series A No. 395, Institute of Economic Research, Hitotsubashi University and Department of Economics, Yeungnam University, August 2000.
27. Ellen Brown, *Web of Debt*, London: Third Millennium, 2008.
28. Josh Ryan-Collins et al., 'Strategic Quantitative Easing', New Economics Foundation, 2013. For other examples see Frank van Lerven, 'A Guide to Public Money Creation', Positive Money, 2016.
29. Richard Koo, *The Escape From Balance Sheet Recession and the QE Trap*, Singapore: Wiley, 2014.
30. Lerner, 'Functional Finance and Federal Debt'.
31. L. Randall Wray, *Understanding Modern Money: The Key to Full Employment and Price Stability*, Cheltenham: Edward Elgar, 1998, p. 81.
32. Wynne Godley and Alex Izurieta, 'The US Economy: Weaknesses of the "Strong" Recovery', *Banca Nazionale del Lavoro Quarterly Review*, Vol. 57 (June 2004), pp. 131–9.
33. Steve Suranovic, 'International Finance: Theory and Policy, v. 1.0.1', Flat World, 2017.

34. Ibid.
35. Ibid.
36. Ibid.
37. Ibid. (emphasis added).
38. Atish Ghosh and Uma Ramakrishnan, 'Current Account Deficits: Is There a Problem?', *Finance & Development*, 28 March 2012.
39. Suranovic, 'International Finance'.
40. Marcel Fratzscher, *Die Deutschland Illusion*, Munich: Carl Hanser, 2014.
41. 'Germany's Ailing Infrastructure', *Spiegel*, 18 September 2014.
42. Ibid.
43. Philippe Legrain, 'Germany's Economic Mirage', *Project Syndicate*, 23 September 2014.
44. We are aware that many countries don't employ fully floating exchange rates. However, as noted, this is a voluntary constraint.
45. Ghosh and Ramakrishnan, 'Current Account Deficits'.
46. Anthony Kryger, 'Australia's Foreign Debt: A Quick Guide', Parliament of Australia, 28 October 2014.
47. Ibid.
48. Fernando Eguren-Martin, 'Friedman Was Right: Flexible Exchange Rates Do Help External Rebalancing', *Bank Underground*, 15 April 2016.
49. Jeannine Bailliu et al., 'Has Exchange Rate Pass-Through Really Declined? Some Recent Insights from the Literature', *Bank of Canada Review*, Autumn 2010, p. 4.
50. Kristin Forbes, 'Much Ado About Something Important: How Do Exchange Rate Movements Affect Inflation?', speech given at the 47th Money, Macro and Finance Research Group Annual Conference, Cardiff, 11 September.
51. Eguren-Martin, 'Friedman Was Right'.
52. Carmen M. Reinhart and Kenneth S. Rogoff, *This Time Is Different: Eight Centuries of Financial Folly*, Princeton, NJ: Princeton University Press, 2009, p. 205.
53. Jonathan D. Ostry et al., 'Capital Inflows: The Role of Controls', IMF Staff Position Note SPN/10/04, 19 February 2010.
54. Ibid., p. 6.
55. Ibid., p. 5.
56. Jonathan D. Ostry et al., 'Neoliberalism: Oversold?', *Finance & Development*, Vol. 53, No. 2 (2016), p. 39.
57. M. Ayhan Kose and Eswar Prasad, 'Capital Accounts: Liberalize or Not?', *Finance & Development*, 28 March 2012.
58. Ostry et al., 'Capital Inflows'.
59. Giovanni Andrea Cornia et al., *Adjustment with a Human Face: Protecting the Vulnerable and Promoting Growth, Volume 1*, Oxford: Clarendon, 1987.
60. Adam Lerrick and Allan H. Meltzer, 'Grants: A Better Way to Deliver Aid', *Quarterly International Economics Report*, January 2002.
61. Paul Krugman, 'Increasing Returns, Monopolistic Competition, and International Trade', *Journal of International Economics*, Vol. 9, No. 4 (1979), pp. 469–79.

62. Dani Rodrik, *The Global Governance of Trade as if Development Really Mattered*, report submitted to the UNDP, July 2001.

63. Ibid.

64. Ha-Joon Chang, *Bad Samaritans*, New York: Bloomsbury, 2008.

65. Ibid.

CHAPTER 9

1. Andrew Berg et al., 'Robots, Growth, and Inequality', *Finance & Development*, Vol. 53, No. 3 (2016), p. 10.

2. David H. Autor, 'Polanyi's Paradox and the Shape of Employment Growth', in Federal Reserve Bank of St. Louis, *Re-Evaluating Labor Market Dynamics*, 2015, pp. 135–6.

3. Michael Polanyi, *The Tacit Dimension*, New York: Doubleday, 1966, p. 4.

4. Ibid.

5. David Autor, 'Why Are There Still So Many Jobs? The History and Future of Workplace Automation', *Journal of Economic Perspectives*, Vol. 29, No. 3 (2015), p. 11.

6. Ibid., p. 22.

7. Ibid., p. 27.

8. Erik Brynjolfsson and Andrew McAfee, 'Jobs, Productivity and the Great Decoupling', *New York Times*, 11 December 2012.

9. Juliet Rhys-Williams, *Taxation and Incentive*, New York: Oxford University Press, 1953.

10. Milton Friedman, *Capitalism and Freedom*, Chicago: University of Chicago Press, 1962.

11. Ibid., p. 193.

12. William Mitchell and Martin Watts, 'The Right to Income versus the Right to Work', CofFEE Working Paper 03-08, University of Newcastle, 2003, p. 3.

13. Ibid.

14. Ibid.

15. Philippe Van Parijs, 'Why Surfers Should be Fed: The Liberal Case for an Unconditional Basic Income', *Philosophy and Public Affairs*, Vol. 20 (1991), pp. 101–31.

16. There are some exceptions. For example, the recently rejected Swiss proposal spoke of a basic income that would have allowed 'a humane existence and participation in public life for the whole population'.

17. Karl Widerquist and Michael A. Lewis, 'An Efficiency Argument for the Guaranteed Income', Working Paper No. 212, The Jerome Levy Economics Institute, 1997.

18. Robert J. Van der Veen, 'Real Freedom versus Reciprocity: Competing Views on the Justice of Unconditional Basic Income', *Political Studies*, Vol. 61, No. 1 (1998), pp. 140–63.

19. Mitchell and Watts, 'The Right to Income', p. 11.

20. Arjun Kharpal, 'Tech CEOs Back Call for Basic Income as AI Job Losses Threaten Industry Backlash', *CNBC*, 21 February 2017.

21. Ibid.
22. Paul Gregg and Richard Layard, 'A Job Guarantee', London School of Economics, 16 March 2009, p. 2.
23. CofFEE, 'Creating Effective Local Labour Markets: A New Framework for Regional Employment Policy', November 2008.
24. Anat Shenker-Osorio, *Don't Buy It: The Trouble with Talking Nonsense About the Economy*, New York: Public Affairs, 1987.
25. Meeting of the Federal Open Market Committee, 1–2 November 2011, p. 39.
26. Margaret Thatcher, interview in *Women's Own*, 1987.
27. Shenker-Osorio, *Don't Buy It*.
28. David L. Blustein, 'The Role of Work in Psychological Health and Well-Being: A Conceptual, Historical, and Public Policy Perspective', *American Psychologist*, Vol. 63 (2008), pp. 230.
29. Ibid.
30. Ibid.
31. Ibid., p. 232.
32. Ibid., p. 330.
33. Robert J. Van der Veen and Philippe Van Parijs, 'A Capitalist Road to Communism', *Theory and Society*, Vol. 15, No. 5 (1987), p. 642.
34. Ibid., pp. 644–5.
35. Louis Blanc, *Plus de Girondins*, Paris: Charles Joubert, 1851, p. 92.
36. Ibid. (authors' translation).
37. Karl Marx, *Critique of the Gotha Program*, Moscow: Progress Publishers, 1875.
38. Amartya Sen, *Development as Freedom*, New York: Random House, 1999.
39. Lester Thurow, *Dangerous Currents*, Sydney: Allen and Unwin, 1983, p. 216.
40. Peter Kriesler and Joseph Halevi, 'Political Aspects of Buffer Stock Employment', Working Paper 2001/02, Centre for Applied Economic Research, 2001, pp. 11–12.
41. Stuart Hall, 'The Great Moving Right Show', *Marxism Today*, January 1979, p. 18.

CHAPTER 10

1. Paul Cohen, 'Lessons from the Nationalization Nation: State-Owned Enterprises in France', *Dissent*, Winter 2010.
2. Ibid.
3. Ibid.
4. Ibid.
5. Ibid.
6. Mario Pianta et al., 'Industrial Policy in Europe, Report for the Rosa Luxemburg Foundation', April 2016, p. 12.
7. Cohen, 'Lessons from the Nationalization Nation'.
8. Ibid.
9. Ibid.

10. TNI, 'The Privatising Industry in Europe', 2016.
11. Dinyar Godrej, 'Myth 5: The Private Sector Is More Efficient than the Public Sector', *New Internationalist*, No. 488, 2015.
12. IMF, *Public-Private Partnerships*, Washington, DC: IMF, 2004.
13. New Economics Foundation, 'A New Ecological Macroeconomic Model', 2015.
14. Cohen, 'Lessons from the Nationalization Nation'.
15. Ibid.
16. Ibid.
17. Ibid.
18. John Maynard Keynes, 'National Self-Sufficiency', *The Yale Review*, Vol. 22, No. 4 (June 1933), pp. 755–69.
19. Trond Andersen, 'A Modern Revival of Import Substitution is the Needed Solution', *Real-World Economics Review Blog*, 15 March 2016.
20. Ibid.
21. Mary Amiti and David Weinstein, 'Do Bank Shocks Affect Aggregate Investment?', *Liberty Street Economics*, 8 July 2013; see also Mary Amiti and David Weinstein 'How Much Do Bank Shocks Affect Investment? Evidence from Matched Bank-Firm Loan Data', Federal Reserve Bank of New York Staff Report No. 604, 2013.
22. Speech by Adair Turner at the South African Reserve Bank, 2 November 2012.
23. Eric Toussaint et al., 'What is to be Done with the Banks? Radical Proposals for Radical Changes', CADTM, 13 April 2016.
24. Ibid.
25. Frédéric Lordon, 'L'effarante passivité de la "re-régulation financière"', in Les Économistes Atterrés, *Changer d'économie*, Paris: Les liens qui libèrent, 2011, p. 242 (authors' translation).
26. Nuno Teles, 'Socialize the Banks', *Jacobin*, 27 April 2016.
27. Toussaint et al., 'What is to be Done with the Banks?'
28. Stephen Schulmeister, *A General Financial Transaction Tax: A Short Cut of the Pros, the Cons and a Proposal*, WIFO Working Paper No. 344, 2009.
29. Ibid., p.5.
30. Ibid.

CONCLUSION

1. Perry Anderson, 'Why the System Will Win', *Le Monde diplomatique*, March 2017.
2. Becky Bond and Zack Exley, *Rules for Revolutionaries: How Big Organizing Can Change Everything*, White River Junction, VT: Chelsea Green, 2016.
3. Wolfgang Streeck, 'The Return of the Repressed', *New Left Review*, Vol. 104 (March–April 2017).
4. Michael Ignatieff, 'Sovereignty and the Crisis of Democratic Politics', *Demos Quarterly*, 17 January 2014.
5. Wolfgang Streeck et al., 'Where Are We Now? Responses to the Referendum', *London Review of Books*, Vol. 38, No. 14 (14 July 2016).

Index

Compiled by Melinda Hannan

Printed and bound by CPI Group (UK) Ltd, Croydon, CR0 4YY

09/06/2025

14685867-0002